Constitutional Reform
Of School Finance

Edited by
Kern Alexander
and
K. Forbis Jordan

Lexington Books
D. C. Heath and Company
Lexington, Massachusetts
Toronto   London

Lexington Books Politics of Education Series
Frederick M. Wirt, Editor

Michael W. Kirst, Ed., *State, School, and Politics*: *Research Directions*

Joel S. Berke and Michael W. Kirst, *Federal Aid to Education*: *Who Benefits? Who Governs?*

Al J. Smith, Anthony Downs, M. Leanne Lackman, *Achieving Effective Desegregation*

Kern Alexander, K. Forbis Jordan, *Constitutional Reform of School Finance*

Published simultaneously in Canada.

Printed in the United States of America.

International Standard Book Number: 0 - 669 - 86702 - 0

Library of Congress Catalog Card Number: 73 - 242

TABLE OF CONTENTS

CHAPTER 1

Page

Preface

Today as never before the courts are being called upon to solve the perplexing problems of school finance. Although the legal questions are many and complex, two major thrusts of cases are apparent, one is toward establishment of judicial standards for equal treatment of children attending public schools and the other involves the pervasive question of public aid for parochial schools. It is these two important issues to which the authors of this book address themselves. Chapters one through six are devoted to a legal analysis of fiscal inequality among school attendance units, among school districts and among states. Chapters seven through nine provide a pro and con discussion of public aid to parochial schools. Both the legal and economic aspects of alternative financing schemes are brought into play.

The authors have been drawn from various fields and represent a wide range of perspectives and interests. Professors Alexander, Holmes, Johns, Jordan and Rossmiller are from the field of educational administration in general, and school finance in particular. All have been deeply involved in the analysis and design of state school support programs for several years. Professors Hornby and Lucas are faculty members in outstanding colleges of law. Professors Goddard and Goffman are from the field of economics and participated in various efforts of the National Educational Finance Project and the President's Commission on School Finance. The chapters concerning financing of non-public schools written by McManus and Doerr, two articulate spokesmen on the issue, represent different points of view.

In this discussion of equity in financing the public schools and the constitutionality of aid to parochial schools, certain authors are obviously advocates for particular positions, the reader is cautioned to keep this in mind as he reads each chapter. The goal of the editors has been to present a resource book which will provide guidance for school fiscal planners as they develop state school support programs.

This volume is a compilation of papers presented to a conference on law and education held in Indianapolis, Indiana in the Spring of 1972. The conference was sponsored by the National Educational Finance Project in cooperation with Phi Delta Kappa, The University Council of Educational Administration, The University of Florida, The University of Virginia and Indiana University.

Kern Alexander
K. Forbis Jordan

November, 1972

CHAPTER 1

Constitutional Methods of Financing
Public Schools

K. FORBIS JORDAN AND KERN ALEXANDER

During the past few years the constitutional rights of students have been continually expanded, placing new limitations and restrictions on the police power of the state to regulate and control education.[1] Courts once obliquely maintained that education was a privilege bestowed upon the individual by the goodwill of the state and that it could be altered or even taken away at state discretion. Today, however, this judicial attitude has changed to the concept that the student now possesses a constitutional right to an education. The theory that education is a right has manifested itself in constitutional protections for students in both the substantive and procedural aspects of constitutional law.

The equal protection clause of the 14th Amendment has been the primary vehicle by which the courts have expanded individual rights. With the desegregation cases as the basic source of precedent, the courts have recently reached the point of invoking equal protection rights as a means of forcing redistribution of state tax funds for education. The cases harbor vast legal implications, not the least of which is their impact on the traditional role of the legislature with regard to govern-

The authors are respectively: Professor, Educational Administration, University of Florida, and Research Director, National Educational Finance Project; and Professor, Educational Administration, University of Florida, and Director, National Educational Finance Project.

mental finance. Of all of the powers possessed by the legislative branch of government, the discretionary power to tax and distribute resources is the most fundamental and jealously guarded.

These cases, therefore, represent a giant step in constitutional legal precedent because they involve limitations not only on the police power of the state to regulate and control education but also restrict a state's power to devise and regulate its own system of taxation. Both of these issues have traditionally formed almost entirely separate precedents in constitutional law. This discussion will give the reader a view of these precedents as they affect both the police power of the state to provide for education and the constitutional limitations on state taxation as they impact on alternative methods for state school financing.

The unique feature of the early cases is that they contested the constitutionality of state school finance programs only from the position of taxation. In these situations the taxpayer was usually the agrieved party and was, in the tradition of most taxpayers, simply instituting the action to save himself a few tax dollars. The most recent cases depart generally from the taxpayer equity argument and approach the issue of equalization of resources from that of the aggrieved student, the student maintaining that his educational opportunity should not be dependent on the fiscal ability of his school district. This issue cannot, of course, be totally removed from the purview of taxation and the power of the state to set up whatever tax system it chooses. In addition to the issue of equalization of resources, other legal and educational questions are raised which ask, does the state have an affirmative constitutional duty to compensate for variations in educational needs among children? Must the state correct for educational disabilities and disparities which may be the result of social, economic, or individual mental or physical deficiencies?

THE COURTS' TRADITIONAL POSITION

Nonintervention has been the password for decades when courts have been asked to examine the constitutionality of legislatively prescribed methods of taxation for financing of education. The courts have steadfastly adhered to the philosophy that an act of the legislature will not be rendered invalid unless the act without a doubt violates certain prescribed constitutional standards. With regard to the constitutionality of state school finance programs, the courts have only been asked to determine whether such programs create unconstitutional classifications or violate equality and uniformity of taxation requirements. The equal protection clause of the 14th Amendment encompasses, but is not limited to, the same protections as the equality and uniformity of taxation provisions of most state constitutions. Even though the federal equal protection clause encompasses much more than mere equality and uniformity of taxation, its broader aspects were not invoked to challenge state school finance programs until recently.

Practically all state constitutions have the equivalent of an "equal protection" provision — that is, some constitutional restriction against "unreasonable classifications." While the United States Supreme Court has the last word regarding "reasonableness" under the federal equal protection clause, state courts have the last word as to the meaning of reasonableness under their respective state constitutions. The primary problem is, of course, the definition of reasonableness with regard to appropriate classification. There are apparently no universally applicable tests by which to determine the reasonableness or unreasonablenesss of a classification. The cases merely indicate a vague outline and in some instances a given basis may be valid with respect to one tax and invalid with another.

The equal protection clause of the 14th Amendment is no stranger to disputes over the distribution of school funds. As early as 1912 the Supreme Court of Maine in *Sawyer v. Gilmore*[2] handed down an opinion which drew a hard and fast line between judicial and legislative prerogative saying that:

> The method of distributing the proceeds of such a tax rests in the wise discretion and sound judgment of the Legislature. If this discretion is unwisely exercised, the remedy is with the people, and not with the court, . . . We are not to substitute our judgment for that of a coordinate branch of government working within its constitutional limits.
> . . . In order that taxation may be equal and uniform in the constitutional sense, it is not necessary that the benefits arising therefrom should be enjoyed by all the people in equal degree, nor that each one of the people should participate in each particular benefit.

The court in *Sawyer* dismissed the federal equal protection

question rather curtly by pointing out that the object of the
14th Amendment was to prohibit discriminatory legislation and
did not apply where all persons subject to a law are treated
alike in both privileges conferred and liabilities imposed. Further, the court quoting the United States Supreme Court said:

> The provision in the Fourteenth Amendment that no state
> shall deny any person within its jurisdiction the equal
> protection of the laws was not intended to prevent a state
> from adjusting its system of taxation in all proper and
> reasonable ways.[3]

The logic conveyed in this case reflected a judicial philosophy
which was relied upon for over half a century. The courts steadfastly refused to apply state constitutional uniformity and
equality of taxing provisions to school fund distribution formulas. In all fairness to the courts, however, seldom if ever was
a statute challenged where the legislature was not attempting
itself to move toward greater equity in distribution of resources
among school districts. Plaintiffs were typically attempting to
retard such progress. Indeed, in most cases, state equality of
taxation and the federal Constitution were invoked in an attempt to prevent the equalization of resources among school
districts.

In a relatively recent case in South Dakota, *Dean v. Coddington,*[4] the constitutional equality and uniformity arguments were
again raised in an attempt to prevent the initiation of a foundation or equalization program. The plaintiff, a taxpayer, asserted
that the state foundation program act was unconstitutional,
violating both the equal and uniform provision of the South
Dakota constitution and the equal protection clause of the 14th
Amendment.

The plaintiff admitted that the taxes were probably uniformly raised, but contended that the uniformity requirement
is not satisfied unless the funds derived from the taxes are
uniformly distributed. The court, in upholding the constitutionality of the foundation program, commented on equality and
uniformity of taxation of both the state and federal constitutions and then laid down guidelines to govern the legislature's
apportionment of public funds. First, the court pointed out that
the test of the uniformity of taxation provision under the South
Dakota constitution was substantially the same as that required

by the 14th Amendment to the United States Constitution. The rule was stated by the court as:

> It is generally held that the constitutional provisions requiring equality and uniformity relate to the levy of taxes and not to the distribution or application of the revenue derived therefrom; and hence statutes relative to the distribution or application of such money cannot be held invalid on this ground.[5]

In justifying state taxation programs the courts have not always adhered strictly to their philosophy of separation between taxation and distribution of revenues. Indeed, a court is forced into this very dilemma when it seeks to justify a legislative act on the basis of its rationality. In fact, the court in seeking to determine the reasonableness of a classification cannot avoid analyzing the impact of tax revenues on local school districts. Such an analysis forces a court to look at such things as fiscal ability, educational needs, high costs of programs, and other conditions peculiar to particular school districts.

Courts have been hesitant to invalidate legislative acts on the basis of unconstitutional classification because the source of taxation is often tightly interwoven with the government's plan for distribution of funds to local districts.[6] The essence of an illegal constitutional classification is to arbitrarily classify local districts or persons with no regard for their actual conditions or needs. The United States Court of Appeals, Ninth Circuit speaks of this as fitting tax programs to needs:

> Traditionally classification has been a device for fitting tax programs to local needs and usages in order to achieve an equitable distribution of the tax burden. It has, because of this, been pointed out that in taxation, even more than in other fields, legislatures possess the greatest freedom of classification. Since the members of a legislature necessarily enjoy a familiarity with local conditions which this court cannot have, the presumption of constitutionality can be overcome only by the most explicit demonstration that a classification is a hostile and oppressive discrimination against particular persons and classes. The burden is on the one attacking the legislative arrangement to negative every conceivable basis which might support it.[7]

The Ninth Circuit Court of Appeals made this statement with reference to a case testing an Alaskan statute which levied property taxes among various types of governmental units for the purpose of supporting municipal and public school functions. The principal claim of inequality arose essentially not from lack of uniformity in the taxation but rather from the fact that the property tax collected in a municipality or school district could be retained by the collecting entity while such property taxes collected outside the designated municipalities and school districts reverted to the territorial treasurer. The court, in answering this charge, said that in the absence of unquestionable systematic geographical discrimination,[8] no requirements of equality and uniformity of the Organic Act of Alaska or the equal protection clause of the 14th Amendment limit the power of the legislature in respect to allocation and distribution of public funds.[9]

Even though the court denied that equality and uniformity of taxation requirements of both state and federal constitutions applied to the distribution of funds, the court proceeded nevertheless to lay down "guiding principles" which govern the legislatures' distribution of tax funds.

Quoting *Corpus Juris Secundum*,[10] the court said:

> In the absence of contitutional regulation the method of apportioning and distributing a school fund, accruing from taxes or other revenue, rests in the wise discretion of the state legislature, which method, in the absence of abuse of discretion or violation of some constitutional provision, cannot be interferred with by the courts. . . . the fact that the fund is distributed unequally among the different districts or political subdivisions does not render it invalid.[11]

In other words, the needs of the various types of school districts and the resulting impact of methods of taxation are matters which are to be determined by the legislature.

SCHOOL DISTRICT WEALTH AND THE CHILD'S EDUCATION

The importance of an education has been presumed to be a constitutionally protected right at least since the Supreme Court in *Brown*[12] said:

> Today, education is perhaps the most important function of state and local government. . . . In these days, it is

doubtful that any child may reasonably be expected to succeed in life if he is denied the opportunity of an education. Such an opportunity, where the state has undertaken to provide it, is a right which must be made available to all on equal terms.

This statement by the court has two important aspects: first, it confirmed the Supreme Court's recognition of the state's responsibility to provide education; second, it also pointed out that education was of such importance that it was a constitutionally protected right which must be provided to all on equal terms. This philosophy has been echoed several times since by the Court.[13]

Arthur Wise in 1965 advanced the theory that since education was a constitutionally protected right and must be provided to all on equal terms, a state which gives fewer dollars for the child in a poorer school district may be denying the child his constitutional rights.[14] Wise argued that the state had no reasonable constitutional basis on which to justify making a child's education contingent on the wealth of his school district. The United States Supreme Court had laid the groundwork for such a conclusion by previously holding that to classify persons on either the basis of poverty[15] or on the basis of their location, homesite, or occupation was unreasonable.[16]

This rationale characterizes most of the recent school finance decisions, that is, the quality of a child's education cannot be contingent upon the wealth of his school district. A state and local taxing and fund distribution system which is based on the property wealth of the local school district is unconstitutional.

In *Serrano v. Priest*[17] in 1971, the California Supreme Court handed down a well reasoned decision which strongly documents the establishment of the new equal protection precedent. The court here spoke of equalization only in terms of the relative wealth or fiscal ability of the local school districts as measured in terms of property valuation. It did not attempt to define the equal protection argument in terms of educational needs of children or educational programs. In fact, the court was forced to distinguish cases which had sought to relate equal protection to educational needs to avoid adverse precedent previously established by the United States Supreme Court.

After reviewing precedents established in desegregation,[18] criminal law,[19] and voting rights [20] cases, the court concluded, "we are convinced that the distinctive and priceless function of education in our society warrants, indeed compels, our treating it as a fundamental interest." With regard to wealth as a "suspect classification" the court relied on inferences made by the United States Supreme Court to the effect that "lines drawn on the basis of wealth or property, like those of race, are trationally disfavored."[21] This established, to the satisfaction of the court, that wealth was a "suspect classification." The court then critically analyzed the present California finance system and pointed out that although the basic state aid program in California tends to equalize among school districts, the total system, including state and local funds combined, creates great disparities in school revenues and the system as a whole generates school revenue proportional to the wealth of the individual school district.

Finally, after concluding that education was a "fundamental interest" and property wealth was a "suspect classification," the court then applied the "strict scrutiny" standard to determine if the financing system was "necessary to accomplish a compelling state interest." The defendant sought to establish a compelling state interest by alleging that the state school finance program in California "strengthened and encouraged local responsibility for control of public education," essentially maintaining that local control of education was inseparable from local discretion in financing. The court acknowledged that local administrative control of education may be a compelling state interest but denied that the present system of financing was necessary to further that interest. The court said, "No matter how the state decides to finance its system of public education, it can still leave this decision-making power in the hands of local districts."

The defense also asserted that a "compelling interest" of the state is to allow the local school district the authority to choose how much it wishes to spend for education of its children. Countering this argument, the court pointed out that the poor school district did not have such a choice and could not so long as the assessed valuation of property was the major determinant of how much it could spend for schools.

The poor district cannot freely choose to tax itself into an excellence which its tax rolls cannot provide. Far from being necessary to promote local fiscal choice, the present financing system actually deprives the less wealthy districts of that option.

Striking down this and other arguments by the defense, the court held that the state did not have a "compelling interest" in classifying children according to the wealth of the school district. Said another way, a statutory classification which makes the quality of a child's education dependent on the wealth of the school district is unconstitutional.

Closely following *Serrano,* a United States District Court in Minnesota entertained a class action suit[22] wherein plaintiffs alleged denial of equal protection and violation of the Civil Rights Act.[23] Plaintiffs showed that rich districts in Minnesota enjoy both lower rates and higher spending. The court, in viewing the facts, arrived at the inescapable conclusions that, "The level of spending for publicly financed education in Minnesota is profoundly affected by the wealth of each school district." Education was considered to be a "fundamental interest" and wealth to be a "suspect classification" as held in *Serrano.*

When the state defended its finance system by claiming that local control was a "compelling interest," the court pointed out that the state by creating erratic disparities in the economic power of the local district has itself limited local initiative, with poor districts having to spend low with high taxes and rich districts spending high with low taxes. The court further observed that local control and local financing are not inexplicably intertwined; local administrative control and local effort can be maintained even though wealth is held neutral. Finally, the court concluded that the plaintiffs stated an appropriate cause of action and that a "system of public school financing which makes spending per pupil a function of the school district's wealth violates the equal protection guarantee of the Fourteenth Amendment."

A significant decision by a federal three-judge court in Texas followed both the California and Minnesota cases and reached the same conclusion.[24] Here it was held that plaintiffs had been denied equal protection of the laws by the Texas system of financing its public schools. Plaintiffs contended that the educational finance system of the state makes education a function of the local property tax base. In "strict scrutiny" of the Texas system, a survey of 110 school districts in Texas indicated that the school districts with over $100,000 market value of property enjoyed a tax rate per $100 of only thirty-one cents, while the poorest four districts with less than $10,000 in property per pupil had more than double the tax burden of seventy cents per $100 property valuation. The lower rate of the rich districts yielded $585 per pupil while the higher rate in the poorer districts yielded only $60 per pupil. Relying on these data the court observed that the school finance system of Texas erroneously assumes that the value of property in various districts will be sufficiently equal to maintain comparable expenditures among districts. This inequality is not corrected to any substantial degree by state funds, because when all state and local funds were combined, the poor district of Edgewood had only $231 per pupil while the rich district of Alamo Heights had $543. Expert testimony substantiated that the Texas system of school finance "tends to subsidize the rich at the expense of the poor."

To correct this unconstitutional inequality, *Rodriguez* established a standard of "fiscal neutrality." As was the case in both *Serrano* and *Van Dusartz*, the court maintained that fiscal neutrality did not require that all educational expenditures be equal for each child. The standard simply requires that "the quality of public education may not be a function of wealth, other than the wealth of the state as a whole."

In commenting further on educational expenditures, *Rodriguez* made it clear that the "fiscal neutrality" standard does not involve the court in the intricacies of affirmatively requiring expenditures be made in a certain manner. "On the contrary, the state may adopt the financial scheme desired so long as the variations in wealth among the governmentally chosen units do not effect spending for the education of any child."

The *Rodriguez* court made it very clear that it would not become involved in the nebulous concept of educational needs. Such an undertaking would involve the court in "endless research and evaluation for which the judiciary is ill-suited." To the court, judicially manageable standards could only be established along the definable lines of valuation of property wealth.

AFFIRMATIVE DUTY TO CORRECT FOR EDUCATIONAL NEEDS

Contemporaneous with and even preceding the fiscal neutrality cases is another type of case which promises to be the focal point of much litigation in the future. Educators for some time have recognized that all children cannot be educated equally with equal resources. Some children with special learning deficiencies caused by cultural deprivation or mental or physical incapacities must be given special educational services. On reflection, no one can sensibly contend that a non-English speaking child or a child with speech or hearing difficulties does not need special instructional programs. Such programs cost more than regular programs geared to normal children possessing no particular learning disorders or deficiencies. The higher costs of such programs have been documented by the National Educational Finance Project.[25] Today, some state aid programs partially take into account the differences in educational needs of children with high cost learning problems. Most state finance programs, however, do not adequately measure or compensate such educational needs by providing proportionately greater funds to school districts with high incidences of high cost children. Since education is generally considered by the courts today to be a "fundamental right," can state legislatures constitutionally avoid recognizing special learning problems? Is a child denied his constitutional right of an equal education if he cannot hear the teacher, cannot enunciate his words clearly enough to progress in school normally or his cultural background has placed him at such a learning deficit that he will be unable ever to catch up or compete? In such cases, equal expenditures or regular programs for all children may provide equal learning opportunity for normal, middle class children but attendance in such regular middle class educational programs by the physically, mentally or culturally deprived provides for less than equal educational opportunity.

A fundamental legal question is whether a state's responsibility to provide a child with an opportunity for equal education is successfully discharged where no recognition is given to individual needs and deficiencies. Should a state's constitutional responsibility to the child be elevated from simply providing equal access to dollars to a level of giving children equal access to educational programs as mandated by the educational needs of children?

The courts to date have dealt only superficially with the pervasive problems of educational needs. Two cases represent, at this time, the judicial precedent in this realm. In both cases the courts declined to place constitutional limitations on the legislative power to allocate funds for education. In the first of these decisions, *McInnis v. Shapiro*[26] the United States District Court for the Northern District of Illinois held that the Illinois state system of school finance was not unconstitutional as violative of the Equal Protection and due process clauses of the Fourteenth Amendment. Since *McInnis* was summarily affirmed by the Supreme Court of the United States,[27] this statement probably represents precedent at this time.[28] This is true in spite of the California Supreme Court's attempt to distinguish *McInnis* solely on the contention that *McInnis* involved only a plea for equalization in terms of educational needs. The plaintiffs in *McInnis* did not clearly state either the fiscal equalization issue or the educational need issue. With regard to variation in property wealth, the plaintiff was probably intentionally evasive since the four districts involved were not, in fact, property poor. As far as educational needs were concerned the plaintiff districts claimed high incidence of high need children, but did not adequately support their claim with data showing precisely the additional costs of special programs for high need children. In view of the lack of information and standards provided by the plaintiffs, the court held that the Illinois system of financing was not unconstitutional. In so holding, the court quoted Justice Holmes who once said that "the 14th Amendment is not a pedagogical requirement of the impractical."[29] The position in *McInnis* was summed by saying that there were no "discoverable and manageable standards by which a court can determine when the Constitution is satisfied and when it is violated."

The decision in Illinois was closely followed by a similar case in Virginia.[30] In *Burruss,* the plaintiffs instead of being from suburban school districts were from a rural county in western Virginia. Plaintiffs in this suit relied more directly on the educational needs argument than did the plaintiffs in *McInnis.* Bath County, the county in which plaintiffs resided and attended school, had higher than the state average assessed valuation of property per pupil but had a very high incidence of low income families. In terms of property wealth per pupil, Bath County ranked 14th in the state, but when wealth was measured in terms of family income it ranked 55th among counties in the state. With the state aid formula relying almost entirely on property wealth as the chief allocation determinant,

Bath consistently received fewer funds per pupil than it needed to provide adequate educational services for the children from low income families. Specifically, plaintiffs claimed the state formula created and perpetuated substantial disparities in educational opportunities throughout the state of Virginia and failed to relate to any of the variety of education needs present in the several counties and cities of Virginia.

To the former charge, *Burruss* found that the system of finance was not discriminatory as it operated under a uniform and consistent state plan. With regard to educational needs, the court commended the equalization of educational opportunity as worthy and desirable but refused to interject the wisdom of the court in ascertaining what constituted educational need disparities. In the following the hands-off course of the *McInnis,* the court said:

> . . . the courts have neither the knowledge, nor the means, nor the power to tailor the public moneys to fit the varying needs of these students throughout the state. We can only see to it that the outlays on one group are not invidiously greater or less than that of another. No such arbitrariness is manifest here.[31]

Accordingly, *Burruss* denied relief to plaintiffs under either the "efficiency" provision of the Virginia Constitution or the equal protection clause of the 14th Amendment. The United States Supreme Court summarily affirmed this decision.

In neither *McInnis* nor *Burruss* could the school districts in which plaintiffs attended school be classified as fiscally poor if wealth were measured in terms of assessed valuation of property. However, in both instances claims were made that the high incidence of deprived children created excessive unmet educational needs which denied children equal access to educational programs. In both instances, the courts recognized the existence of varying educational needs and costs but refused to elevate the disparity to a plane of constitutional discrimination.

The most recent case to acknowledge the problem of educational needs as a possible criterion for measuring the constitutionality of state school finance programs was handed down by a Superior Court in New Jersey.[32] This court viewed approvingly a New Jersey report which stated:

It is now recognized that children from lower socio-economic level homes require more educational attention if they are to progress normally through school. When the additional compensatory education is provided, it results in *substantially higher costs. The weighting* of the children from the lower income families *compensates in part* for the larger expenditure necessary to provide them with an adequate educational program so they may overcome their lack of educational background. [Emphasis added][33]

Unfortunately, the New Jersey court's discussion of educational needs did not progress to the point of establishing standards or guidelines, but one could extrapolate from the court's discussion that if educational needs and cost weightings had not been previously included in the state aid formula, the court might quite possibly have imposed them. This is, of course, conjecture, but the decision of this court gave the fullest recognition to varying educational needs and costs of any court to date. It is significant to note that the court gave such credence to educational needs while holding that portions of the state school finance formula of New Jersey violated both the "thorough and efficient" provisions of the state constitution along with the equal protection clause of the 14th Amendment. Such judicial acknowledgment of educational needs and costs variations suggests the distinct possibility of a judicial formulation of acceptable standards for legislative identification and funding of special educational needs among children.

IMPLICATIONS OF THE COURT DECISIONS FOR STATE SCHOOL SUPPORT PROGRAMS

The millennium in school finance may appear to have arrived for those who have advocated greater equalization for years and for others who have recently become interested in the extension of the equal protection clause of the Fourteenth Amendment to the Federal Constitution into the state school finance area. Both groups see their goal in sight as several courts have recently ruled that the state has a responsibility to provide local districts with equal access to dollars for education irrespective of the wealth of the local district. The harsh facts are that "Rome was not built in a day" and the revolution in school finance programs will not be accomplished over night. Such mundane matters as state appropriations, local school budgets and available revenues will in the final analysis be the determinants which will dictate when the theories and court decisions become operational.

Orderly planning is a prerequisite of any plan, for state legislatures must make budgetary projections so that the state appropriation may be determined. The end result may be that the relative differences in expenditure levels among districts will be maintained for several years, especially if legislatures impose a maximum percentage of increase on local districts as they prepare budgets for subsequent years. As the Fleishmann Commission[34] recently recommended in New York, most states will in all probability phase into higher levels of equalization rather than moving in one bold step.

Even though the recent court decisions and the current furor appear to offer great hopes to taxpayers and educators, there are some pitfalls. If the concept of "fiscal neutrality" should result in a "one scholar-one dollar" funding system, the effect on local school districts which are presently spending more than the state average would be obvious. Immediately, they would be required to reduce their per pupil expenditures to the prescribed level for the state irrespective of the educational programs which they might be providing or the cost of living in the local districts. Therefore, the high expenditure districts would be required to reduce their per pupil expenditures to the state average, and the low expenditure districts would be provided with sufficient funds to raise their expenditure level to the state average. In the first instance, the districts would have to restrict their educational program because of reduced funds; in the second instance, the districts would be provided with an immediate windfall but would not have had the opportunity to engage in sufficient advanced planning to assure fiscal accountability. Granted, the principal court decisions have stated that their rulings should not be interpreted as requiring equal levels of expenditures per pupil throughout the state. The problem is that they have provided no substantive guidelines other than the concept of fiscal neutrality—that the wealth base must be the wealth of the state as a whole rather than that of the local district.

In responding to the mandate of the courts in the present social, economic and political climate, legislatures will be faced with the obvious temptation to provide for equal levels of expenditures per pupil in all districts. Then comes the question of leveling all up to the expenditure level of the high spending districts, leveling down to the expenditure level of the low spending district or seeking some magic point between the two extremes. (That point might be the state average referred to in the previous paragraph.)

The question of how much, if any, local leeway for enrichment will be permitted has not been resolved. Also the question of whether a state will be required to correct its program immediately or permitted to move toward full and complete "equal access" at a deliberate pace under a "constitutional plan" has not been answered. Such issues will only be resolved through experience and further litigation. If the present trend of court decisions continues there seems to be little question but that most states will be required to make significant changes in their present methods of financing schools.

Many members of the educational community view the recent court decisions with a degree of skepticism. Rather than being a great promise for the future in the field of educational finance, the end results of *Serrano* may bring a leveling of the growth curve of revenues provided for education. The possibilities of a period of retrenchment may not be too remote. Taxpayers throughout the nation are rebelling against the local property tax. The cost of, and demand for, all governmental services are increasing; and many citizens are quite concerned about the spiraling costs of educational programs and services.

In their current state, the court decisions appear to be leaving as many questions unanswered as they are answering. For example, do the decisions apply to school transportation programs, the need for which varies from school district to school district? Do they apply to capital outlay and debt service programs? Within the context of current practice, these two latter programs rely more on the local property tax as a revenue source than do other school programs. In the absence of greater specificity, will the courts permit local districts to have any local "leeway" for enrichment or individuality in financing their school programs? If so, to what degree? Will the courts require an immediate shift in the state school support program to provide for full and complete "equal access," or will states be permitted to enact statutes providing for an orderly transition? Will the courts recognize that certain groups of pupils require different types of educational services and programs, and that the costs for these services and programs are higher than for normal programs? Will the concept of "equal access" be extended to include equal access to education programs and thereby require that educational expenditures per pupil be unequal among school districts within a state.

When viewed in an evolutionary context the court cases may be classified as being in "three generations." Plaintiffs in the first generation cases sought to provide taxpayer relief by striking down legislation appropriating state aid on a per pupil basis which resulted in a sharing of tax resources among school districts within a state. Through the precedent of this litigation the courts established the constitutionality of using the equalization method in distributing state aid to local school districts; e.g., funds may be distributed in inverse relationship to the wealth of the local school district.

In the second generation cases, the courts have established that any child in the state is deprived of "equal protection" if the state school support program does not provide him (or his local school district) with equal access to dollars for the support of the local school program. The second generation court decisions emphasize two basic points: (1) the funding of a child's educational program is to be based on the wealth of the state as a whole rather than the wealth of the district of residence; and (2) the decisions do not require that expenditures throughout a state be uniform or equal. Due to the recency of these decisions, their true impact has not been assessed; however, litigation has been initiated in several states and recent decisions in four states have been essentially consistent.

The comprehensive pattern has been established through the third generation cases which have added the additional concept that a child cannot be denied equal access to education programs as well as equal access to dollars. Current cases have focused on the relationship between the allocation of revenues and the capacity of local school districts to provide programs with those revenues. The contention has been that certain children have educational needs which result in local districts having to provide high cost educational programs if those needs are to be met. In these third generation cases, the courts have reviewed the dimensions and problems associated with providing revenues on the basis of educational need and have also questioned the *appropriateness of local district educational expenditures being dependent upon the mood or aspirations of the parents or the taxpayers of the local districts.*

The ultimate extension of this principle of educational need would result in local districts being mandated to provide pupils with access to those educational programs needed by the pupils in the district. State legislative actions mandating special education programs are examples of statutory recognition of differing educational needs of pupils, and state intervention to assure that those educational programs are being provided.

The *McInnis* decision rejected the contention that available educational revenues should be determined on the basis of pupil's educational needs because of the absence of discoverable or judicially manageable standards. In *Robinson* the court recognized that educational programs for different groups of children will have different levels of costs, and it considered the inclusion of cost differentials in the computation of state school support programs to be a reasonable extension of the "equal protection" clause.

In projecting the future, the basic question is whether the courts will maintain their traditional posture of subjecting state school finance programs to the test of "reasonableness" and requiring that the legislature not exercise its authority in an arbitrary or capricious manner, or subjecting state school finance programs to "strict scrutiny" which may result in an extension of the "fiscal neutrality" doctrine to state school finance programs throughout the nation. In any event, the fact remains that current state school finance statutes in virtually all states contain provisions which result in the amount of dollars available for local educational programs being dependent upon the wealth of the local district.

The research conducted by the National Educational Finance Project[35] (NEFP) provides additional support of the cost differential concept. NEFP researchers have reported that costs for "representative best practice" educational programs varied significantly from a ratio of 1.00 for basic elementary grades 1-6 to a ratio of 2.06 for compensatory education programs, with broad categories of vocational education and special education having a ratio of 1.81. Within special education, cost differentials for specific categories varied extensively from 1.20 for children in programs for the speech handicapped to 3.25 for children in programs for the physically handicapped. In analyzing the conditions contributing to the differences in costs among programs, the researchers reported that the principal contributing factors were:

1. Pupil-teacher ratio in the particular class.
2. Percentage of pupil's day or week spent in the class.
3. Non-teaching support personnel provided for the class.
4. Equipment and materials provided for the class.
5. Salary level of the teacher.

In addition to those additional costs associated with the incidence of pupils who require or seek educational programs with higher cost ratios, local district per pupil expenditures will also be influenced by transportation requirements. Rather than being a unform cost in all districts, transportation expenditures will vary in terms of the percent of pupils transported, population density, labor costs in the community, and road conditions.

Even though one might agree that certain groups of pupils require educational programs which are different from those required by others, and that these programs have varying levels of costs, the theory of incorporating cost differentials into state school support computation might be rejected if it were not for the additional research findings that some districts have higher percentages of pupils with need for higher cost programs than other districts. This condition results in the requirement of additional financial resources in those districts with high incidences of pupils with special needs if those districts are to provide pupils with "equal access" to educational programs. The concept of spending different amounts of money on the education of various pupils was supported in *Robinson* when the court recognized that the educational programs required for different groups of pupils dictated different levels of expenditure. The focus was on programs for pupils of low socio-economic status, but the same concept may be applied to vocational education and special education programs.

As a part of the NEFP basic research, a data bank for a prototype state was developed so that simulated application of various state school programs could be analyzed in terms of their impact on "real world" situations. The data base for the prototype state was developed from a selected number of actual districts whose characteristics are generally representative of typical school districts found throughout the nation. The lone exception is that none of the districts had an average daily membership of less than 1,500 pupils. In Table 1, selected data for each of the 32 districts in the prototype state have been presented to illustrate the impact of the cost differentials when the weighted pupil approach is used in determining the incidence of educational needs as contrasted with using an unweighted pupil approach or assuming that there are no differences in the educational programs required by different groups of pupils. The impact of cost differentials is reflected in the increase in the number of program units over the number of ADM (Average Daily Membership) pupil units.

In the following table, district number 24, with the highest incidence of high cost pupils, is rural and agricultural. The district with second highest incidence is the largest city and can be classified as having a core ghetto and a typical large city pupil population. District number 2, with the lowest impact of incidence of high cost pupils, is essentially a high income suburban area.

In making more detailed analysis of the impact of the weighted pupil approach, the NEFP staff found that the incidence of pupils with need for high cost programs varied among the types of districts, e.g., rural-small town, suburban and independent city, as well as among all districts in the prototype states.

As a further illustration of the impact of using the cost differential approach in allocating state funds, Tables 2-5 were computed using the data from the prototype state as in Table 1. There is a difference in the number of pupils and program units between Table 1 and Tables 2-5 because kindergarten pupils were included in this computation.

The total value of the basic state school support is identical in each of the four tables. In Tables 2 and 4 a full state support model is shown, but the weighted pupil approach was used in Table 4. The differences in the incidence of pupils and the resultant impact on funding are illustrated by District No. 1. In Table 2 District No. 1 was provided with a state support of $800 per pupil; however, in Table 4 the amount of support per pupil was reduced to $752 per pupil because District No. 1 had a lower incidence of high cost pupils. District No. 25, the urban core city in the prototype state, experienced the opposite effect; the weighted pupil approach provided this district with $931 per pupil as contrasted with $800 per pupil using the unweighted pupil approach. Depending upon the incidence of high cost pupils the basic program for each district will vary, Dis-

TABLE 1

IMPACT OF COST DIFFERENTIALS ON VARIOUS TYPES OF SCHOOL DISTRICTS
IN THE PROTOTYPE STATE (Grades 1-12 Only)

District	ADM Units[a]	Program Units[b]	Percent of Impact	Type of District[c]
1	8,243	10,700	29.8	City/Suburb
2	12,905	16,174	25.3	City/Suburb
3	28,801	37,318	29.6	City
4	107,024	138,545	29.5	City/Rural
5	4,485	6,670	48.7	Rural/Town
6	6,218	9,659	55.3	Rural/Town
7	9,022	11,450	26.9	City
8	1,624	2,105	29.6	Rural/Town
9	13,246	17,141	29.4	Suburban
10	3,718	4,725	27.1	Town
11	3,534	5,230	48.0	Rural/Town
12	118,514	152,277	28.5	Suburban/Town
13	4,208	6,387	51.8	Rural
14	2,959	3,700	25.0	Suburban/Town
15	137,177	172,194	25.5	City/Rural
16	18,235	26,107	43.2	City/Rural
17	14,430	19,245	33.4	Rural/Town
18	63,561	83,297	31.1	City/Rural
19	21,491	29,622	37.8	City/Rural
20	13,066	18,584	42.2	Rural/Town
21	25,626	33,286	29.9	Rural/Town
22	16,370	23,995	46.6	City/Rural
23	5,305	8,081	52.3	Rural/Town
24	6,364	10,301	61.9	Rural/Town
25	174,927	282,798	61.7	City
26	11,816	16,296	37.9	Rural/Town
27	11,671	16,872	44.6	Rural
28	9,164	14,024	53.0	Rural
29	2,392	2,992	25.1	Suburban
30	5,297	8,010	51.2	Rural
31	4,866	7,256	49.1	Rural
32	4,425	6,181	39.7	Rural
TOTAL	870,684	1,201,222		

[a]Total pupils in average daily membership in grades 1-12.
[b]District entitlement computed by using a weighted pupil approach to recognize incidence of pupils in high cost programs.
[c]In this classification: cities have populations of over 25,000 and towns between 2,500 and 25,000.

tricts 19 and 26 were the only ones which were not affected to some degree.

In Tables 3 and 5 an equalization program was used to provide local districts with funds. The same total amount of dollars was used as in Tables 2 and 4, but a 12 mill local effort was required. The basic program per pupil was the same as in

TABLE 2

FULL STATE SUPPORT

$800 PER ADM UNWEIGHTED PUPIL, GRADES K-12

Dist. No.	Basic Prog. $	Total Pupils	Program Units	Basic Prog. St. $/Pup.	Basic Prog. Loc. $/Pup.	Basic Prog. $/Pup.
1	7343200	9179	9179	800	0	800
2	10875200	13595	13594	800	0	800
3	24291200	30364	30364	800	0	800
4	91129600	113912	113912	800	0	800
5	3829600	4787	4787	800	0	800
6	5259200	6574	6574	800	0	800
7	7610400	9513	9513	800	0	800
8	1363200	1704	1704	800	0	800
9	11301600	14127	14127	800	0	800
10	3152800	3941	3941	800	0	800
11	3000800	3751	3751	800	0	800
12	101202400	126503	126503	800	0	800
13	3548800	4436	4436	800	0	800
14	2484800	3106	3106	800	0	800
15	119302400	149128	149128	800	0	800
16	15608800	19511	19511	800	0	800
17	12297600	15372	15372	800	0	800
18	54876000	67970	67970	800	0	800
19	18387200	22984	22984	800	0	800
20	11062400	13828	13828	800	0	800
21	21992000	27490	27490	800	0	800
22	13978400	17473	17473	800	0	800
23	4522400	5653	5653	800	0	800
24	5390400	6738	6738	800	0	800
25	151192000	188990	188990	800	0	800
26	10167200	12709	12709	800	0	800
27	9984000	12480	12480	800	0	800
28	8051200	10064	10064	800	0	800
29	1986400	2483	2483	800	0	800
30	4497600	5622	5622	800	0	800
31	4118400	5148	5148	800	0	800
32	3730400	4663	4663	800	0	800
	747037600	933797	933797			

TABLE 3

EQUALIZATION PROGRAM WITH 12 MILL LOCAL CHARGEBACK
$800 PER ADM UNWEIGHTED PUPIL, GRADES K-12

Dist. No.	Basic Prog. $	Total Pupils	Program Units	Basic Prog. St. $/Pup.	Basic Prog. Loc. $/Pup.	Basic Prog. $/Pup.
1	7343200	9179	9179	67	733	800
2	10875200	13595	13594	119	681	800
3	24291200	30364	30364	292	508	800
4	91129600	113912	113912	313	487	800
5	3829600	4787	4787	346	454	800
6	5259200	6574	6574	386	414	800
7	7610400	9513	9513	430	370	800
8	1363200	1704	1704	434	366	800
9	11301600	14127	14127	435	365	800
10	3152800	3941	3941	440	360	800
11	3000800	3751	3751	456	344	800
12	101202400	126503	126503	460	340	800
13	3548800	4436	4436	470	330	800
14	2484800	3106	3106	498	302	800
15	119302400	149128	149128	501	299	800
16	15608800	19511	19511	518	282	800
17	12297600	15372	15372	528	272	800
18	54376000	67970	67970	533	267	800
19	18387200	22984	22984	541	259	800
20	11062400	13828	13828	547	253	800
21	21992000	27490	BGDTJ	558	242	800
22	13978400	17473	17473	565	235	800
23	4522400	5653	5653	566	234	800
24	5390400	6738	6738	569	231	800
25	151192000	188990	188990	573	227	800
26	10167200	12709	12709	602	198	800
27	9984000	12480	12480	607	193	800
28	8051200	10064	10064	632	168	800
29	1986400	2483	2483	644	156	800
30	4497600	5622	5622	659	141	800
31	4118400	5148	5148	660	140	800
32	3730400	4663	4663	670	130	800
	747037600	933797	933797			

TABLE 4
FULL STATE SUPPORT WEIGHTED PUPILS
GRADES K-12

Dist. No.	Basic Prog. $	Total Pupils	Program Units	Basic Prog. St. $/Pup.	Basic Prog. Loc. $/Pup.	Basic Prog. $/Pup.
1	6905668	9179	11757	752	0	752
2	9928429	13594	16903	730	0	730
3	22941947	30364	39058	756	0	756
4	85674035	113912	145857	752	0	752
5	4119000	4787	7012	860	0	860
6	5912697	6574	10066	899	0	899
7	7027221	9513	11964	739	0	739
8	1284965	1704	2188	754	0	754
9	10629958	14127	18097	752	0	752
10	2914101	3941	4961	739	0	739
11	3217056	3751	5477	858	0	858
12	94512011	126503	106904	747	0	747
13	389935	4436	6640	879	0	879
14	2263663	3106	3854	729	0	729
15	109001587	149128	185572	731	0	731
16	16161996	19511	27515	828	0	828
17	11913155	15372	20282	775	0	775
18	51774858	67970	88145	762	0	762
19	18372994	22984	31279	799	0	799
20	11415430	13828	19434	826	0	826
21	20758245	27490	35340	755	0	755
22	14828331	17473	25245	849	0	849
23	4978359	5653	8475	881	0	881
24	6303742	6738	10732	936	0	936
25	175856493	188990	299390	931	0	931
26	10158748	12709	17295	799	0	799
27	10453027	12480	17796	838	0	838
28	8857789	10064	15080	880	0	880
29	1811765	2483	3084	730	0	730
30	4925494	5622	8385	876	0	876
31	4447323	5148	7571	864	0	864
32	3787575	4663	6448	812	0	812
	747037600	933797	1271807			

TABLE 5

EQUALIZATION PROGRAM WITH 12 MILL LOCAL CHARGEBACK
WEIGHTED PUPILS, GRADES K-12

Dist. No.	Basic Prog. $	Total Pupils	Program Units	Basic Prog. St. $/Pup.	Basic Prog. Loc. $/Pup.	Basic Prog. $/Pup.
1	6905668	9179	11757	20	733	752
2	9928429	13594	16903	49	681	730
3	22941947	30364	39058	247	508	756
4	85674035	113912	145857	265	487	752
5	4119000	4787	7012	407	454	860
6	5912697	6574	10066	485	414	899
7	7027221	9513	11964	369	370	739
8	1284965	1704	2188	388	366	754
9	10629958	14127	18097	387	365	752
10	2914101	3941	4961	379	360	739
11	3217056	3751	5477	514	344	858
12	94512011	126503	106904	407	340	747
13	389935	4436	6640	549	330	879
14	2263363	3106	3854	427	302	729
15	109001587	149128	185572	432	299	731
16	16161996	19511	27515	547	282	828
17	11913155	15372	20282	503	272	775
18	51774858	67970	88145	495	267	762
19	18372994	22984	31279	541	259	799
20	11415430	13828	19434	572	253	826
21	20758245	27490	35340	513	242	755
22	14828331	17473	25245	614	235	849
23	4978359	5653	8475	646	234	881
24	6303742	6738	10732	703	231	936
25	175856493	188990	299390	704	227	931
26	10158748	12709	17295	601	198	799
27	10453027	12480	17796	645	193	838
28	8857789	10064	15080	712	168	880
29	1811765	2483	3084	574	156	730
30	4925494	5622	8385	735	141	876
31	4447323	5148	7571	724	140	864
32	3787575	4663	6448	682	130	812
	747037600	937797	1271807			

74-15759

the other examples, and the impact of using the weighted pupil approach was identical. In the previous discussion attention has been given to "equal access to dollars", and this concept of equalization is shown in the "Basic Program—Local Dollars Per Pupil" column. The required local share is identical in both tables because the measure of local taxpaying capacity was equalized assessed valuation per pupil. Some shift would have taken place if the measure of local taxpaying capacity had been equalized assessed valuation per program unit, or weighted pupil. Various measures of local taxpaying capacity may be used to meet the "equal access to dollars" criterion, provided that the amount of funds per pupil in the local district does not become a function of the wealth of the local district.

The contention of the NEFP is that the cost differential approach through either the weighted pupil or weighted instructional unit recognizes the differences in the "educational need" of the pupils among school districts. Through this approach local school districts will have sufficient funds to support broadened educational programs so that the criterion of "equal access to educational programs" may be met.

The previous discussion illustrates that techniques can be utilized to determine the "educational needs" of different subgroups of pupils and that these pupils are not uniformly distributed among school districts. Through the application of the research techniques discussed above, an individual state can determine its cost differentials, incorporate either the weighted pupil or instruction unit into its state school support computation, and then begin to meet the thrust of the third generation of equal protection cases, that is, providing pupils with equal access to educational programs as well as equal access to dollars.

CONSTITUTIONALLY ACCEPTABLE ALTERNATIVES

The courts have not identified specific operational state school support programs which are considered to be constitutionally acceptable; however, sufficient guidelines have been stated which suggest the following four basic alternatives.

1. Full state funding—fixed level program.
2. Equalization with no leeway—fixed level program.
3. Equalization with minimal leeway—fixed level program.
4. Incentive—variable level program.

In each of the suggested alternatives, cost differentials have been incorporated so that pupils would be provided with "equal access to educational programs" as suggested by the third generation cases. To increase the level of equity, the costs of necessary services such as pupil transportation have not been recognized in the tabular material which accompanies each of the graphical presentations contained in the previous chapter. Additional adjustments could be provided to recognize capital outlay and debt service expenditures. To meet the test of the second generation cases, it does not appear as though the courts would require the inclusion of the cost differentials to recognize the differences in educational need among pupils and among school districts. However, to meet the test of the third generation cases, the courts would require inclusion of the educational needs measures in the state school support program.

Full State Funding

This alternative meets the test of "the wealth being dependent upon the total wealth of the state." In operation, educational programs could be identified with accompanying cost differentials. The allocation for the total program could then be computed by multiplying the program units by the state allocation with whatever additional modifications might be incorporated into the state school support program. The key consideration is that the local district's, and thereby the pupil's, access to wealth is dependent upon the total wealth of the state. Revenue for the program could be obtained completely from the general fund of the state or from state tax earmarked for this purpose. A graphical presentation of this alternative is shown in Figure 1. All of the funds come from the state sources, thereby meeting the court test of the access to dollars being a function of the total wealth of the entire state rather than the wealth in the individual local school district.

Another alternative under full state funding would be for the legislature to establish a state-level school budget approval agency which would determine the funds to be allocated to each district, with such determination being made after a review of the budget requests of each local district and a consultation with local school district officials. This approach has been referred to as the "negotiated budget." At first glance, the option seems attractive, for it provides an opportunity for recognition

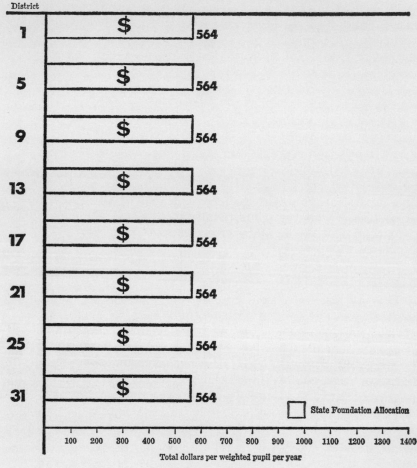

Figure 1
Full State Funding

of the unique local conditions which may influence the level of
local district expenditures, e.g., cost of living, level of teachers'
salaries, variations in the type and quantity of educational
services, and locally-determined differences in instructional programs provided for pupils.

Operationally, the administration of the "negotiated budget"
in allocation of funds to local districts would have several problems. Equity to all parties would require the extensive development of criteria or standards to be used in making the allocations; considerable amounts of time would be consumed in con-
ferring with local school officials in reviewing and approving

their budgets; and considerable power would be concentrated in the state agency with review and approval responsibility. Lingering questions of equity and favoritism would inevitably be raised.

If standards and criteria for programs and cost differentials were to be developed and utilized in apportioning state funds, the budget would no longer be "negotiated" and the program would resemble the basic computation method outlined in the previous alternative in this section. It would be difficult to develop equitable administrative procedures for this approach, and there would be a tendency to centralize educational budgetary decision-making at the state level rather than to provide opportunity for allocation decisions to be made as close to the point of implementation as possible.

Another option under full state funding would be for the legislature to distribute funds through a series of categorical flat grants. If local districts were not permitted to supplement these grants the "equal access to dollars" test would be met. If the flat grants were sufficiently comprehensive and recognized the full range of educational programs needed in local school districts, the test of "equal access to educational programs" would also be met. The chief problems with this approach would be the absence of comprehensive planning in state school support programs and the possibility that decision making would be swayed by special interest groups.

Full state funding obviously meets the "equal access" test and makes the level of expenditures per pupil in the local school district dependent upon the wealth of the entire state rather than on the concentration of wealth in the district. The concept of "equal access to educational programs" can be incorporated through the use of cost differentials. However, full state funding does not provide an opportunity for districts to make higher levels of local effort if they desire to provide or supplement programs or services beyond the level recognized in the computation of the local district's entitlement. Even though considerable support may be found for permitting local school districts to have the option of a "leeway levy" for enrichment, this practice was questioned in *Robinson* when the court emphasized that this practice results in ". . . control for the wealthy, not for the poor." In other discussion of this issue, the *Robinson* decision further stated that, "Education was too important a function to be left to the mood—and in some cases the low aspirations of the taxpayers of a given district, even whose children attend schools in the district."

Even in view of the previous discussion, the courts might permit a state to "phase into" a complete "equal access" state school support program. A gradual reduction could be scheduled in the level of reliance on local revenue resources with an accompanying increase in reliance on state revenue sources. Under this arrangement local school districts might retain the "leeway" option temporarily, but it would be "phased out" within a relatively short period of time, e.g., three to five years. However, in the absence of direct precedent this is pure conjecture, even though the courts have permitted these practices in the area of racial desegregation.

Equalization with no Leeway

This alternative has been referred to as the minimum foundation program and the Strayer-Haig formula as well as the percentage-equalizing, state aid ratio, or guaranteed assessed valuation program for funding state school support programs. Various computational schemes have been devised, but the end result is the same dollar allocation to local school districts if the unit value of the program remains constant for all districts in the state and if the same measures of local fiscal capacity are used for all districts.

Under this alternative, the basic value of units of educational need would have a fixed dollar value for all districts in the state; however, certain modifying factors could be included to permit dollar adjustments for transportation, cost of living, teacher training and experience, and similar items. The allocation of funds per unit of educational need would be uniform whether the distribution be based on a cost differential approach for various programs or on a standard allotment irrespective of the nature of the educational programs provided in the local school districts. In assuring that the local district has funds to support the computed program, the state provides variable amounts of state funds among the districts of a state in inverse relationship to local wealth per unit of need.

As shown in Figure 2, each local district in the state is required to levy a tax on a specified revenue base or bases; the proceeds of this levy are then "charged against" the value of the local school district's computed program and the state

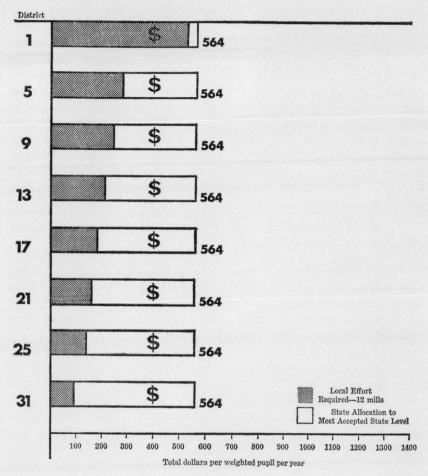

Figure 2
Equalization with no Leeway

then funds the remaining amount. If the yield of the local leeway exceeds the dollar amount of the local school district's
program, the local district retains the amount required to fund
its program and is required to forward the remainder to the
state treasury to be used in meeting the revenue needs of the
less wealthy districts.

In this alternative, locally available revenues would be dependent upon the wealth of the entire state rather than the
wealth of the district; therefore, it would meet the tests established by the courts in the second generation cases. The inclusion of cost differentials in the computation of the fixed

value program would enable the alternative to meet the standards implied in the third generation cases.

Equalization with Minimal Leeway

This alternative could be an adaptation of the "full state support" or "equalization with no leeway" programs. Figure 3 illustrates the effect of an equalization program with a 10 mill rate charged against the local district's state school support program, but the district is permitted to levy an additional two mills to supplement or enrich its educational program.

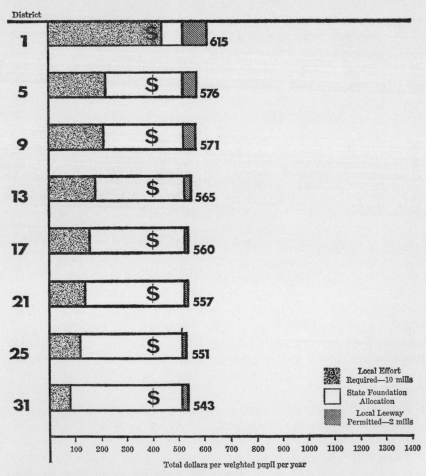

Figure 3
Equalization with Minimal Leeway

In the absence of the courts' having determined the constitutionality of this alternative or having set a standard for leeway, discussion of this alternative might be characterized as pure conjecture. However, *Robinson* did briefly discuss this possibility in reviewing an enacted, but not fully funded state school support program in New Jersey. The court indicated that the level of that program, if it were fully funded for all districts, might meet the test of providing adequate support for a ". . . thorough and efficient system of public schools. . . ." even though the program might result in disparities in access to revenues among school districts within the state.

If the courts should permit states to operate under a "constitutional plan" of orderly progress toward full and complete "equal access," this alternative might be permissible. In the prototype state, the net effect of this alternative is that the richest school district would have access to approximately ten percent more revenue per pupil than the poorest district. From the richest to the poorest district in the prototype state, the range in wealth per pupil is approximately seven to one—a range much less than typically found in states throughout the nation. In other states with greater disparity in per pupil wealth, the inequities of this alternative would be greater.

If the concept of the available revenue being dependent upon the wealth of the state as a whole is accepted and implemented literally, an "equalization with minimal leeway" alternative would not meet the test of the courts. However, the courts have been consistent in stating that their decisions should not be interpreted as mandating uniform expenditures per pupil among districts within the state. Proponents of local control would undoubtedly advocate this alternative, but as *Robinson* has emphasized, ". . . local control is illusory. It is control for wealthy, not for the poor." This alternative provides for a minimal level of disparity and possibly would meet the test of equal access if any variation would be permitted by the courts.

Incentive

Under this alternative local school district officials are permitted to exercise discretionary judgment in determining the level of local effort (beyond a prescribed minimum) to be made in providing school revenues. The total locally available revenues become a function of the effort rather than the wealth of the school district; therefore, the test of equal access to wealth will be met through this alternative. Two critical features characterize the model in the discussion: (1) a fixed level base has been prescribed to assure that all pupils have access to an "adequate" educational program irrespective of their district of residence; and (2) the state's proportional contribution is the same for the last dollar of available revenue as it is for the first dollar.

Various titles have been given to this program from the time it was first proposed by Updegraff[36] until its recent advocacy by Coons *et al.*[37] under the title of "district power equalizing." In computing the relative state and local share, the amount of the local district's state allocation is determined by multiplying the local revenue which a district raises by that district's state aid ratio. As shown in Figure 4 the combination of the state and local funds provides the revenues to support the local district educational program.

The amount of available revenue is dependent upon the "effort" of the district rather than its wealth. As with the previous alternative, this approach meets the court test of equal access to wealth among districts within a state, but does make the quantity of funds dependent upon the mood and aspirations of the taxpayers—thereby creating a disequalized access to educational programs among the state's districts. However, this choice does provide assurance that pupils will be provided with equal access to a predetermined minimal level of revenues to support educational programs.

An adaptation of this alternative would be for local district officials to have the opportunity to exercise full discretionary judgment in determining their level of local effort and in turn the total amount of available revenues would be a function of the effort of the district rather than its wealth. This alternative would meet the test of the courts in the area of equal access to wealth, but would be suspect on other grounds in that the amount of funds available to support education in the school district would be left to the mood and aspirations of the taxpayers, thereby opening the possibility of pupils' having unequal access to educational programs among school districts within a state. This latter possibility is of even greater concern when one recognizes that local school officials could set their level of effort, and thereby their level of available revenue, at whatever level they deemed appropriate. A disequalized access to both revenues and educational program would seem to be an

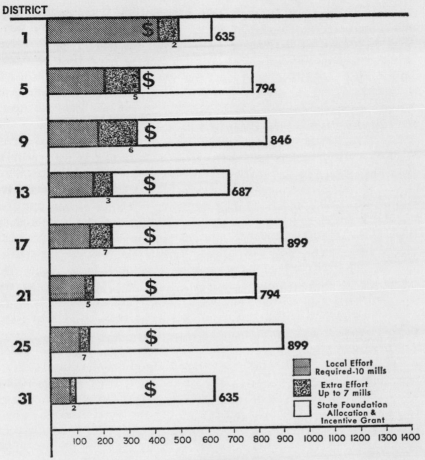

DISTRICT

Total dollars per weighted pupil per year

Figure 4
Incentive

inevitable outgrowth of leaving this range of discretion to local school officials; therefore, this adaptation of the incentive model in all likelihood would not stand the test of the courts.

The "incentive plan" has certain psychological and political attractions because of the traditional methods of financing local schools. Those districts which are presently spending more would be permitted to retain their favored position; of course, other districts could also achieve the same level of expenditures if they made the same levels of effort—in terms of tax rates on the wealth measures to which the local districts have access.

Historical patterns of local school district expenditures suggest certain basic questions concerning the incentive program. Considerable research indicates that high expenditure districts are characterized by patrons with higher than average income and level of education. In other districts with children who should be provided with high cost programs because of special physiological or psychological problems or special occupational goals, levels of per pupil expenditures have often been low. These are the types of situations to which *Robinson* was referring when the statement was made that expenditure levels for education would be dependent upon the "mood or aspirations" of the community rather than educational needs of the children.

Many factors influence the "mood" of the local school district. If high percentages of children attend non-public schools, blocks of citizens may not desire to provide needed resources for the public schools. This is especially evident in parts of the south where segregated academies have been opened to serve the children of those in the local power structure. The end result has been that the public schools have been left with those pupils needing high cost programs, but decision makers have not provided the funds needed to support the programs.

If local property wealth is concentrated in the hands of a few, these property holders may seek to serve their own self-interest by keeping school expenditures low, thereby depriving the pupils in their district of "equal access to educational programs" even though the courts requirement of "equal access to dollars" may be fulfilled.

Free operation of the "incentive program" will be further hampered in local districts which are fiscally dependent upon city councils, city commissions or similar local governmental bodies. These groups have other interests which compete for local revenues, and education may not receive top priority even though there may be great "need."

As presently proposed the incentive programs also rely heavily upon the local property tax as the measure of "effort" which will determine the total revenues available to the district from local and state sources. The end result is that education will continue to rely upon a regressive tax system in determining the total amount of available revenues. In urban areas the combination of a municipal over-burden resulting from a demand for broad governmental services in an educational program based on "the more effort you make, the more you receive from the state", does not offer much promise of tax relief for local governmental units which already consider themselves taxed to the confiscatory level.

From the standpoint of the state assuming its responsibility to insure equal educational opportunity for all children and the general interest that citizens and government have in providing an adequate level of education for all students, the decision making process of the "incentive" program has several short comings. Local school officials can determine their levels of expenditure with no built-in mechanism for assuring that an adequate educational program is being provided for pupils or that desired levels of efficiency are being maintained in the operation of local schools. Many local school districts do not have sufficient enrollments to provide a comprehensive program without excessive cost, and the "incentive" program would permit them to continue operation at a time when most states need to make significant strides in school district reorganization to gain greater efficiency in providing educational programs and services and in expending public funds.

With the present rate of mobility which characterizes the American population, a state cannot afford the luxury of permitting each local school district to "do its own thing." Some guarantees must be provided that attention is given to the programmatic needs of the pupils in local school districts. Irrespective of their district of residence, pupils should have access to special education, vocational education and compensatory education programs if those programs are appropriate in terms of the student's current physiological problems or occupational goals.

If a state accepts and enacts a pure "incentive" or district power equalizing program, it not only is saying "the more effort you make, the more revenues you receive", but also is abdicating its responsibility to provide for equal educational opportunity in any aspect other than equal access to wealth among districts within a state.

Immediate movement from existing school expenditure patterns to a fixed level program for an entire state would be somewhat disruptive and distasteful but equal access to educational programs should be one of the primary goals. As an alternative, consideration might be given to determining the per pupil expenditure level which would be needed to support an "adequate" educational program in all districts, and then permit each local district to "power equalize" through additional effort.

Summary

Of the third generation cases, only *Robinson* was concerned with the issues of fiscal neutrality as well as educational needs. If the earlier precedent in the federal courts concerning educational need should be reversed, this additional dimension will be added to the current litigation issues. As the school finance issues are subjected to further litigation, most observers will be quite interested in the degree to which the courts become involved in providing either dicta or direct mandates for state legislatures. On other occasions the courts have contended that the members of the legislature necessarily enjoy a familiarity with local conditions which the court cannot have, and have presumed statutes to be constitutional unless the one attacking the legislative arrangement could demonstrate that a classification was hostile or oppressive against particular persons or classes.[38] Under this type of interpretation the state school finance program would be subjected to a test of rationality or reasonableness rather than strict scrutiny.

The previously discussed alternatives can be grouped into two broad categories—fixed level and variable level programs. Under the former, each district has access to the same quantity of dollars per unit of educational need. Adjustments may be made for cost of living, sparsity, level of training and experience of teachers or educational programs provided by the local school district; but each district will have access to the same amount of dollars. Under the variable level program each district determines through its decision making process the revenues which will be provided for the local educational program. Rather than local wealth being the primary determinent, the "effort" being made by the district is the critical factor.

The "full state support" and "equalization with no leeway" alternatives are the only two which meet the full set of requirements set forth by the courts. The "incentive" program might be permissible, but the problem of educational expenditures in a district being left to the mood and aspirations of the taxpayers would obviously result in some degree of unequal access to educational programs for pupils in districts which chose to make a minimum level of local effort. In absence of more precise guidelines from the courts, the exact status of the incentive program remains undetermined, for it meets the criterion of "equal access to wealth" but fails to guarantee "equal access to educational programs."

The judicial fate of "equalization with minimal leeway" is also somewhat uncertain because of the absence of precise guidelines from the courts. A literal reading of the court decisions would suggest that this alternative would not meet the test of the courts, but some minimal disparity in access to wealth might be permitted.

Under any of the alternatives discussed above, the interest of the third generation cases in the varying "educational need" among districts in a state could be ignored, thereby depriving certain groups of pupils of the ultimate form of "equal protection." The concept that varying educational programs are required to meet the educational needs of different groups of pupils appears to have been accepted, but previously the question of judicially manageable standards has been a barrier which discouraged the courts from entering into this area. The *Robinson* decision, recent research by the National Educational Finance Project, and other studies made in particular states support the basic concept and provide data which indicate that these programs do have different levels of costs and that these pupils are not uniformly distributed among school districts within a state. With this recent research, it is possible that the precedent of *McInnis* and *Burruss* might be reversed by further litigation.

The question of local determination of the level of effort to be made in support of education remains essentially unresolved, for the recent decisions have uniformly stated that their interpretation of equal protection should not be extended to require equal levels of educational expenditure for all pupils in a given state.

If a subsequent court action should uphold *Robinson* by holding that "Education is too important a function to leave it also to the mood—in some cases the low aspirations—of the taxpayers of a given district. . . ." the result will be a form of fixed level program for all districts in the state. Revenues may be raised at the state level or be a combination of local and state and federal funds, but the wealth base will be that of the state as a whole. The key factor in the further extension of the "equal protection" will be to provide for equal access to educational programs so that the level of expenditures and the range of educational opportunities will be substantially equal for all pupils irrespective of their school district or residence and the incidence of wealth in that district.

FOOTNOTES

1. See: *Tinker v. Des Moines School District,* 393 U.S. 503 (1969); *School District of Abington Township v. Schempp,* 374 U.S. 203 (1963) and *Brown v. Board of Education of Topeka,* 347 U.S. 483 (1954). In the matter of Gault, 87 S. Ct. 1428 (1967); *Madera v. Board of Education of the City of New York,* 386 F. 2d 778 (1968).
2. *Sawyer v. Gilmore,* 109 Me. 169, 83 A 673 (1912).
3. *Bell's Gap Railroad Co. v. Pennsylvania,* 134 U.S. 232 (1890).
4. *Dean v. Coddington,* 81 S.D. 140, 131 N.W. 2d 700 (1964).
5. *Ibid.*
6. *Miller v. Nunnelley,* 468 S.W. 2d 298 (Ky. 1971).
7. *Hess v. Mullaney,* 15 Alaska 40, 213 F. 2d 635 (U.S.C.A. 9th Cir. 1954), Cert. Denied *Hess v. Dewey,* 348 U.S. 836, 75 S. Ct. 50 (1954).
8. See: *Cumberland Coal Co. v. Board of Revision of Tax Assessments of Green County,* 284 U.S. 23, 52 S. Ct. 48 (1931).
9. See: *Gen. Amer. Tank Car Corp. v. Day,* 270 U.S. 367, 46 S. Ct. 234 (1926); *Carmichael v. Southern Coal Co.,* 301 U.S. 495, 57 S. Ct. 868 (1937).
10. 79 C.J.S. § 411.
11. *Hess v. Mullaney, supra.*
12. *Brown v. Board of Education,* 347 U.S. 483 (1954).
13. *Tinker v. Des Moines School District,* 393 U.S. 503 (1969); *Palmer v. Thompson,* 39 U.S. L. Week 4759 (1971); *Griffin v. County School Board of Prince Edward County,* 84 S. Ct. 1226 (1964).
14. "Is Denial of Equal Educational Opportunity Constitutional?" *Administrator's Notebook,* No. 6. XIII (University of Chicago, Feb. 1965). See also: Arthur E. Wise, *Rich Schools Poor Schools* (Chicago: The University of Chicago Press, 1968).
15. *Griffin v. Illinois,* 351 U.S. 12 (1956).
16. *Baker v. Carr,* 369 U.S. 186 (1962); *Gray v. Sanders,* 372 U.S. 368 (1963).
17. Serrano v. Priest, 5 Cal. 3d 584, 487 P. 2d 1241 (1971).
18. *Brown v. Board of Education, supra.*
19. *Griffin v. Illinois,* 351 U.S. 12, 76 S. Ct. 585 (1956); *Williams v. Illinois,* 399 U.S. 235, 90 S. Ct. 2018 (1970); *Douglas v. California,* 372 U.S. 353, 83 S. Ct. 814 (1963).
20. *Harper v. Virginia State Board of Elections,* 383 U.S. 663, 86 S. Ct. 1079 (1966); *Cipriano v. City of Houma,* 395 U.S. 701, 89 S. Ct. 1897 (1969); *Kramer v. Union School District,* 395 U.S. 621, 89 S. Ct. 1886 (1969).
21. *Harper v. Virginia State Board of Elections, supra.*
22. *Van Dusartz v. Hatfield,* 334 F. Supp. 870 (D. Minn. 1971).
23. Also raised issue of discrimination under Civil Rights Act, 42 U.S.C. §1983.
24. *Rodriguez v. San Antonio Independent School District,* 337 F. Supp. 280 (W.D. Texas, 1971). See also: *Hollins v. Shofstall,* No. C-253 652, Superior Court of the State of Arizona, County of Maricopa (1972).
25. R.L. Johns, Kern Alexander, Forbis Jordan, *Planning to Finance Education,* 3 National Educational Finance Project, (Gainesville, Fla: 1971).
26. 293 F. Supp. 327 (N.D. Ill., E.D., Nov. 15, 1968); Affirmed mem. 89 S. Ct. 1197 (March 24, 1969).
27. 89 S. Ct. 1197 (March 24, 1969).

28. See: *Spano v. Board of Ed. of Lakeland Cent. Sch. Dist.*, 68 Misc. 2d 804, 328 N.Y.S. 2d 229 (1972).

29. *Dominion Hotel v. Arizona*, 249 U.S. 265, 39 S. Ct. 273 (1919).

30 *Burruss v. Wilkerson*, 310 F. Supp. 572 (May 23, 1969) affirmed mem., 397 U.S. 44, 90 S. Ct. 812 (1970).

31. *Burruss v. Wilkerson, supra.*

32. *Robinson v. Cahill*, Superior Court of New Jersey Law Division - Hudson County Docket No. L-18704-69.

33. *The Bateman Report*, State Aid to School Districts Study Commission, N.J., December 19, 1968, p. 48.

34. *Report of New York State Commission on the Quality, Cost and Financing of Elementary and Secondary Education*, The State Department of Education, (Albany, New York) 1972.

35. *Alternative Programs for Financing Education*, 5 National Educational Project, (Gainesville, Florida: 1971).

36. Harland Updegraff, *Rural School Survey of New York State: Financial Support* (Ithaca, N.Y.: by the author, 1922).

37. John E. Coons, *et al. Private Wealth and Public Education* (Cambridge, Mass.: The Belknap Press of Harvard University Press, 1970).

38. *Hess v. Mullaney*, 15 Alaska 40, 213 F. 2d 635 (U.S.C.A. 9th Cir. 1954), Cert. Denied *Hess v. Dewey*, 348 U.S. 836, 75 S. Ct. 50 (1954).

CHAPTER 2

Full State Funding: An Analysis and Critique

RICHARD A. ROSSMILLER

The question of how schools should be financed has become one of the critical issues of our time. Although specialists in educational finance have long been aware of the developing crisis, recent events have thrust the problems of educational finance into the forefront of contemporary legal, economic and political debate. The constantly rising cost of educating America's school age population; the increasing "crunch" as an over worked local property tax base has been burdened with the task of providing even more revenue; and the growing legal and ethical concern for providing equal educational opportunities for all children without regard for their race, their place of residence, or the social station of their parents, all have contributed to growing dissatisfaction with current methods of financing public schools.

One proposed solution to the problem of financing schools which has attracted growing interest is that of full state funding of education. Proponents of this approach would have the state provide from state revenue sources all or nearly all of the money required to finance public elementary and secondary schools. Although Morrison advanced a similar proposition in 1930, it is only in recent years that the idea of complete state

The author is Professor and Chairman of the Department of Educational Administration at the University of Wisconsin-Madison.

support of education has attracted serious attention.[1] During the late 1960's both James B. Conant and the late James Allen suggested that full state funding of education be given serious attention.[2] In 1969, the Advisory Commission on Intergovernmental Relations recommended that the states assume major responsibility for financing education.[3] More recently, the President's Commission on School Finance strongly urged that the states assume major responsibility for financing public elementary and secondary schools.[4]

Considerable confusion exists as to the meaning of the term "full state funding." In this paper, full state funding is defined as any arrangement in which the state provides all, or nearly all, of the money needed to finance public elementary and secondary schools. This definition does not preclude modest optional local school taxes, but revenue from such taxes could provide only a very small percentage of the total state and local revenue available for support of schools.

During the past few years three major trends have converged to place increasing pressure on current methods of financing public elementary and secondary schools. The overall impact of these trends has been to generate increasing dissatisfaction with current methods of financing education, as well as stimulating a search for other alternatives which are better suited to meet contemporary needs.

Expenditures for public elementary and secondary schools have increased more than 2½ fold during the 1960's. Total expenditures increased from 15.6 billion dollars to 42.4 billion dollars during the decade and expenditure per pupil increased from $393 to $839.[5] One important reason for this growth in expenditures was inflation, which has eaten away the purchasing power of the educational dollar to the point where during the 1971-72 school year an expenditure of nearly $185 was required to purchase the equivalent of $100 worth of 1957-59 educational services.[6] Growth in school enrollments also contributed to the rising level of expenditures. Enrollment increased by more than 25 percent between the fall of 1960 and the fall of 1970.[7] The percentage of children and young adults attending school also increased so that by 1970, nearly 90 percent of all five and six year olds and close to 48 percent of all 18 and 19 year olds were enrolled in school.[8] Although population growth apparently has stabilized, some growth in school enrollments will continue as educational programs are extended to meet the needs of children who have not been served adequately in the past. For example, programs of early childhood education are likely to expand substantially over the next decade. Special educational programs for physically, mentally, and emotionally handicapped pupils also are likely to be expanded, as are educational programs tailored specifically for socially and/or economically disadvantaged pupils. Career education is attracting a great deal of attention and additional efforts in job-related educational programs, especially at the postsecondary level, can be expected.

Revenue obtained from taxes levied by local school districts has always been the major source of funds for education in the United States. Revenue from local governmental sources, most of it provided by local property taxes, still provides about 52 percent of all revenue for public elementary and secondary schools. The rapidly growing revenue needs of the schools during the past decade placed increasing pressure on the property tax base. The result was increasing tax friction as taxpayers became more and more reluctant to approve additional school tax levies. While the percentage of total revenue obtained from local school taxes varies greatly among the states, only 14 states provided more than 50 percent of the revenue for their public school operation in 1970-71.[9] Heavy reliance on the property tax as a source of revenue for education has led to a taxpayer rebellion in many states. Bond issues have been defeated, school taxes have been withheld or placed in escrow, and schools in several states have been forced to close when their funds ran out and no additional tax levy had been approved. Since the property tax is the only major tax that can be used successfully by most local units of government, growing dissatisfaction with the property tax has produced increasing pressure for a higher level of state support for education.

A concern for equality of educational opportunity has always characterized American education. This concern finds expression today in the thrust to improve educational opportunities for the handicapped and the disadvantaged, as well as in the concern of the courts for equality of educational opportunity. A long series of cases contesting the constitutionality of racially segregated schools culminated in the decision by the U.S. Supreme Court in 1954 that racially segregated schools are inherently unequal and violate rights guaranteed by the Fourteenth Amendment. More recently, state provisions for financing education have been the subject of litigation and in many states the constitutionality of the state's method of financing education is being contested. Thus, the courts are now being called upon to determine whether or not existing state support systems violate state and/or federal constitutional guarantees. Decisions by courts in California, Minnesota, Texas, New Jersey, Wyoming, and Arizona which have declared that the level of educational spending may be a function only of the wealth of the entire state, not the wealth of the school district in which a pupil happens to reside, have served to focus attention on the feasibility and desirability of full state funding as an alternative financing arrangement.

PROBLEMS AND ISSUES IN FULL STATE FUNDING

A number of issues inevitably will arise in any state where the alternative of full state funding is considered seriously. Some of these issues are philosophical in nature; others involve operational procedures. The following discussion will identify some of the issues that are most likely to arise in any debate on this subject.

Political Feasibility

Decisions with regard to financing education must be accomplished through our democratic political process. This process will, of course, bring to bear upon legislators and the executive all of the pressures which can be exerted by special interest groups. These groups will view any proposed legislation in terms of the possible impact it will have upon their own interests. Any proposal for full state funding must survive this political gauntlet before it can be enacted into law.

It appears that full state funding is more likely to be adopted in states which currently supply a large percentage of the revenue for public schools. The prevailing system of school district organization also will influence the decision. States with a large number of relatively small school districts are likely to encounter greater opposition to the notion of full state funding because of its perceived threat to local control. This threat, whether real or imagined, will create powerful opposition to full state funding by special interest groups who believe their interests are threatened.

The extent to which movement toward full state funding

can be accomplished within a state's existing tax structure will be another important consideration. Few legislators will be willing to support full state funding if this would require substantial increases in existing tax levies or the imposition of new taxes. However, trade-offs are possible. For example, a new or expanded income tax might be more acceptable if, at the same time, property tax rates could be reduced substantially. The political feasibility of full state funding will vary from state to state and will depend upon a number of factors such as the existing tax structure of the state, the state's pattern of school district organization, and the support or opposition of special interest groups.

The Local Role

The concept of local control of education is deeply rooted in the American educational tradition and is one of the unique features of American education. The ideology of local control is especially deep rooted in those states which followed the early New England pattern of educational organization. Many persons argue that if local control of education is to be maintained, it is necessary that the basic education unit, i.e., the local school district, provide a major share of the revenue for support of education. This emphasis on local financial support, together with highly decentralized administrative arrangements, inevitably results in wide variations in wealth among the school districts of a state. Some districts are able to raise large amounts of revenue with a modest tax rate while other districts can raise very little revenue even if they levy a tax rate which is virtually confiscatory. Unless the state utilizes appropriate measures to equalize the amount of revenue which is produced, a given tax rate will yield varying amounts of revenue in each school district which, according to recent court decisions, is unconstitutional.

Full state funding does not necessarily rule out all revenue from local school taxes, but the revenue obtained from such taxes could provide only a very small percentage of the total school revenue. Thus, fear has been expressed that adoption of full state funding would weaken, if not destroy, local control of education. It is argued that unless a substantial share of school revenue is obtained from taxes levied by local school districts, local control of education inevitably will be lost.

It may be argued, on the other hand, that true local control of education cannot exist as long as there exist wide disparities in the amount of revenue available per pupil among the state's school districts. The range of decisions available to local boards of education and administrators is directly related to the resources available to them. If a school district has a very limited property tax base, its range of alternatives for educational programming is much more restricted than is the range of alternatives available to a district where the tax base is very large. Using this argument, it has been asserted that full state funding will, in fact, strengthen local control of education by giving local educational decision makers access to the resources needed to provide adequate educational programs for all children.

The Federal Role

Although federal financial support for education dates from the original land grants in the 1780's, it is only during the past decade that substantial amounts of federal funds have been made available to support elementary and secondary schools. Even now, the federal government provides only about 7 percent of all revenue for elementary and secondary schools and most of this is in the form of categorical aids for specific purposes. Unfortunately, these categorical aids tend to disrupt state equalization efforts. Unless federal aid distributions are carefully orchestrated with state aid programs, the objectives of the state aid program may be frustrated or circumvented by federal categorical aids. Federal categorical aids are, in many respects, incompatible with the objectives claimed for full state funding of elementary and secondary schools.

General federal aids or revenues shared with the states by the federal government could easily be accommodated in a full state funding program. Such revenue could be dealt with as if it were state revenue and distributed in accordance with the criteria and procedures developed by the state. In fact, relatively small amounts of federal revenue might be instrumental in persuading a state to move in the direction of full state funding. In most states abandonment of the property tax for support of education is out of the question, for it would require too great an increase in other taxes to be politically feasible, as well as resulting in substantial windfall gains to current owners of property. Federal revenue could be used to replace local revenue for school support and thus make it possible for the states to reduce their reliance on revenue from property taxes levied by local school districts. General federal aid also might be employed to encourage the states to develop school support programs which will meet the test enunciated in the Serrano decision, i.e., school support programs in which the amount of revenue per pupil is a function of the wealth of the entire state, not the wealth of the local school district.

Just as it is argued that local support is essential to local control of education, so is it argued that greater reliance on federal support would lead inevitably to federal control of education. Either general federal aid or a program of sharing federal revenues with the states would be much less likely to result in federal control than would federal categorical aids. Federal categorical aids for specific purposes are much more likely to distort local and state educational decisions than are federal general aids. Federal programs which require matching expenditures by state or local governments also are likely to distort local and state decisions. Even more important, general federal aid or revenue sharing is much more likely to produce equality of educational opportunity than will federal categorical or matching aids.

Delivery Systems

State educational systems exist for the primary purpose of delivering educational services to students. The states have created local school districts and have granted them authority to levy taxes. Delegation of taxing authority to small units of government almost inevitably produces variations in tax bases and, as a general rule, the smaller the taxing units the wider the variations in size of tax base which will exist. This results in substantial differences in the ability of local school districts to raise revenue and produces a situation in which the revenue available in a local school district is a function of the wealth of that district rather than the wealth of the entire state.

In many states school district reorganization could reduce greatly the range between the wealth of the poorest and richest school districts. In fact, reorganizing school districts so that each district would have the same amount of property tax base per pupil would be one way of meeting the test applied in the *Serrano* case.

The existing pattern of school district organization in many states represents far from the most efficient way of delivering educational services. Many school districts are too small to achieve economies of scale and, from an equity standpoint, can provide educational programs of only marginal quality—and these at a very high cost per pupil. It is difficult to see how a state could long permit the continued existence of inefficient delivery systems under a program of full state funding. A substantial amount of reorganization to eliminate small, inefficient school districts could be expected. Alternative arrangements which would more efficiently provide educational services for certain types of pupils might also be developed. In sparsely populated areas, for example, residential schools for deaf or blind students may be the most efficient way to deliver the needed educational services. In other situations intermediate agencies or consortiums of local school districts may represent the most efficient way to guarantee delivery of adequate educational services for all children.

Adoption of full state funding is likely to result in substantial changes in a state's pattern of school district organization as alternative delivery systems are developed. However, with full state funding there may be less resistance to school district reorganization, since the economic advantages presently enjoyed by districts that are enclaves of high value property would no longer exist.

Program Determination

A number of the issues which will arise in any serious consideration of full state funding are program-related. They involve such questions as the nature of the program to be supported, the level at which programs will be supported, the extent to which differences in the cost of educational programs will be recognized, and the way in which expenditures for education will be controlled.

Program Definition

One critical problem which will arise under full state funding is that of the defining the program which is to be funded by the state. Since the educational programs offered by school districts within a state tend to vary widely—partly as a result of differences in fiscal capacity and partly because of local preferences—

simply funding school districts at their present operating level will not produce equality of educational opportunity. Thus, the question becomes, "What components are to be included in the educational program funded by the state?"

One possible approach is to allocate a certain amount of money per pupil to be expended at the discretion of the local operating unit. Using this approach, one would simply multiply the number of pupils by the allocation per pupil to obtain the total amount of revenue to which a district is entitled. At least two problems inhere in this approach. First, there is the matter of determining the amount per pupil to be allocated. Should the amount per pupil be equivalent to that currently available in the highest expenditure district in the state, or at the expenditure level of some other district—perhaps the expenditure per pupil made by the district at 65th percentile? Second, legislators might be reluctant to accept this approach, for it gives them no control over the specific programs to be funded, leaving this decision at the local level.

A second alternative would be to define carefully the components of the educational program which would be eligible for funding by the state. The approximate cost of such program components could then be identified and aggregated to determine each district's allocation. This approach would place maximum control over educational programs in the hands of the legislature. A number of sticky questions would remain, however. For example, how would local preferences be honored? If, for example, a district wished to offer four foreign languages rather than three, would this be permitted and under what circumstances? Also, program costs vary among school districts for the same educational program and such variations would need to be considered if program equality is to be attained. Arguments concerning the components which would be included in the state-funded program could be expected. Some persons would feel strongly that program components such as interscholastic athletics and uniforms for the marching band are "frills" and should not be eligible for state funding. Others would argue strongly that interscholastic athletics and music are integral components of a well rounded educational program and must be funded by the state.

Level of Support

The matter of program definition leads directly to the question of whether full state funding would result in a "leveling up" or "leveling down" of expenditure for education. The answer to this question will depend, in part, on how the program is defined. It will also depend upon the range in expenditure per district which the courts ultimately determine to be constitutionally permissible, and upon the philosophy which prevails in a given state. Leveling up of expenditures would occur if a state placed emphasis upon increasing expenditures in low expenditure districts to a point where they more nearly approximate the current level of spending in high expenditure districts. Leveling down would occur if the state emphasized reducing the current expenditure level in high expenditure districts, thus bringing them closer to the state average. The strategy which would be most appealing to a state legislature would undoubtedly depend to a large extent on the amount of additional state revenue which would be required. Maintaining the current state average expenditure level would require no increase in revenue, although a redistribution of the revenue among the school districts of the state would be required. A reduction in state average expenditure would, of course, reduce the total revenue required and any increase in state average expenditure would increase revenue requirements.

It must be recognized that a state average is just that; many districts are above and many are below the average. Thus, any attempt to impose a program in which all districts would be permitted to spend at the state average would attract bitter opposition from at least one-half the school districts in the state— those currently spending above the state average. High expenditure districts can be expected to oppose any attempt to reduce the quality of their schools. Low expenditure districts can be expected to support an increase in their present expenditure level. Thus, it seems likely that state average expenditure per pupil would increase under a full state funding program, although the range of expenditure between the highest and lowest spending district would narrow substantially as the program is phased in.

Variations in Program Costs

The same number of dollars will not purchase an equal amount of educational services in every school district. The "educational cost of living" varies from one school district to another. Thus, unless some means of providing for differences in the purchasing power of an educational dollar among the state's school district is developed, equality of treatment will not be attained.

An even more serious problem, however, is the difference in the cost of educational programs for various types of pupils. Research conducted by the National Education Finance Project has demonstrated that the educational programs needed by some pupils are much more expensive than the programs needed by others. Programs for mentally handicapped pupils are, on the average, about 1.9 times more costly than programs for children in regular classrooms; programs for physically handicapped pupils are about 3.5 times as expensive as programs for normal children; and programs of compensatory education are nearly twice as costly as programs for normal children in regular classes. These cost differentials would pose no serious problem if pupils who require high cost programs were distributed equally among all of the state's school districts, but they are not! Some school districts have relatively high concentrations of pupils who require costly special programs; other school districts have a very low percentage of such pupils. Although large cities tend to have a higher-than-average percentage of pupils who need costly special educational programs, such programs are not confined to large cities. High concentrations of pupils who require special programs also have been found in rural districts and in suburban districts. Unless the additional cost involved in providing adequate educational programs for pupils with special needs is recognized in a full state funding program, equalization of educational opportunity will not be achieved.

Expenditure Controls

During the past decade state legislators have been increasingly unwilling to allow all expenditure decisions to remain in the hands of local school boards. In a number of states the state support program has been modified to include "cost control" features. Cost control has been accomplished by placing a lid on local school tax rates, by refusing to provide state support for any expenditures which exceed the statewide average, and by eliminating "open-ended" programs where the state's financial obligation is determined by the decisions of local spending units.

Attempts by state legislators to control expenditures of local school districts are not surprising in view of the very rapid increase in expenditures for education during the past ten years.

Many legislators feel that local school boards and administrators have not been fiscally responsible; that they have too easily acceded to the demands of teacher organizations for reduction in class size and increases in salary. One feature of full state funding which may appeal to legislators is the opportunity to control directly the level of spending for education in the school districts of the state.

Compensation of Personnel

The advent of organized bargaining activities in education has created a new set of pressures which are reflected in school expenditure levels. Collective action by teachers, together with the teacher shortages which prevailed during the 1960's, resulted in substantial increases in the salaries paid certificated personnel. Salary gains by noncertificated personnel employed by school districts also have been impressive. Since 75 percent or more of expenditures for current operation go to pay the salaries of teachers and other personnel, the effect on school operating costs has been significant.

Implementation of full state funding could easily lead to adoption of statewide salary schedules for teachers. Many legislators fear that any additional money appropriated for education will quickly find its way into the pay checks of teachers without regard for their individual merit. Thus, state policy makers might be reluctant to adopt a full state funding unless they could be guaranteed some control over teacher salary schedules.

State teacher organizations have generally followed a "divide and conquer" strategy in their negotiations with local boards of education. The state teacher organization works closely with its local affiliates in the bargaining process. It is common practice for the state organization to select a few key school districts and try to negotiate substantial increases in wages and fringe benefits for teachers in these districts. If breakthroughs can be achieved in these districts, the teacher organization has gained leverage which can then be applied in bargaining with other districts. Boards of education, on the other hand, have tended to go it alone rather than attempting to present a united front. Thus, a local board of education often can be "whipsawed" into acceding to the demands made by the teacher organization.

If a statewide salary schedule is adopted, bargaining on teacher salaries and fringe benefits would shift to the state level (although working conditions might still be bargained locally). Bargaining at the state level would involve state teacher organizations, the state legislature, and the governor. A basic state salary schedule likely would be established with some provision for slight departures from the schedule to adjust for variations in cost of living, attractiveness of working conditions, and similar factors. Although it may appear at first glance that teacher organizations would be somewhat disadvantaged in bargaining at the state level, this would not necessarily be the case. A statewide work stoppage or teacher strike represents a powerful threat, particularly if the threat is exercised judiciously. It is conceivable that it would be as difficult for policy makers at the state level to hold the line on teacher salaries as it has been for policy makers at the local level to do so.

Non-current Expenditures

Expenditures by local school districts for capital outlay and debt service are classified as non-current expenditures, since they represent payments for durable capital goods which will continue in use over a period of several years. Current provisions for state support of expenditures for capital outlay and debt service vary widely. In some states the local school district is expected to finance such expenditures entirely from its own resources; in others, the state has developed extensive provisions for helping local districts finance such expenditures.

It is difficult to deny that the quality of buildings and equipment available to support a child's education will affect the quality of his educational opportunity. It is evident that children who must attend school in overcrowded, poorly ventilated, improperly lighted or inadequately equipped classrooms do not enjoy the same quality of educational opportunity as is enjoyed by children who attend school in well designed, properly equipped facilities.

Expenditures for capital outlay will require special consideration in any program of full state funding. Capital outlay requirements are likely to vary widely from year to year in school districts, particularly small school districts. For a state, however, capital outlay requirements are much more regular and predictable than they are for a single school district. A more difficult problem arises from the fact that some school districts will have an extensive backlog of capital outlay needs while others have met such needs when they arose. A full state funding program certainly should not penalize districts which have met their capital outlay needs and reward districts which have failed to provide adequate buildings and equipment.

Paying for capital outlay expenditures from local tax sources creates the same problems that arise when expenditures for current operations are financed from local taxes. Some districts have a much larger tax base than others, thus enabling them to provide fine buildings and equipment while maintaining relatively low tax rates. In districts where the tax base is small, on the other hand, the tax burden required to support expenditures for current operation may be so heavy that taxpayers are not willing to accept the additional burden which would be required to provide needed buildings or equipment. The situation is further aggravated by the fact that districts where the tax base is small and the tax rate is high generally receive a lower credit rating and must pay higher interest rates on any money they borrow. Such districts are not only hard pressed to afford the necessary capital outlay expenditures, but they must pay more for them.

The problem of how to handle existing debt is closely related to the problem of financing capital outlay. Most school districts finance major capital outlay expenditures by issuing bonds. Revenue from local property taxes often is pledged to guarantee that the principal and interest on these bonds will be paid as it comes due. If authority to levy local school taxes is reduced or eliminated through adoption of full state funding, it will be necessary for the state to protect bondholders by guaranteeing that the existing obligations of local school districts will be honored. Failure to do this would be fatal, for bondholders are protected by a constitutional guarantee that the obligations entailed in their contract with the school district will not be impaired. If a full state funding program does not provide support for capital outlay and debt service, then some type of local tax levy will still be required.

Transportation

Many methods of providing state support for transportation are now found among the 50 states. These range from flat grants per pupil transported at one extreme to complete state operation of the pupil transportation system at the other extreme. Expenditure for transportation is often a major component of the school district budget in sparsely populated districts where a complicated transportation network is needed to bring pupils to school. On the other hand, in school districts where public transportation systems are well developed the school system typically provides transportation only for special categories of pupils such as the mentally retarded or the physically handicapped.

The pupil transportation area involves problems of program definition. Pupil transportation could be accommodated within the general state financing plan by applying weightings which would reflect the variations in cost involved in transporting pupils. In fact, variable transportation grants designed to reflect differing transportation costs are now employed in some states. It also would be possible to treat pupil transportation as a separate component of the total educational program. This might permit the state to maintain greater flexibility in dealing with pupil transportation needs.

The possibility that pupil transportation could most efficiently be provided through a state-operated system, or through systems operated by agencies, is worthy of investigation. In pupil transportation, maximum operating efficiency consistent with pupil safety is the primary goal. Thus, it is appropriate to apply operations research techniques and procedures to identify the most efficient possible system for providing pupil transportation.

Accountability

The concept of accountability has taken on new meaning for educators in recent years. Educators have for many years been held accountable, but in the sense of insuring that school funds were not lost or stolen. In recent years, however, the definition of accountability has been expanded to include providing evidence that expenditures for education are achieving the desired objectives.

The "new" concept of accountability in education is closely linked to the economic concept of productivity, i.e., maximizing the output obtained from a given level of input. Full state funding would offer greater opportunity for state policymakers to require, as a condition of increased appropriations for education, evidence that previous expenditures were effective in achieving the desired results. Thus, full state funding might enable state policymakers to exercise considerable control over the nature of local educational programs.

If demands for accountability are to be met, state education agencies and local school districts will need to develop assessment procedures, build information systems, and apply analytical techniques which will yield the required data. Most local school districts do not have the resources and personnel needed to do this job. Consequently, the state education agency may need to assume much greater responsibility in the area of assessment and evaluation of educational programs.

SOME FULL STATE FUNDING MODELS

Although the permutations of full state funding models are virtually unlimited, there are at least three general approaches which may be taken. In this section we shall examine three general models, discuss how they might operate in practice, and identify some of their strengths and weaknesses. The three models are as follows:

1. Complete state funding of education with no provision for local school tax levies.
2. Provision by the state of a basic flat grant per pupil with local districts permitted to supplement the basic state grant by a small local tax levy.
3. Provision by the state of a basic flat grant per pupil with each local district permitted to supplement this by a local tax levy. In this model, however, the state will compensate for deficiencies in a local district's tax base by supplementing local tax revenue with additional state aid so that each district that levies a given tax rate is assured of receiving the same amount of revenue per pupil.

The National Educational Finance Project (NEFP) developed a prototype state to illustrate the operation of various state support models. The Project's prototype state contains 32 school districts which each operate K-12 educational programs and enroll at least 1800 pupils. The basic data developed by the NEFP staff to illustrate the operation of various state support models will be employed to show how the three full state funding models operate. In each model, pupils were weighted to incorporate the cost differentials discovered by National Educational Finance Project researchers.[10] The weights assigned to various types of pupils are shown in Table 1 and reflect the average cost of educating various categories of pupils in comparison with the

TABLE 1
SCALES USED IN WEIGHTING PUPILS

Programs	Weighting for Cost Differential
Early Childhood	
3 year olds	1.40
4 year olds	1.40
Kindergarten (5 year olds)	1.30
Non-Isolated Basic Elementary and Secondary	
Grades 1-6	1.00
Grades 7-9	1.20
Grades 10-12	1.40
Isolated Basic Elementary and Secondary[a]	
Elementary Size	
150-200	1.10
100-149	1.20
less than 100	1.30
Junior High	
150-200	1.30
100-149	1.40
less than 100	1.50
Senior High	
150-200	1.50
100-149	1.60
less than 100	1.70
Special (exceptional)	
Mentally Handicapped	1.90
Physically Handicapped	3.25
Emotionally Handicapped	2.80
Special Learning Disorder	2.40
Speech Handicapped	1.20
Compensatory Education	
Basic: Income under $4,000	2.00
Vocational-Technical	1.80

[a] Elementary schools must be 10 miles or more by road from another elementary school in order to be weighted for isolation; junior high schools 15 or more miles from another junior high school and senior high schools, 20 miles or more from another senior high school.
*Source: R. L. Johns, et al., ALTERNATIVE PROGRAMS FOR FINANCING EDUCATION. (Gainesville, Fla.: National Educational Finance Project, 1971), p. 272.

cost of providing education for pupils in grades 1-6 of the regular school program. Complete descriptions of each school district included in the prototype state are available in publications of National Educational Finance Project.[11]

To facilitate comparisons, it was assumed that the same total amount of revenue was available for distribution in each model except Model III, where some additional revenue was required to equalize the revenue obtained from the district's optional local tax levy. It also was assumed that the funds provided by the state would be appropriated from the state's general fund and would be obtained from several sources, including a statewide property tax. Each model involves only full state funding of expenditures for current operation. No provision is made for transportation, capital outlay or debt service.

Model I: Complete State Funding

In this model there is no local school tax levy. All revenue is provided by the state from state sources. Figure 1 shows the revenue per weighted pupil which would be received by the odd numbered districts in the prototype state. Note that the revenue per weighted pupil is identical in each district. (It will be recalled that the use of weighted pupils automatically adjusts for differences in the cost of educational programs required by various types of pupils.) The state allocation is $565 per weighted pupil. This model clearly meets the *Serrano* test, for the expenditure per pupil is a function only of the total wealth of the state.

Model II: Full State Funding with a Minimal Optional Local Tax

This model provides that, in addition to the basic state grant, a small optional local school tax may be levied by each district. For purposes of illustration, we shall assume that the maximum optional local tax is four mills, and that each district chooses to levy the maximum permissible tax. In Figure 2 the amount available per weighted pupil in each of the odd numbered school districts is graphically portrayed. The same total amount of money will be allocated as in Model I, but in this model some of the revenue is derived from the optional four mill local tax, thus reducing the basic state grant to $494 per weighted pupil.

In District 1, the four mill local levy will produce $173 per weighted pupil, giving the district a total of $667 per weighted pupil. In District 31, the four mill local tax will yield only $64 per weighted pupil and the district will have a total revenue of $558 per weighted pupil.

It can readily be seen that District 1 will have available $119 more per weighted pupil than will District 31. Thus, District 1 will be able to spend about 20 percent more per weighted pupil than can be spent in District 31. Whether or not this much variation in spending would be permissible under the standard applied in *Serrano* remains to be decided. It is important to note,

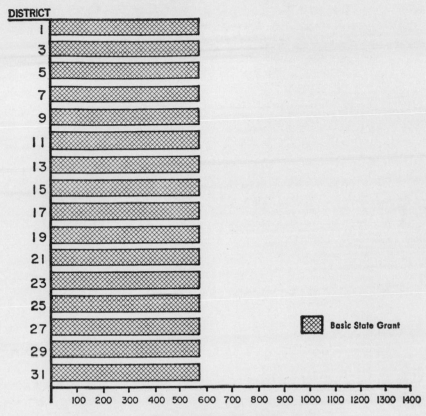

Figure 1
Full State Funding

that the entire difference in available revenue per pupil is a function of the wealth of the local school district.

Model III: Basic State Grant and Optional Local Tax with Equalized Yield *(Power Equalizing)*

The third model combines a basic state grant with an optional local tax of not more than six mills. In contrast to Model II, however, in this model the yield of the local tax is equalized by having the state guarantee a minimum yield for each mill of local school tax. In this model we shall assume that the basic state grant is $500 per weighted pupil. We also shall assume that each district is guaranteed $50 of revenue per weighted pupil for each mill of tax that it levies. The state will make up the

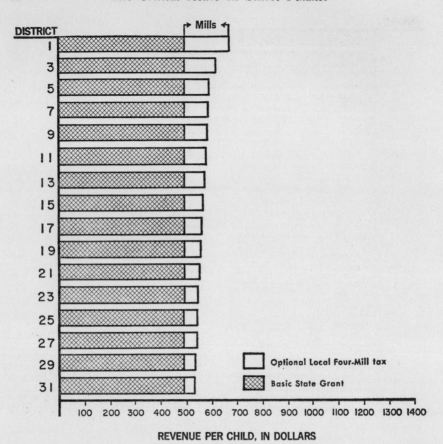

Figure 2
Full State Funding With Minimal Local Tax

difference between the actual yield of the district's local tax
and the guaranteed amount of revenue. The resulting distribution is shown in Figure 3 with the optional local tax levied by
each district shown in parentheses.

Note that District 1, District 19, and District 31 each elected
to levy one mill of local tax. Thus, each district was guaranteed
$50 per weighted pupil in addition to the $500 basic grant provided by the state. In District 1, the one mill local tax produced
$43 per weighted pupil with the state providing an additional $7
to make up the $50 per pupil which was guaranteed. In District
31, the one mill local tax produced only $7 per weighted pupil
and the state provided an additional $43 per pupil. District 3,

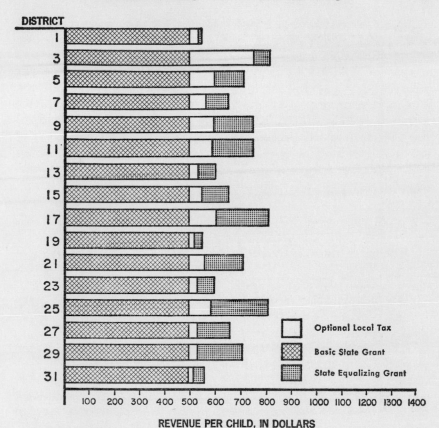

Figure 3
Basic State Grant and Optional Local Tax With
Equalized Yield (Power Equalizing)

District 17, and District 25 each chose to levy the full six mills permitted. Thus, each district was guaranteed $300 per weighted pupil in addition to the $500 basic state grant. In District 3, the six mill local tax produced $246 per weighted pupil with the state providing and additional $54. In District 17, the six mill local tax produced $94 with the state providing an additional $206. In District 25, the six mill local levy produced only $66 per weighted pupil with the state providing an additional $234 to make up the $300 guaranteed.

A critical consideration in this alternative is that *Serrano*-type decisions appear to require that the state confiscate any revenue produced by the optional local tax which exceeds the amount of revenue guaranteed by the state.

It also should be noted that in Model III, the amount of revenue available to a district is a function of the district's tax *effort*, not its tax base. Although this model could result in considerable variation in revenue per weighted pupil among the school districts of a state, it does not violate the principle that the amount of money available for a child's education must be a function of the wealth of the state. It does, however, make the amount of money available for a child's education a function of the willingness of his parents and neighbors to take on a heavier tax burden in order to increase the revenue available for education.

An Evaluation of the Three Models

The three models presented and discussed above do not exhaust the possibilities. They do represent three major approaches to full state funding. Each model has certain strengths and weaknesses and the merits of each model will depend to some extent upon the specific methods and procedures employed in implementing a full state funding program.

The following comments may be made with regard to Model I—complete state funding:

1. This model would eliminate any relationship between the wealth of an individual school district and the amount of revenue available to educate pupils in that district. If pupils are weighted appropriately with respect to differences in the cost of the program in which they are enrolled, equality of educational opportunity would be greater than if pupils are not weighted.

2. The extent to which the tax burden would be equalized under this model would depend upon the extent to which the state's tax system is more equitable than the present combination of state and local financing. In general, however, state taxes are less regressive than a property tax levied by local school districts.

3. The range in quality of educational offerings among the school districts of the state would certainly be narrowed. There is no guarantee, however, that the overall quality of education in the state would be improved.

4. The nature of local decision making would be altered, with local decision makers devoting much less attention to how to raise the necessary revenue and much more attention to efficient use of the available revenue. There exists the possibility

that local decision making could be diluted or impaired, although there is no reason why a high level of state funding is not compatible with substantial local control over such basic educational concerns as curriculum, personnel and the like.

5.   A complete state funding model is more likely to be accepted in states where a high level of state funding currently exists. In states where the percentage of revenue from the state is low there undoubtedly will be much greater resistance to the notion of complete state funding. The extent to which this model might be used to achieve substantial local property tax relief undoubtedly would be an important factor affecting its political acceptability.

Model II—a basic state grant combined with an optional local tax levy of not more than four mills—may be evaluated as follows:

1.   This model will reduce, but not eliminate, the relationship between the amount of revenue available for a child's education and the wealth of the district in which he resides. Revenue produced by the optional local tax levy will be entirely a function of the wealth of the local district. Wealthy districts will be able to raise much more revenue by levying one mill of tax than will poor districts. Whether or not the approximately 20 percent differential in revenue per weighted pupil between the lowest spending district and the highest spending district would be considered an unconstitutional denial of equal protection has yet to be determined. The bulk of the revenue available for school support, 80 percent or more, would be provided from the general revenues of the state. Since state taxes tend to be less regressive than local property taxes, there would be a tendency toward equalization of the tax burden but to a lesser degree than would be achieved under Model I.

2.   The range in educational opportunity among school districts of the state would be narrowed under this model, although not to as great an extent as would be achieved under Model I. Equality of educational opportunity would be increased if appropriate weightings which reflect the cost differentials associated with various types of educational programs are used as a basis for the distribution of funds.

3.   It would appear that greater potential for retention of local control of education exists under this model than under

Model I. The four mill optional local tax will afford some opportunity for local preferences to be expressed.

4.   This model undoubtedly will be more popular than Model I in states where there exists a strong tradition of local financing and local control of education. It should again be emphasized that the revenue produced by the local tax is purely a function of local district wealth. If the principle enunciated in *Serrano* is adhered to strictly, this model may not be acceptable.

Model III—a basic state grant with an equalized optional local tax—is a variation of what generally is termed "power equalizing." A tax yield equalizing approach was used to illustrate this model, but either tax base equalizing or percentage equalizing could have been used. The following comments may be made with regard to Model III:

1.   This model, like Model I, would sever the tie between the wealth of a school district and the amount of revenue available to educate pupils within that district. The amount of money available for a child's education would depend upon the willingness of his parents and neighbors to levy a local school tax. Nevertheless, a one mill tax would raise the same amount of revenue in each district.

2.   Equalization of the tax burden for support of education would be nearly as great as under Model I. The use of a regressive local property tax would, however, make this model slightly less equitable than Model I.

3.   The same degree of equalization of educational opportunity could be achieved under this model as could be achieved under Model I *if* two conditions are met: (1) every district chooses to levy the maximum permitted local tax and (2) appropriately weighted pupil units are used as a basis for distribution of funds. If the range in local property tax rates were as great as those used in the example, the highest taxing districts would have about 45 percent more revenue per weighted pupil than would the lowest taxing districts. This variation, however, would be a function of local tax effort, not local wealth.

4.   Under this model local school districts can influence the level of expenditure for education in each district—the claimed *sine qua non* of local control. The fully equalized optional local tax levy places every district on equal footing with regard to its tax effort. However, if the level of spending for a child's educa-

tion is too important to be a function of the wealth of the district in which he resides, perhaps it is also too important to be a function of local preferences for educational spending.

5. The provision of an optional local tax levy for education, when viewed in the context of the strong tradition of local control which exists in many states, should lend appeal to this model. From a political point of view, the model has one severe disadvantage. That is, the amount of state revenue required beyond the basic state grant will depend upon local decisions and thus is somewhat resistant to cost control efforts. This feature also makes state budgeting more difficult.

SOME PROS AND CONS OF FULL STATE FUNDING[12]

Proposals for full state funding of expenditures for elementary and secondary education are sure to provoke heated debate. In this section some of the major arguments which are likely to be advanced on each side of the issue will be identified and discussed.

Advantages Claimed for Full State Funding

Proponents of full state funding claim several advantages for this approach to financing education. Among the major arguments are those related to equalization of educational opportunity, tax equity, interdistrict competition, school district organization, and local priorities.

Equalization of Educational Opportunity

The present disparities in spending among the school districts of a state can no longer be tolerated in a country which has long been espoused the principle of equality of educational opportunity. Advocates of full state funding point out that under most current state support programs the discrepancy between the level of spending in wealthy districts and poor districts tends to increase rather than decrease over time. Although the relationship between expenditure level and educational quality is not perfect, both common sense and research indicate that a positive relationship does exist. While money alone is not sufficient to guarantee educational quality, it is undoubtedly necessary. Full state funding would reduce the range between the spending level of the highest and lowest expenditure districts in a state.

Adoption of full state funding could greatly increase the quality of educational opportunity available within a state if it were accompanied by a successful effort to raise the expenditure level in districts which currently are at the low end of the expenditure continuum. Few would argue that this should be an abrupt change, for it is likely that such districts would not be able to spend wisely sudden large amounts of additional revenue. A systematic effort to raise the level of expenditure in low expenditure districts is likely to be accompanied by monitoring by the state to insure the wise use of the additional funds. While this may infringe on traditional local prerogatives, it will probably be necessary to assure state policy makers that school funds provided from the general revenues of the state are not being wasted.

Greater Tax Equity

Another advantage claimed for full state funding is that it will provide greater equity for taxpayers, especially if it is tied to property tax relief. It is generally conceded that property ownership does not always accurately reflect taxpaying ability, and that the property tax bears more heavily on the elderly and upon low income groups. Even the most ardent advocates of full state funding recognize that in many states it will be impossible to abandon the property tax as a source of revenue for education. However, they claim that use of a statewide property tax for school support would reduce the present inequities in tax rates among districts and also would lead to improved administration of the property tax. Property assessments leave much to be desired in most states and it is argued that adoption of the property tax as a source of state revenue should lead to improved administration of the tax.

It is also claimed that full state funding would modernize the tax base used for support of education. The property tax admittedly is poorly related to ability to pay and to benefits received, at least insofar as the benefits of education are concerned. It also is not very responsive to changes in economic conditions. It is argued that full state funding would result in greater reliance on more productive and less regressive taxes and thus would lead to greater equity for taxpayers.

Reduction of Interdistrict Competition

The existing decentralized system for financing education often produces intense competition between school districts. This competition is particularly apparent when one looks closely at what is happening in the more affluent districts. Districts which are able to raise large amounts of local revenue while maintaining a relatively low tax rate have an unfair advantage in competing for the most able teachers because they are able to offer higher salaries, smaller classes and wider range of fringe benefits. It is argued that full state funding, accompanied by a statewide teacher salary schedule, would reduce or eliminate the whipsaw effect of interdistrict competition. It must be acknowledged, however, that bargaining on teacher salary schedules at the state level could easily result in statewide work stoppages if a satisfactory agreement could not be reached.

More Efficient District Organization

Full state funding undoubtedly would result in the elimination of school districts which are unable to offer adequate educational programs at reasonable cost. For one reason, it is unlikely that the state would continue to support school districts of this type. A second reason would be the inability of such districts to provide educational programs adequate to meet the needs of students, thus leading to increasing pressure from parents for reorganization or consolidation.

Changing Local Priorities

It is argued that present funding arrangements force local school boards and administrators to spend the bulk of their time attempting to obtain the resources they need. With full state funding, all school districts would have about the same amount of revenue per pupil and local policy makers could turn their full attention to determining how best to use the resources available to them. Under a full state funding program, a school administrator's success would be judged by his ability to use efficiently the resources at his disposal rather than by his ability to promote career moves to more affluent districts.

Disadvantages of Full State Funding

Among the arguments advanced by those who do not look

with favor on full state funding are those related to educational quality, local control, innovation, flexibility and competition for revenue.

Regression Toward Mediocrity

Those who are not sold on the advantages of full state funding point out that although equalization of educational opportunity might be achieved, the equalization may be at a level of mediocrity. They fear that major attention will be directed toward reducing the revenue available to high expenditure districts rather than increasing the revenue available to low expenditure districts, i.e., "leveling down" rather than "leveling up." Leveling down would certainly require less new revenue than leveling up. However, a number of studies indicate that wealthy districts wield greater political influence than do poor districts. If this is true, then it is not likely that leveling down will occur, for most wealthy districts will not wish to have their current expenditure level reduced to any marked degree.

Dilution of Local Control

It has long been contended that control is so closely related to support that the two are inseparable. Thus, opponents of full state funding fear that the control over education traditionally exercised at the local district level eventually will be lost under a full state funding program. It is undoubtedly true that constant vigilance will be required if local control is to be retained. However, some persons argue that local control without access to adequate resources is meaningless and is but a cruel hoax. It is also argued that freeing local decision makers from responsibility for raising revenue will permit them to concentrate on other important educational concerns. Even those who advocate full state funding most strongly usually advocate retention of local control over decisions concerning the employment and retention of staff, the content of the curriculum, and other matters relating to the day-to-day operation of the schools.

Innovation and Experimentation

Opponents of full state funding often point to the diversity which is possible under current financing arrangements. They argue that the existence of high expenditure school districts provides numerous "laboratories" for educational experimentation and innovation. They fear that full state funding would eliminate these "light house" schools. Advocates of full state funding question whether light house schools really are effective laboratories for experimentation and innovation. They note that light house schools invariably are high expenditure schools, and that their programs are tailored for a particular type of student population. They question whether such programs are equally appropriate in a rural area or in an urban ghetto, arguing that other approaches to research and development would be more effective in promoting desirable educational change.

Flexibility

Centralized financing could lead to the imposition of rigid allocation formulas and operating rules which would frustrate attempts to respond appropriately to the widely varying conditions found among the school districts of a state. Bureaucratic rigidity is, of course, not an unavoidable adjunct of full state funding. Care will be required, however, to make sure that local school systems are not hamstrung in their attempts to deal with the educational problems which confront them by inflexible rules and procedures imposed by the state.

Competition for Revenue

Those who fear the adverse affects of full state funding often point to the fact that elementary and secondary education will be placed in direct competition with all other functions of state government. They fear that the elementary and secondary schools would fare poorly in this competition. They point out that representatives of higher education, as well as all other state agencies, have years of experience with the political processes of state decision making and are fearful that those who represent elementary and secondary schools will be out-maneuvered by the more experienced representatives of other state agencies.

Advocates of full state funding recognize this possibility, but claim it is remote. They claim that those who represent elementary and secondary education have in the past been at least as effective as the representatives of other governmental agencies. They also argue that the allocation of scarce public resources will be accomplished more efficiently if all competing demands are debated and resolved through the political process.

CONCLUSION

Movement toward a much higher level of state support for public elementary and secondary schools appears inevitable. It should be evident, however, that full state funding will not be a panacea for all the ills which afflict elementary and secondary education. Full state funding would eliminate or reduce some problems but probably would aggravate other problems. In fact, full state funding might create problems which do not presently exist. It also should be evident that full state funding can be accomplished in a variety of ways. Each model has advantages and disadvantages and none are perfect. This nation has 50 state school systems and each is somewhat unique. Movement toward full state funding undoubtedly will occur on a broken front, and is likely to vary according to the situation which confronts each state.

FOOTNOTES

1. Henry C. Morrison, *School Revenue* (Chicago: University of Chicago Press, 1930).
2. James E. Allen, Jr., "Educational Priorities and the Handicap of Local Financing" (Address before the School Superintendent's Work Conference, Teacher's College, Columbia University, July 11, 1968).
3. Advisory Commission on Intergovernmental Relations, *State Aid to Local Government* (Washington, D.C.: Government Printing Office, 1969).
4. The President's Commission on School Finance, *Schools, People, and Money: The Need for Educational Reform* (Washington, D.C.: Government Printing Office, 1972).
5. Committee on Educational Finance, National Education Association, *Financial Status of the Public Schools, 1971* (Washington D.C.: National Educational Association, 1971), pp. 28-29.
6. *School Management*, "Cost of Education Index," Jan., 1971, p. 21.
7. Committee on Educational Finance, *op. cit.*, p. 5.
8. *Ibid*, p. 8.
9. Research Division, National Education Association, *Rankings of the States, 1971* (Washington, D.C.: National Education Association, 1971), p. 49.
10. R. L. Johns, et al., *Alternative Programs for Financing Education* (Gainesville, Fla.: National Educational Finance Project, 1971), p. 2/2.
11. *Ibid*, pp. 353-63.
12. Much of the material in this section appeared in an earlier paper on full state funding prepared by the author for the National Association of State Boards of Education.

CHAPTER 3

Constitutionality of Federal School Aid Formulas

Kern Alexander

Recent court decisions testing the constitutionality of state school finance programs open a new era of civil rights adjudication. The major cases in this area holding state systems of financing unconstitutional pose corollary questions with regard to federal mechanisms for financing education. Whether the courts will apply similar standards to federal programs as they have to state school finance provisions is argumentative at this point in time, but it is certainly a current legal question which deserves attention.

The purpose of this paper is to apply the legal rationale of equal protection and due process to two selected federal aid programs. Underlying this basic purpose are questions of whether the selected federal programs do now disequalize among the states in terms of their target populations. Broken down sequentially, the issues appear to be (1) what is the equality standard as propounded in *Serrano*[1] and *Rodriguez*,[2] (2) does the federal government have a constitutional responsibility to treat children equally, and (3) do the methods of allocation of the selected federal programs disequalize among children in targeted populations?

It should be emphasized that the constitutional standard

The author is Professor of Educational Administration, University of Florida and Director, National Educational Finance Project.

enunciated here is not a requirement that the federal government equalize among states, but merely that the resources of the federal government not be used to disequalize. In other words, is the federal government bound to treat all children in like circumstances alike?

TREATING ALL CHILDREN EQUALLY

The cases contesting governmental distribution of funds for the purposes of education are premised on equal protection of the law. Equal protection of the law means the protection of equal laws.[3] It requires that all persons in like circumstances be treated equally. "The concept of equal protection has been traditionally viewed as requiring the uniform treatment of persons standing in the same relation to the governmental action questioned or challenged."[4] In other words, government action cannot create unconstitutional classifications of persons similarly situated. States do not have the power to legislate "that different treatment be accorded to persons placed by a statute into different classes on the basis of criteria wholly unrelated to the objective of that statute."[5] The Supreme Court, many years ago, said that a classification:

> "must be reasonable, not arbitrary, and must rest upon some ground of difference having a fair and substantial relation to the object of the legislation, so that all persons similarly circumstanced shall be treated alike."[6]

The question of constitutional classification is the standard to which the courts are now addressing themselves in the issues of school finance.

UNCONSTITUTIONAL STATE SCHOOL
FINANCE PROGRAMS

A child's education cannot be a function of the wealth of the parents or neighbors or the state must be "fiscally neutral." These are the standards adopted by the courts in *Serrano* and *Rodriguez.* The courts in these cases found that the chief determinant of expenditures for a child's education was the fiscal ability or wealth of the local school district. The systems of financing created situations where children attending school in poor school districts were uniformly denied equal tax resources for education, thus violating the equal protection clause of the Fourteenth Amendment.

The Supreme Court of California developed a very persuasive argument based on three legal suppositions, first, wealth is a "suspect classification," second, education is a "fundamental interest," and third, the state must have a "compelling interest" to justify a system of financing which makes the revenues available per pupil dependent on wealth.

In the first instance the court placed heavy reliance on the U. S. Supreme Court's demonstrated antipathy toward legislative classifications which discriminate on the basis of "suspect" personal classifications. Wealth is such a suspect classification. In *Harper v. Virginia State Board of Elections*,[7] the U. S. Supreme Court said:

"Lines drawn on the basis of wealth or property, like those of race, are traditionally disfavored."

In this case, the Supreme Court in invalidating the poll tax further stated:

"To introduce wealth or payment of a fee as a measure of a voter's qualification is to introduce a capricious or irrelevant factor . . . [A] careful examination on our part is especially warranted where lines are drawn on the basis of wealth . . . [a] factor which would independently render a classification highly suspect and thereby demand a more exacting judicial scrutiny."[8]

The California Court found it irrefutable that the California system of financing public schools classified children on the basis of wealth[9] creating a "wealth-oriented" discrimination.[10] Among other arguments, the defense in *Serrano* maintained that classifiication by wealth is constitutional so long as the wealth is that of the district, not the individual. Answering this assertion the court said:

"We think that discrimination on the basis of district wealth is equally invalid. . . . To allot more educational dollars to the children of one district than to those of another merely because of the fortuitous presence of such property is to make the quality of a child's education dependent upon the location of private commercial and industrial establishments. Surely, this is to rely on the most irrelevant of factors as the basis for educational financing."

Plaintiffs pressed further that not only does the California system of financing classify on the basis of wealth, but also such classification "touches upon" a "fundamental interest," education. To show that education is a "fundamental interest" is necessary, since the U. S. Supreme Court has in the past only invalidated wealth classifications in conjunction with a limited number of fundamental interests, rights of defendants in criminal cases[11] and voting rights cases.[12] The court adopted the plaintiffs argument that education is a "fundamental interest" and noted that education holds an indispensable role in the modern industrial state,

> "first, education is a major determinant of an individual's chances for economic and social success in our competitive society;" [and] "second, education is a unique influence on a child's development as a citizen and his participation in political and community life."[13]

Buttressing this argument the court cited the U. S. Supreme Court in *Brown v. Board of Education*[14] which said: "In these days, it is doubtful that any child may reasonably be expected to succeed in life if he is denied the opportunity of an education."

By establishing that "wealth is a suspect classification" and education is a "fundamental interest," the court brought the case within the "strict scrutiny" test established by the U. S. Supreme Court in the previously cited criminal and voter rights cases. This standard requires that the state show a "compelling state interest" to justify a "suspect classification." This standard is much more restrictive on the legislature and requires more than a mere "rational relationship" between the legislative objective and the classification, and it tends to place the burden of proof on the legislature. In spite of attempts by the defense to justify the California finance machinery in terms of a compelling state interest, the court held that the California school finance system could not withstand the "strict scrutiny" test. The court said:

> "For reasons we have explained in detail, this system conditions the full entitlement to such [fundamental] interest on wealth, classified its recipients on the basis of their collective affluence and makes the quality of a child's education depend upon the resources of his school district. . . ."[15]

The principal of "fiscal neutrality" was introduced in *Rodriguez*,[16] a Texas decision. The court here said:

". . . plaintiffs have not advocated that educational expenditures be equal for each child." ". . . they (plaintiffs) have recommended the application of the principle of 'fiscal neutrality.' Briefly summarized, this standard requires that the quality of public education may not be a function of wealth, other than the wealth of the state as a whole."

DUE PROCESS AND THE FEDERAL GOVERNMENT

Since the Fourteenth Amendment provides that *"no state shall . . .* deny equal protection," (emphasis added) one might at first glance assume there is no constitutional basis on which to rely in applying the equal protection rationale of *Serrano* and *Rodriguez* to the federal government. However, it would be constitutionally inconsistent to assume that Congress could deny equal protection and unconstitutionally classify persons while state governments could not. After all, the Bill of Rights was originally written to protect the people against the central government. It was not until years later that individual protections of the Bill of Rights were brought into play against the states.[17]

The problem of not having an "equal protection clause" which directly applies to discriminations by the federal government was first faced squarely by the United States Supreme Court in 1954. In *Bolling v. Sharpe*,[18] companion case to the famous *Brown v. Board of Education*,[19] the United States Supreme Court was asked to desegregate the federally controlled schools in the District of Columbia, the Court was forced to seek constitutional authority other than the Fourteenth Amendment in order to overthrow federally promulgated segregation. The Court found its rationale in the "due process clause" of the Fifth Amendment.

The Court said:

"We have this day held that the Equal Protection Clause of the Fourteenth Amendment prohibits the states from maintaining racially segregated public schools. The legal problem in the District of Columbia is somewhat different, however, the Fifth Amendment, which is applicable in the District of Columbia, does not contain an equal protection clause as does the Fourteenth Amendment which applies only to the states. But the concepts of equal protection and due process, both stemming from our American ideal of fairness, are not mutually exclusive. The 'equal protection of the laws' is a more explicit safeguard of prohibited unfairness than 'due process of law' and, therefore, we do not imply that the two are always interchangeable phrases. But, as this Court has recognized, discrimination may be so unjustifiable as to be violative of due process.

****In view of our decision that the Constitution prohibits the states from maintaining racially segregated public schools, *it would be unthinkable that the same Constitution would impose a lesser duty on the Federal Government.*"[20]

In 1964, the Supreme Court held that a statute by Congress providing for denationalization of a naturalized citizen of the United States constituted unconstitutional discrimination, saying, "Moreover, while the Fifth Amendment contains no equal protection clause, it does forbid discrimination that is 'so unjustifiable as to be violative of due process.' "[21]

In 1969, the Supreme Court held that welfare assistance waiting-period requirements in the District of Columbia were unconstitutional even though they were adopted by Congress as an exercise of federal power.[22] The discrimination created by a one-year residency requirement violated the due process clause of the Fifth Amendment. The Court said:

"—The Due Process Clause of the Fifth Amendment prohibits Congress from denying public assistance to poor persons otherwise eligible solely on the grounds that they have not been residents of the District of Columbia for one year at the time their application was filed."[23]

It should be noted that in this case the court held that an individual's right to travel was *fundamental* and that a residency law unconstitutionally restricted that right. In a concurring opinion, Justice Stewart pointed out that government must show a *compelling interest* before it can impinge on the right of interstate travel.

"This is necessarily true whether the impinging law be a classification statute to be tested against the Equal Protection Clause, or a state or federal regulatory law, to be tested against the Due Process Clause of the Fourteenth or Fifth Amendment."[24]

In 1971, the United States Court of Appeals for the Seventh Circuit held that the United States Department of Housing and Urban Development violated both the Civil Rights Act and the Fifth Amendment by its approval and funding of construction for a segregated public housing system in Chicago.[25] In applying the strictures of the due process clause of the Fifth Amendment to the federal agency the court partially quoting *Bolling v. Sharpe*[26] said:

"Moreover, the fact that it is a *federal* agency or officer charged with an act of racial discrimination does not alter the pertinent standards, since *** it would be unthinkable that the same Constitution would impose a lesser duty on the Federal Government.[27]

Other courts have also applied the due process clause to the federal government. In *Hobson v. Hansen*,[28] a case involving the public schools of the District of Columbia, the court held that "the equal protection clause in its application to public school education — is in its full sweep a component of due process binding on the District under the due process clause of the Fifth Amendment." In this case, the court held the operation of the schools of Washington, D. C. violated the Fifth and Fourteenth Amendments.

In a subsequent *Hobson* case[29] the Federal District Court in the District of Columbia examined the expenditure levels of the elementary schools in Washington, D. C., and found variations in teacher expenditures per pupil as great as 40 percent. The court concluded that such variations denied black and poor children equal access to dollars therefore constituting racial and economic discrimination. The court ordered that per pupil expenditures for teachers' salaries and benefits in any elementary school should not deviate more than 5 percent from the mean per pupil expenditure for teachers' salaries and benefits at all elementary schools in the District of Columbia.[30]

In each of the instances cited above the courts applied the "due process clause" of the Fifth Amendment to prevent unconstitutional classification and discrimination on the part of the federal government. The same application may certainly be made to controversies which challenge the lack of equalization of federal school aid provisions among children in the various states.

EDUCATION AS A FEDERAL RESPONSIBILITY

Education has been traditionally and legally controlled by the laws of the states.[31] The federal government derives its powers from constitutional delegation, and since education was not so delegated, the Tenth Amendment reserved it "to the states respectively, or to the people." However, it has long been established that the Congress through the "general welfare" clause[32] can "authorize the expenditure of public moneys for public purposes [and] is not limited by the direct grants of legislative power found in the Constitution."[33] The discretion to tax and spend for general welfare "belongs to Congress, unless the choice is clearly wrong, a display of arbitrary power, not an exercise of judgment."[34] The Congress has not been restricted in its use of the "general welfare" clause. The Supreme Court has said that:

"Nor is the concept of the general welfare static. Needs that were narrow or parochial a century ago may be interwoven in our day with the well-being of the Nation. What is critical and urgent changes with the times."[35]

On the strength of these precedents the United States Congress has entered the field of education through numerous financing mechanisms. Attention of major committees in Congress is devoted to education. Laws providing various types of aid to education fill a 748 page volume published by the Congress each year.[36] There is little doubt that Congress has assumed a responsibility for education and is actively exercising it. This entry into the field of education is documented by the Declaration of Policy set forth under Title I of the Elementary and Secondary Education Act of 1965:

"In recognition of the special educational needs of children of low-income families and the impact that concentrations of low-income families have on the ability of local educational agencies to support adequate educational programs, the Congress hereby declares *it to be the policy of the United States to provide financial assistance* to local educational agencies serving areas with concentrations of children from low-income families to expand and improve their educational programs by various means which contribute particularly to meeting the special educational needs of educationally deprived children."[37] [Emphasis added]

This type of declaration of national policy is either expressed or implied in the numerous acts which provide federal support for education. By expending public tax dollars and by asserting control over the expenditure of those moneys, the federal government currently exercises vast responsibility for various phases of education, including programs in higher education, adult education, elementary and secondary education, vocational education, educational research, and educational professional development. Although these programs exhibit more scope than depth in terms of dollars, they nevertheless indicate a substantial federal commitment and responsibility for education.

With this assumption of responsibility for educational programs coupled with the "compelling interest" standard of *Serrano* and *Rodriguez,* a valid question can be raised as to the constitutionality of formula allocations which tend to treat children in certain target groups unequally, or make the funds available a function of the wealth of the state.

CONSTITUTIONAL CRITERIA APPLIED TO FEDERAL DISTRIBUTIONS

Application of constitutional criteria may be made to two large federal subventions, Title I of the Elementary and Secondary Education Act of 1965 and Public Law 81-874. These two programs account for over two billion[38] dollars and comprise the major portion of all U.S. Office of Education funds for elementary and secondary education.

Title I, ESEA. The purpose of Title I is to provide funds to meet the special educational needs of educationally deprived children. The distribution formula allocates funds in the following manner:

> "The maximum grant which a local educational agency in a state shall be eligible to receive under this part for any fiscal year shall be an amount equal to the federal percentage* of the average per pupil** expenditure in that state, or, if greater, in the United States multiplied by the number of children in the school district of such agency who are aged five to seventeen, inclusive, and are (a) in families having an annual income of less than the low-income factor,*** (b) in families receiving an annual in-

---

* "Federal percentage" is 50 percent
** Average Daily Attendance
*** The"low-income factor" is $3,000 for the four years, 1969 through 1972.

come in excess of the low-income factor from payments under the program of aid to families with dependent children under a state plan approved under Title IV of the Social Security Act, or (c) living in institutions for neglected or delinquent children (other than institutions operated by the United States) but not counted pursuant to paragraph (7) of this subsection for the purpose of a grant to a state agency, or being supported in foster homes with public funds."[39]

More simply, this formula provides for grants to the states on the basis of the number of educationally deprived children times 50 percent of the average state or federal expenditure, whichever is greater.

In fiscal year 1971 Title I allotments to local education agencies amounted to $1,299 billion.[40] When the allotments were finally calculated, New York received $273 per educationally deprived pupil. The poorest state, Mississippi, with comparable fiscal effort, received only $164 per educationally deprived pupil (See Figure 1). This disparity of $109 per educationally deprived pupil is *prima facie* evidence of the federal government's "unequal treatment of equals." While this amount of funds is not

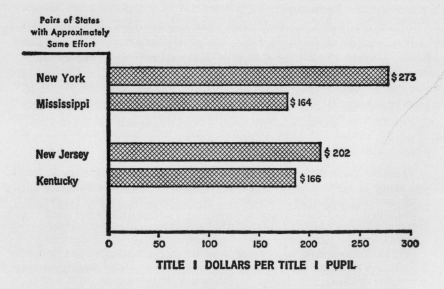

Figure 1
Title I Allotment Per Title I Pupil

particularly striking when expressed in terms of pupil units, it is more impressive when viewed on a statewide basis. If, for example, the federal government did not disequalize in the allotment formula and the Mississippi child received the same amount as the New York child, then, the state of Mississippi's Title I allotment would be increased by about $28 million.[41] In 1971 the entire Title I allotment to local education agencies in Mississippi amounted to only $42,074,152. (See Table 1).

TABLE 1

TITLE I, ESEA ALLOTMENTS PER TITLE I CHILD TO LOCAL EDUCATION
AGENCIES, FISCAL YEAR, 1971

(Selected States Paired Rich and Poor with Comparable Effort)*

State	Total Local Agency Title I Allotment, 1971	Title I Allotment Per Title I Child
New York	$ 191,230,096	$ 273
Mississippi	42,074,152	164
Maryland	19,393,856	177
South Carolina	34,313,120	163
New Jersey	39,674,083	202
Kentucky	37,131,906	166
Connecticut	11,101,653	185
Alabama	40,257,134	164

Source: *Title I, Assistance for Educationally Deprived Children, Allotments for Fiscal Year, 1971,* Office of Education, H.E.W.

* Effort of states determined by dividing state per capita personal income into state and local revenue per pupil for education.

Using another example, to correct the disequalization of the formula and bring the state of Kentucky up to that of New York, would require a $107 increase per educationally deprived child in Kentucky. This would increase Kentucky's allocation by nearly $24 million.[42]

Public Law 874 (Impact Aid). The purpose of this federal program is to "provide financial assistance for those local educational agencies upon which the United States has placed financial burdens by reason of the fact that:

"(1)   The revenues available to such agencies have been reduced as a result of the acquisition of real property by the United States; or

(2)   Such agencies provide education for children residing on federal property; or

(3)   Such agencies provide education for children whose
        parents are employed on federal property; or
(4)   There has been a sudden and substantial increase in
        school attendance as the result of federal activities."[43]

The formula used to distribute the impact aid funds is the
"local contribution rate" times the number of eligible children
in average daily attendance in the school district. The "local
contribution rate" is the local expenditure per pupil as determined by *groupings* or *comparable* school districts in the state
or by the district taking *one-half the national* or *one-half the
state average per pupil operating costs* whichever is higher. The
use of one-half the federal or state average tends to prevent
discrimination against districts in states which have a high
percentage of state funds for elementary and secondary education. A state may have some districts that obtain funds on the
basis of groupings or comparable districts while others in the
same state obtain funds based on one-half the federal or state
average.

It is in this formula that a possible constitutional challenge
lies. Even though the school district has alternatives of groupings, comparable districts, one-half federal* or one-half state*
expenditures per pupil, the impacted child in a low-wealth school
district in a poor state can only hope to receive at most one-half
the federal average expenditure per pupil. This means that a
federal installation child in Alabama will receive substantially
less impact aid than a child similarly situated in Massachusetts.

Although some studies[44] have pointed out several inequitable
and inconsistent features in the P.L. 874 formula, the net effect
of the formula is that it favors the impacted children in school
districts in wealthy states over impacted children in districts
in poorer states. The formula discriminates within the target
population class and the discrimination is based on "wealth." A
recent Battelle study of impact aid moneys concluded that the
methods of calculating the local contribution rate results in substantial variation among the states. These data show that generally the poorer southern states, with the lowest expenditures
per pupil must select one-half the national average local contribution rate, while the wealthier states merely needed to rely on
their own resources to exceed the national rate. Although, the
national average option raises the poorer states in some degree,

* Federal funds excluded.

the impact of the entire formula is to discriminate against impact aid children in poorer states in favor of those in wealthier states.

In Table 2, it can be seen that for fiscal year 1970, in the poorer states, including Mississippi, Alabama and Arkansas, maximum allowable local contribution rate was the national average which amounted to only $307 per pupil. This amount is much less than the local contribution rate allowed for New York which obtained $576. The wealthy states of Massachusetts and New Jersey had $545 and $532 respectively.

The use of the local contribution rate makes aid to impact children a function of the wealth of the state. This can easily be shown by correlating the average local contribution rate of all 50 states against the net per capita personal income of the states.[45] Results indicate that the Pearson Correlation coefficient is .6575 and is significant at the .01 level. This correlation is particularly strong even though the 13 poorest states were entered at one-half the national average, tending to create a randomness which detracts from the relationship. (See Figure 2).

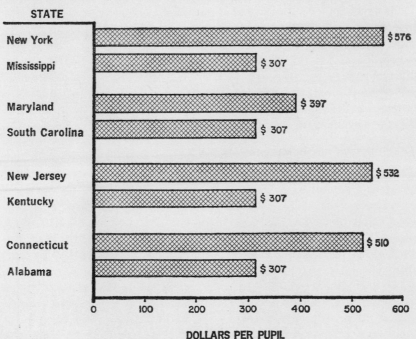

Figure 2
P.L. 874 Average Local Contribution Rate 1970
For Pairs Of States Having Same Approximate Effort

TABLE 2

AVERAGE (TO NEAREST DOLLAR) LOCAL CONTRIBUTION RATES BY
STATE, FISCAL 1970

State	Contribution	State	Contribution	State	Contribution
1/2 National Average		*From 350 - 399*		*From 450 - 500*	
Alabama	307	Arizona	350	Illinois	475
Arkansas	307	California	368	Nebraska	480
Florida	307	Kansas	362	New Hampshire	482
Georgia	307	Maryland	397	Rhode Island	479
Kentucky	307	Michigan	376		
Louisiana	307	Ohio	375		
Mississippi	307	Pennsylvania	393		
New Mexico	307	Virginia	395		
North Carolina	307				
South Carolina	307				
Tennessee	307				
Utah	307				
West Virginia	307				
From 308 - 349		*From 400 -449*		*Over 500*	
Delaware	346	Colorado	419	Alaska	736
Hawaii	316	Iowa	419	Connecticut	510
Idaho	343	Maine	414	Massachusetts	545
Indiana	343	Montana	411	New Jersey	532
Minnesota	341	North Dakota	412	New York	576
Missouri	342	South Dakota	400	Oregon	531
Nevada	326	Vermont	410		
Oklahoma	336	Wisconsin	433		
Texas	315	Wyoming	448		
Washington	329				

For fiscal 1971, the P.L. 874 formula produced a revenue disparity between New York and Mississippi of $83 per impacted pupil.[46] To treat the Mississippi child equally, and raise the allotment of Mississippi rather than lowering the New York allotment, would require that Mississippi's total allotment be increased by $1,442,706. Mississippi in 1971 received $3,991,200. To similarly erase the disequalization between Alabama and Connecticut[47] would require that Alabama be allotted an additional $112 per impact child or a total additional for the state of $6,055,728.

Since the wealth of the state is the significant determiner of the state expenditures per pupil, it is quite evident that "the amount of P.L. 874 dollars per impact child is a function of the *wealth* of the state." The formula, because of wealth and geographic circumstance, discriminates against impacted children in poorer states. The Congress would he hard pressed to show a compelling interest in creating a wealth distinction within a nationally identified target population of federally impacted children.

THE FEDERAL GOVERNMENT'S COMPELLING INTEREST IN THE PRESENT FORMULAS

In keeping with *Serrano* and *Rodriguez,* when a fundamental interest such as education is at stake, the government must show a "compelling interest" to withstand a strict scrutiny of the method of classification. Does the federal government have a "compelling interest" for classifying educationally deprived and impacted children on the basis of wealth? It may be assumed that the federal government would cite a number of compelling interest arguments including the ones discussed in the following paragraphs.

(a) *Education is not a federal function, therefore, equalization is not a valid constitutional requirement of the federal government.* In response to this argument it should be observed that it is irrelevant where the basic responsibility for education lies. The fact is that the federal government has assumed the responsibility for financing a portion of the educational program. It may be true that the federal government does not have an overall responsibility for equalization of educational opportunity for all children, but it certainly has a legal responsibility not to disequalize among the children it has identified in a specific target population. Put another way the federal government does not have a responsibility to equalize among regular children in basic educational programs either among school districts or among states, but where it has assumed the responsibility for providing assistance to a certain type of child, it must treat them all equally regardless of where they are located or what their economic circumstance may be.

Of course, the federal government cannot assume that the disequalization created by the federal program be remedied by the states themselves, since it is impossible for states to fiscally equalize among themselves without the assistance of the federal government.

(b) *Equalization is not the purpose of the grant.* Every state or federal aid formula has both a purpose and a method of allocation. The purpose may be and usually is completely separate from the method of allocation. A grant can have almost any purpose and still treat the children in the target group equally.

At any rate, here, there is no suggestion that federal funds must equalize, the standard is merely that the federal allocation formula not disequalize. The minimum standard is simply that all target children be treated equally in terms of resources. This would mean that the allocations per pupil when correlated with the wealth of the state must at least be neutral or have no correlation, meaning no disequalization. Of course, a high positive correlation, as is now found in the two formulas discussed above between allocation per targeted pupil and state wealth, falls short of this minimum.

(c) *High and low expenditures are not related to wealth of the state.* If this assertion is true then it could plausibly be maintained that the federal allocation formulas in question are not constitutionally invalid since wealth is the "suspect classification" not expenditures. However, expenditures are related to wealth and as simple correlations indicate, there is a positive correlation between wealth (per capita net personal income) and expenditures ($+ .7854$ significant at .01 level). High wealth states are also high expenditure states.

(d) *More money per pupil doesn't necessarily mean a better education.* This argument may be made, particularly in view of variations in costs of living throughout the country. However, recently an Associate U. S. Commissioner of Education commented in a speech before the Council of Great City Schools in reference to expenditure variations.

"Wide variations in school expenditures exist within states and among states. These variations often result from the differences in financial resources available to different communities . . . . Although research has not demonstrated the precise relationship between the amount of money a community spends on education and the quality of its schools, it is *assumed that larger expenditures generally produce better education.*" [Emphasis added][48]

Commenting on the question of comparable expenditures, the three judge federal court in *McInnis v. Shapiro* stated:

"Presumably, students receiving a $1,000 education are better educated than those acquiring a $600 education."

In *Hargrave v. Kirk,*[49] the court stated with regard to the outcomes of various expenditure levels:

"It may be that in the abstract the difference in dollars available does not necessarily produce a difference in the quality of education. But this abstract statement must give way to proof to the contrary."

Regardless, the "compelling interest" standard would require more than mere speculation on the subject. Today, data just do not show that the low expenditure level of Alabama produces the same educational output as the higher expenditure level in New York or Illinois.

(e) *Effort of states vary, the richer may be putting forth higher effort thus creating greater expenditures. The federal allocation formula is simply rewarding higher effort and not classifying states according to wealth.*

As a matter of fact, higher effort does not accompany higher wealth, just the opposite is true. When ability is correlated against effort there is a negative correlation (-2.088) significant at .05 level.

In quoting the *Serrano* court and substituting the word *states* for the word *districts* the logic of the *Serrano* reasoning can be conveyed interstate as well as intrastate.

". . . Expenditure doesn't accurately reflect the [state's] wealth because that expenditure is partly determined by [state's] tax rate."

"This argument is . . . meritless. Obviously, the richer [state] is favored when it can provide the same educational quality for its children with less tax effort. Furthermore, as a statistical matter, the poorer [states] are financially unable to raise their taxes high enough to match the educational offerings of wealthier [states]. Thus, affluent [states] can have their cake and eat it too: they can provide a high quality education for their children while paying lower taxes. Poor [states], by contrast, have no cake at all."

IN SUMMARY

In the absence of better educational fiscal data, it appears that the federal government would be hard pressed to show a "compelling interest" defending allocation formulas which make the "targeted child's education a function of the wealth of the state."

If the rationale of *Serrano* and *Rodriguez* is sound, and state systems of school finance are unconstitutional because they unconstitutionally classify children on the basis of wealth, then again quoting the U.S. Supreme Court in *Bolling v. Sharpe:*
"It would be unthinkable that the same Constitution would impose a lesser duty on the Federal Government."

FOOTNOTES

1. *Serrano v. Priest*, 5 Calif. 3rd 615, 96 Cal. Rptr. 601, 487 P.2d 1241 (1971).
2. *Rodriguez v. San Antonio Ind. School Dist.*, 337 F. Supp. 280 (W.D. Tex. 1971), probable jurisdiction noted, S. Ct. 40 U.S.L.W. 3576, (June 6, 1972).
3. *Yick Wo v. Hopkins*, 118 U.S. 356 (1886).
4. *Reynolds v. Sims*, 377 U.S. 533, 84 S. Ct. 1362 (1964).
5. *Reed v. Reed*, 92 S. Ct. 251 (1971).
6. *Royster v. Guano Co. v. Virginia*, 353 U.S. 412, 40 S. Ct. 560 (1920).
7. 383 U.S. 663, 86, S. Ct. 1079 (1966).
8. *Ibid.*
9. *Serrano v. Priest, supra.*
10. See: *Briggs v. Kerrigan*, 307 F. Supp. 295, aff'd. (1st Cir. 1970) 431 F. 2d 967 (1970).
11. *Griffin v. Illinois*, 351 U.S. 12, 76 S. Ct. 585 (1956); *Douglas v. California*, 372 U.S. 353, 83 S. Ct. 814 (1963); *Williams v. Illinois*, 399 U.S. 235, 905 Ct. 2018 (1970).
12. *Harper*; *Cipriano v. City*, Houma, 395 U.S. 701 S. Ct. 1897 (1969); *Kramer v. Union School District*, 395 U.S. 621, 89 S. Ct. 1886 (1969).
13. *Serrano v. Priest, supra.*
14. 347 U.S. 483, 74 S. Ct. 686 (1954).
15. *Serrano v. Priest, supra.*
16. *Rodriguez v. San Antonio Ind. School Dist., supra.*
17. Edward S. Corwin, ed., *The Constitution of the United States of America*, U.S. Government Printing Office, Wash., D.C. 1964, p. 845.
18. 347 U.S. 497 (1954)
19. 347 U.S. 483, 74 S. Ct. 686 (1954).
20. *Bolling v. Sharpe, supra*, 499; See also: *Gibson v. Mississippi*, 162 U.S. 565 (1896).

21. *Schneider v. Rusk*, 377 U.S. 163, 84 S. Ct. 1187 (1964); See also: *U.S. v. Jones*, 384 F. 2d 781 (1967), "Lack of equal treatment of selective service registrants by the federal government can be so discriminatory as to violate Fifth Amendment due process.

22. Shapiro v. Thompson, 394 U.S. 618, 89 S. Ct. 1322 (1969).

23. *Ibid.*

24. *Ibid.*

25. *Gautreaux v. Romney*, 448 F. 2d 731 (1971).

26. *Ibid.*

27. *Ibid.*

28. *Hobson v. Hansen*, 269 F. Supp. 401 (1967); *Smuck v. Hobson*, 408 F. 2d 174, (U.S.C.A.D.C.) (1969). See also: *Harrell v. Tobriner*, 279 F. Supp. 22 (1967) "Equal protection of laws guaranteed by the Fourteenth Amendment is applicable to the District of Columbia by reason of the due process clause of the Fifth Amendment."

29. 327 F. Supp. 844 (1971).

30. *Ibid.*

31. *Serrano v. Priest, supra.*

32. Constitution of the United States of America, Article I, Section 8.

33. *United States v. Butler*, 297 U.S. 1, 56 S. Ct. 312 (1936).

34. *Helvering v. Davis*, 301 U.S. 619 (1937).

35. *Ibid.*

36. *A Compilation of Federal Education Laws*, Committee on Education and Labor, House of Representatives, October, 1971, U.S. Government Printing Office, Washington, D.C.

37. 20 U.S.C. 241a.

38. Title I, ESEA all portions, $1.5 billion and P.L. 81-874, $536,068,000. (Fy 1971).

39. 20 U.S.C. 241c.

40. This excludes allotments for handicapped children, juvenile delinquents, dependent and neglected children, and migratory children.

41. $109 times the total number of culturally deprived (Title I) children in Mississippi.

42. The issue raised here is the basis for a complaint recently filed in the United States District Court, Western District of Kentucky, Louisville. *Mary Louise Downs v. Sidney P. Marland*, No. 7396-B (Sept. 11, 1972).

43. Section 1, Title I, P.L. 874. *Financial Assistance for Local Educational Agencies in Areas Affected by Federal Activity.*

44. Harold A. Hovey, et al. *School Assistance in Federally Affected Areas, A Study of Public Laws 81-874 and 81-815*, Battelle Memorial Institute, Committee on Education and Labor, House of Representatives, U.S. Government Printing Office, Washington, D.C.

45. Net Per Capita Personal Income used is the Per Capita Personal Income in 1969 minus $750 allowance per person. Source: *Alternative Programs for Financing Education*, National Educational Finance Project, Gainesville, Florida, 1971, p. 68.

46. New York receives $313 per impact pupil to Mississippi's $230 per impact pupil ($83 x 17,383 Impact Pupils = $1,442,706).

47. Connecticut received in 1971 $278 per impact child to Alabama's $166 per impact child ($112 x 54,069 = $6,055,728).

48. Duane J. Mattheis, *The Emergency in School Finance*, Council of Great City Schools, March 15, 1972, Washington, D.C., p. 4.

49. 313 F. Supp. 944 (1970); vacated and remanded on other grounds sub. nom.; *Askew v. Hargrave*, 401 U.S. 476, 91 S. Ct. 856 (1971).

CHAPTER 4

Equalization of Resources Within School Districts

D. BROCK HORNBY AND GEORGE W. HOLMES, III*

INTRODUCTION

The drive for equal educational opportunity has invaded the field of public school finance. Together with the President's Commission on School Finance[1] and the National Educational Finance Project,[2] recent judicial activity has focused attention on the problem of distributing resources[3] in public elementary and secondary education. Courts in California,[4] Texas,[5] Minnesota,[6] and New Jersey[7] have ordered those states to end the practice of affording poor districts less access to resources than wealthy districts within the same state, and the Supreme Court has now agreed to decide the Texas case.[8] This "wave" of court cases, however, has focused constitutional attack exclusively on comparison *among* school districts. Explicit reference to allocation of resources *within* school districts has been significantly absent. Even much of the scholarly literature on equalization explicitly avoids the problem of intra-district distribution.[9] But if the concern for resource equalization bears any relation to the quality of education students receive, getting the money to the school districts is surely only one step. The question remains whether resources are being fairly distributed among the schools within

* The authors are respectively: Assistant Professor of Law, University of Virginia and Professor of Educational Administration, University of Virginia.

the district and, ultimately, among the individual students in those schools. Attention to intra-district inequalities is thus the logical next step of the equalization thrust.

Perhaps one of the reasons that the question of intra-district inequalities has been neglected is that information on the subject is scattered. Although an increasing quantity of evidence on the disparities among school districts has fueled the drive for equalization at that level, firm and comprehensive data are still unavailable on the extent of resource variation within school districts.[10] Historically, patterns of racial discrimination appear to have created resource inequality between black and white schools.[11] Remedial measures—perhaps to blunt the drive for desegregation, perhaps simply to correct past inequities—may have alleviated much of this,[12] but scattered evidence indicates that such disparities do remain.[13] Some investigations, moreover, have discovered divergences on a socio-economic basis. A recent survey of school services in the San Francisco Bay area, for example, demonstrated that within districts, especially the urban Oakland district, more money was spent on schools serving students of high socio-economic status than on schools serving other students.[14] The funding superiority was reflected not in instructional materials, an area in which low socio-economic students actually benefited, but in teacher salaries. Greater experience and higher educational qualifications were characteristic of teachers in schools with student bodies of high socio-economic status.[15] A 1961 study of an unidentified large midwestern city found differences in building age, quality of facilities, class size, teacher certification percentages, even availability of free meals, all tending to benefit those schools whose student bodies had high socio-economic status.[16] A recent study in Chicago[17] and the court records of desegregation suits in Denver[18] and Washington[19] have demonstrated similar relationships. But other available data produce contradictory evidence. For example, one recent study concluded that "in certain facilities presumed to be crucial the children of the poor in large-city high schools were likely to be considerably better off than those of the well-to-do."[20] The Coleman Report, the mammoth 1966 study designed to catalog the state of American educational resources, revealed that differences among individual schools on a nationwide basis were much less extensive than had been expected.[21] It did not, however, furnish much direct information on intra-district disparities.[22] Given such indeterminate data, a definitive statement on the extent of intra-district inequality is impossible. While the evidence suggests that some inequalities exist within some districts, their severity and prevalence are unknown.

The attack on intra-district inequality, however, has already begun through legislative and judicial action, without final proof that the problem is one of national significance. The availability of federal Title I funds, designed to provide extra resources for schools serving educationally deprived children, now depends on a demonstration that project schools receive services and expenditures "comparable" to those of the district as a whole.[23] "Comparable" has been construed to allow only a five percent variation from the district-wide mean.[24] President Nixon's proposed legislation on equal educational opportunity and busing would reaffirm this requirement as a condition for receiving funds under that legislation.[25] The most recent session of the Virginia General Assembly considered legislation requiring each local school board to "maintain the same quality of education in all schools within such school division" and to "adopt and enforce plans, methods and procedures whereby education of the same quality shall uniformly be offered in each school within the school division."[26] There are signs too in recent judicial decisions that intra-district inequalities, at least where they relate to racial separation, may be open to successful challenge on constitutional grounds.[27] If the President is successful in getting Congress to call a halt to busing as a desegregation remedy, courts may be even more ready to apply this new "separate but equal" requirement to a racially imbalanced school district.[28]

In this Article, we confront the question of intra-district resource equalization. First, we survey current educational research for information on the importance of resource variations. Finding significant disagreement on their materiality, we turn to examine and assess Title I of the Elementary and Secondary Education Act, a federal education program concerned with intra-district inequalities. In the same light, we explore recent judicial developments pertaining to intra-district allocation and outline an analysis for reaching a decision on the constitutional demands. We conclude that some demands for equalization are legitimate notwithstanding their uncertain significance for affecting educational achievement.

THE EMPIRICAL RESEARCH

Modern investigators, not content to examine cost and quantity, have shifted their focus to the effectiveness of specific educational services. Yet, if it is difficult to ascertain the extent of inequality in expenditures or the provision of educational services within school districts, it is even more difficult to relate such variations to "effectiveness." Most educational programs serve a number of objectives. In the unlikely event that these are fully articulated and agreed upon, the present state of development of learning theory still makes it impossible to draw final conclusions on how to achieve them.[29] Empirical evidence is not available for firm answers to all questions that seem relevant; what evidence is available occasionally conflicts and often presents considerable difficulties of interpretation.

Pertinent studies measure effectiveness of educational services almost exclusively by student performance on achievement (occasionally aptitude) tests. The conceptual model for assessing the data generally posits a relation of the following sort:[30] a student's achievement at a particular point in time hinges on some combination of (1) his initial endowment; (2) his and his family's characteristics cumulative to that time; (3) the characteristics of his peers; and (4) the quality and quantity of his schooling to that time. Of these four inputs, only the last has seemed subject to practical alteration. A child's initial endowment is still beyond reach. A comprehensive preschool day care program designed to serve children from low- and middle-income families provoked a presidential veto to prevent a weakening of American family influence.[31] Attempts at changing the peer environment through racial or social integration have encouraged massive opposition.[32] Not surprisingly, therefore, much of the research has concentrated on the quantity and quality of school services as means for improving achievement.

Prior to the mid-1960's, research confirmed what intuition would suggest: that the level of expenditures and the services schools provide measurably affect student performance. In 1953, for example, Mollenkopf and Melville found a relatively high correlation between achievement and aptitude test scores on the one hand and the cost of instructional support per pupil and the number of specialists on the school staff on the other.[33] Casual connection does not necessarily follow this correlation;

specialists and higher expenditures might have been attracted to these schools because of the high achieving students or for other reasons. But the results were at least consistent with the belief that these inputs affect performance. In 1957-58 Goodman conducted his Quality Measurement Project for the New York State Education Department.[34] He also found that per pupil expenditure and quantity of specialists were highly related to achievement; but whereas Mollenkopf and Melville had found teacher experience insignificant, Goodman found it most important.[35] Marion F. Shaycoft conducted a longitudinal study of a group of 6,583 students in grade 9 in 1960 and 12 in 1963.[36] She found a statistically significant variation in cognitive learning among schools. H. S. Dyer has pointed out that Shaycoft's study provides no information on the significance of the differences or how they related to specific qualities of the schools, but he concluded that because the pronounced differences were in areas of curriculum content not largely affected by family background, "the hypothesis is rather compelling that qualitative differences in the schools themselves account for much, if not all, of the variation in academic and vocational achievement between one school and another."[37] J. Alan Thomas, in a 1962 study, isolated the quantity of school library books, teacher experience, and level of beginning salaries as significantly related to achievement test scores.[38] Charles S. Benson found in a 1965 California study that per pupil teachers' salaries and instructional expenditures were related to achievement.[39]

Then in 1966 the most important empirical study in the history of American education cast serious doubt on the significance of the relationship between variations in student performance and disparities in the services provided children by schools. The Coleman Report, the product of a study of approximately 645,000 students and their teachers, schools, curricula, and administrations across the United States, concluded that variations in overall per pupil expenditure for staff had no significant independent correlation to performance except for black students in the South, and even then the cause and effect relationship was doubtful.[40] School facilities had so little relation to achievement[41] "as to make it almost possible to say there was none."[42] Even teachers' characteristics ran third behind the more important factors of the student's socio-economic background and his or her peer environment at school.[43]

These surprising findings were greeted at first with a mixture of discomfort and neglect.[44] Then critics began to accumulate arguments to challenge the findings. The design of the study was such, they said, as to underestimate the impact of school facilities. The sample of facilities (school library books and, in high schools, science laboratories)[45] tested for impact, for example, was too narrow.[46] Quality of the facilities was ignored,[47] and the number of schools tested was too small.[48] Where measures of inputs were averaged for entire districts, they failed to show differences among the resources available from school to school within a district;[49] where they were separated by school, differences within the same school[50] that might have demonstrated a significant impact were ignored. Furthermore, if in fact it is true that students of low socio-economic status receive lower quality school resources, critics argued, the regression analysis used in the Coleman Report to interpret the data would accord importance to whatever item was tested first: availability of school resources or socio-economic status. Since the Coleman Report chose socioeconomic status, this factor may have been overrated at the expense of school resources.[51] Together with neglect of the importance of a child's initial endowment, failure to seek longitudinal data accounting for past schooling, and possibly systematic patterns of nonresponse, these factors have been said to preclude use of the Report for policy decisions.[52]

A review by Guthrie, Kleindorfer, Levin, and Stout of several additional studies of the effectiveness of school resources found substantially consistent evidence that variations in the quality of school services did influence the level of student achievement.[53] For example, teacher characteristics such as verbal ability, experience, salary, academic preparation, and tenure appeared significantly associated with student performance. Student performance also correlated with the degree of student-teacher contact measured by items such as class size and pupil/school personnel ratios. Even school building age and the quality of physical facilities had some consequence. An empirical study of Michigan schools, using the Coleman Report's data base, confirmed such conclusions for performance on reading, mathematics, and verbal ability tests.[54] Specifically, the Michigan study found performance related to such factors as school site size, building age, classroom ratios, and the use of makeshift classrooms.[55] Other factors were also relevant. The availability of library books, for example, had particular impact on students from high socio-economic backgrounds. Although the impact of teacher experience was slight, that of teachers' verbal ability was fairly strong. Furthermore, measurements of teacher morale were related to student success.[56]

The most recently published reanalyses of the Coleman Report, however, for the most part reaffirm its original conclusions from continued study of the same data.[57] Addressing the charge that the Coleman Report underestimated the importance of school services through its use of regression analysis, David J. Armor concluded that regardless of the order in which the impact of socio-economic status and school services are measured, family input accounts far more heavily for differences in achievement.[58] Marshall S. Smith concluded from his analyses that the Coleman Report, through an error in calculations, had in fact substantially underestimated the importance of family input.[59] On the significance of teacher competence, Christopher Jencks concluded that salary level does not relate to student achievement and that selection devices, such as the National Teacher Examination or a supervisor's recommendation, either do not correlate with achievement or else show a negative relation.[60] Although his studies confirmed a positive relationship between student achievement and teacher verbal scores and found this relationship particularly strong within school districts, Jencks was quick to point out that the hypothesis that verbally fluent teachers are attracted to schools with good pupils is just as consistent with the evidence as the hypothesis that verbally fluent teachers produce better students.[61] Jencks' study also demonstrated that school facilities had minimal impact on student performance. The slight relationship between performance and the number of pupils per room was "depressingly small." Other physical facilities—rooms per teacher; percentage of makeshift rooms; size of the school site; building age; presence of an auditorium, cafeteria, gym, athletics field, laboratory, typing room, infirmary, kitchen or movie projectors—produced equivalent results.[62] The quantity of library books and textbooks was inconsequential.[63]

In short, although scattered individual studies are consistent with the hypothesis that variations in school resources have an impact on tested student performance, that hypothesis is not sustained by the most comprehensive collection of data, the Coleman Report. The methods and assumptions of this study are in turn under significant attack. Experience to date with compensatory programs, although the evidence is admittedly scant, does not appreciably alter this confusing picture. A selection of 189 programs receiving Title I funds, for example, produced "58 [with] positive gains in reading scores, 50 [with] losses, and 81 [with] no significant change."[64] The initial, favorable Office of Education report on Project Follow Through, a test of twenty educational approaches in 178 different projects, was quickly attacked as "fuzzy writing, meager data."[65] This uncertainty is the context in which we must approach the issue of resource equalization.

THE LEGAL PRINCIPLES

Legislative Equalization Requirements

Doubts concerning the relationship of school services to student achievement have not halted federal activity in the area of education. Title I of the Elementary and Secondary Education Act of 1965 supplies funds to local school systems to meet "the special education needs of educationally deprived children."[66] As of July 1, 1972, statutory restrictions implemented by the Office of Education condition these funds on a guarantee of some degree of equalization of resources within school districts. In order to obtain Title I funds for the 1972-73 school year, a local school board must ensure that:

> State and local funds will be used in the district . . . to provide services in project areas which, taken as a whole, are at least comparable to services being provided in areas in such district which are not receiving funds under this subchapter.[67]

Applications for funds will not be approved unless the state educational agency determines that the district has already achieved comparability, or will achieve comparability by the beginning of the fiscal year in which funds are to be used, and that comparability will be maintained.[68] Together with the statutory requirement that federal funds "supplement" and not "supplant" other available funds,[69] these provisions are designed to ensure that Title I funds do not merely equalize resources, but make superior resources available to areas with concentrations of children from low income families.[70]

A local school board applying for Title I funds must identify specific schools in its district as Title I project schools. For each project school, the school district must compute:

1. The average number of pupils per assigned certified classroom teacher;
2. The average number of pupils per assigned certified instructional staff member (other than teachers);
3. The average number of pupils per assigned noncertified instructional staff member;
4. The amounts expended per pupil for instructional salaries (other than longevity pay);
5. The amounts expended per pupil for other instructional costs, such as textbooks, library resources, and other instructional materials.[71]

The figures computed on the first three items (pupil/staff ratios) for each project school are compared to the average for all nonproject schools in the district serving the same grades. The project school must be not more than five percent over the nonproject school average on these pupil/staff ratios. Figures on the last two items (expenditures per pupil) are compared in the same way, and no project school may be more than five percent under the nonproject school average.[72] Each of the five items must meet the comparability standard; overachievement in one will not justify underachievement in another. Thus, the regulations require comparability both of the resources expended and of the services purchased.[73]

This requirement that project schools closely approach the districtwide mean promises to have wide scope. The five items selected for comparability are among the most important factors affecting a school district's budget. The one major item for which comparability is not required is longevity pay.[74] Even this item must be reported,[75] however, perhaps a sign that there is thought of including it. With longevity pay included, the instructional expenditures covered by comparability requirements would account for approximately sixty-three percent of all school expenditures, and about seventy-five percent of annual operating expenses.[76] Moreover, the program is widespread. In fiscal year 1968, the last year for which data have been published, 10,979 of the 11,862 districts nationwide which enrolled 300 or more pupils received Title I funds.[77]

Were it not for the Coleman Report data, dollars spent and goods and services purchased would no doubt be considered perfectly appropriate for evaluating a school board's distribution practices, and the demand for comparability a logical method of equalizing opportunity. The discussion engendered by that research, however, has raised uncertainty over the significance of such inputs for increasing educational achievement. Programs of racial and socio-economic integration or attention to the home background are advocated and disputed as more promising avenues. If little is to be expected from a re-shuffling of resources, why, it may be asked, should the Title I program occasion the considerable administrative costs of implementing and enforcing its demands for comparability?[78]

Even if no impact on achievement is discernible, available resources are bound to affect the pleasantness of the school from day to day through their determination of such items as pupil/teacher ratios and the quality of physical facilities. Perceptible differences in available services carry strong suggestions of unfairness. Where such inequalities are racially, ethnically, or socially oriented, they affect adversely the attitudes of both students and community. Administrators who prepare budgets and testify at hearings continue to extol the importance of teacher qualifications and small classes,[79] and parents continue to believe them.[80] The announcement that such items no longer matter cannot easily dispel the adverse affects resulting from their unequal distribution.

Title I, moreover, demands comparability not as an end in itself, but as a means of assuring that funds distributed under the program provide special services for the education of disadvantaged children.[81] Thus, the real issue is whether the concentration of extra resources on such children is a worthwhile endeavor. Certainly if that objective is sound, then the prerequisite that project schools first receive average treatment from a district is logical and necessary to ensure that federal funds fulfill their purpose.[82] Although the Coleman Report has made us recognize that current school services cannot fully compensate for other factors that affect achievement, its insensitive measurements of variations in school services and student access to them certainly have not destroyed all basis for the intuitive belief that they produce some impact. As a practical matter, attention to school services appears to be the only realistically available approach at present for affecting student performance. Perhaps a significantly larger quantity of some services can be effective.

More importantly, the fact that tested achievement has furnished an easy measure for empirical studies gauging effectiveness must not elevate it to the only criterion of evaluation. Certainly it is an important measure, but it may be an unreliable approximation of other possible criteria, such as the value of schooling to an individual's future earning capacity or the quality of his future consumption.[83] And education has other important goals not easily measured on achievement tests.[84] What is needed is better definition of the various goals of educational programs and monitored experimentation to test the efficiency of different approaches. Title I, properly administered, can provide the funds to encourage the development of new educational programs with defined objectives for disadvantaged students. Proper monitoring could identify those which efficiently secure their goals.[85] Obviously, the arguments for continuing Title I are not overwhelming. The success to date of compensatory programs has not been particularly encouraging,[86] and Title I is a costly program—$1.1 billion for 1969, $1.34 billion for 1970, $1.5 billion for 1971, $1.5 billion requested for 1972.[87] But until better programs are available,[88] or until the evidence clearly indicates the hopelessness of this approach, the importance of upgrading education for disadvantaged students justifies this legislative experiment—provided, of course, that programs are carefully conceived and closely monitored so that adequate judgments of effectiveness can be made.[89]

CONSTITUTIONAL REQUIREMENTS

Unlike the specificity afforded by Title I's legislative and regulatory requirements, constitutional strictures in the area of school resource distribution are still unsettled. The Fourteenth Amendment directs that no state shall "deny to any person within its jurisdiction the equal protection of the laws."[90] This requirement demands more than the impartial administration of legislation on the books; the Supreme Court has said that it constitutes "a pledge of the protection of equal laws" as well.[91] But the case that can be made for the congressional experiment in reallocating school resources furnishes shaky ground on which to build an argument that the Constitution requires reallocation where inequalities of resources occur among schools.

The Tools of Equal Protection Analysis in the General Area of Educational Finance

A strong attack has nevertheless been mounted against judicial restraint in the area of school finance. Commentators have long observed that the Supreme Court uses two approaches in assessing the constitutionality of measures challenged on equal protection grounds.[92] In the area of general social and economic legislation, the Court has required only that governmental classifications of groups or individuals for different treatment bear a "reasonable" or "rational" relationship to a legitimate state objective. A classification based on race or alienage, on the other hand, is termed "suspect" and requires justification by some "compelling state interest" and, on occasion, proof that no less onerous measures could secure the state's objectives. When constitutional rights such as the franchise or interstate movement are impaired, or when certain criminal defense services are priced at a level that indigents cannot afford, this higher level of scrutiny is again applied. Traditionally, almost any classification has survived the "rational relationship" test;[93] only the most extraordinary circumstances have sustained a classification under the "compelling interest" standard.[94]

In 1966, before the significance of resource variation was under strong attack, Professor Horowitz argued that a constitutional analysis of disparities in educational resources should occasion the stricter equal protection scrutiny by considering education a "fundamental personal interest" to be balanced against the state's justifications (considering the availability of alternative means to the same end) for preserving the differences in treatment.[95] Proof of discriminatory purpose in producing or preserving the inequalities, he contended, was sufficient, but not necessary, to prove a constitutional violation. The analysis he advocated was that:

> Neither administrative convenience, desire to expend funds for other purposes, limited demand, higher costs, nor similar considerations would necessarily make consequent inequalities in educational services the product of constitutionally permissible classifications. In each case,

assuming a "rational basis" for a specific inequality were shown, the controlling issue would be whether the school board can demonstrate that there are not other "rationally based" means of carrying out its programs which would have less adverse impact on the children who are provided the lower quality educational services.[96]

To support his contention that more than a "rational basis" was necessary to sustain disparities, Professor Horowitz analogized school resource inequalities to unequal provision of criminal defense services and unequal availability of the franchise.[97]

Other commentators developed this line of argument in the context of inter-district disparities[98] and achieved a measure of victory in a line of cases beginning in 1971 with the California Supreme Court decision in *Serrano v. Priest.*[99] Adverting to Supreme Court statements regarding the importance of education in the context of school desegregation and similar statements by concurring Justices in decisions invalidating religious instruction and Bible reading in the public schools, *Serrano* detailed several reasons why education should be counted a fundamental interest analogous to voting rights and criminal defenses: its relationship to participation in the "economic marketplace;" its "universal relevance;" its duration; its effect on individual parsonalities; and its compulsory nature.[100] *Serrano* did not rely on the "fundamental interest" argument alone, however; the court accorded special scrutiny to California's financing scheme because in relying on local property taxes the state distributed this "fundamental interest" on the basis of district wealth.[101] *Serrano* concluded that wealth was a suspect" classification which, when it impinged on a fundamental interest, deserved strict scrutiny. It referred for authority to cases like *Griffin v. Illinois*[102] and *Douglas v. California,*[103] requiring respectively a free transcript and a court-appointed lawyer for an indigent defendant who appealed, and *Harper v. Virginia State Board of Elections,*[104] requiring that the right to vote not be dependent upon payment of a tax. Finding no "compelling interest" to support the California scheme, *Serrano* declared that if the plaintiffs proved their allegations, the scheme must be declared unconstitutional.[105]

Some rough spots, however, are evident in this form of the equal protection analysis. The first is the growth of skepticism over the relevance of disparities. *Serrano,* because of its procedural posture, accepted as true the plaintiffs' allegation that "[a]s a *direct result* of the financing scheme . . . substantial disparities in the quality and extent of availability of educational opportunities exist and are perpetuated . . . .[106] That allegation is now an item for proof on remand. A review of the available data suggests that proof will be difficult. If the cause and effect relationship between financing variations and quality of schooling cannot successfully be proved, the "fundamental interest" of education can hardly be said to be distributed on the basis of wealth. Justice Harlan long contended, moreover, that no historical or doctrinal underpinning ever supported the more stringent equal protection scrutiny except in the case of racial classifications, the primary focus of the Fourteenth Amendment.[107] Although the Supreme Court has consistently rejected this argument[108] (Justice Rehnquist appears now to have taken up the cry),[109] it is nevertheless awkward to fit education into the "fundamental interest" category. It is true that the Court has referred broadly to the importance of education in American life,[110] but never has it specifically identified education as a fundamental interest that sparks a special equal protection analysis.[111]

Some recent decisions make unlikely any extension of the fundamental interest category beyond those interests identified as constitutional rights—such as the franchise and interstate movement. In *Dandridge v. Williams*,[112] for example, a case involving welfare assistance and, in the Court's words, "the most basic economic needs of impoverished human beings,"[113] the Court declined to apply a strict standard of review. It stated that in the "area of economics and social welfare" it would impose only the traditional requirement of a legitimate objective and a rational means of implementing the objective.[114] Education is not an independent constitutional right and certainly seems to fall in the "area of . . . social welfare." In *Lindsey v. Normet*,[115] the Court refused to place "decent, safe and sanitary housing" in the fundamental interest category. Again, it was a "social and economic ill" for which the "Constitution does not provide judicial remedies."[116] The Court's statement that "[w]e are unable to perceive in [the Constitution] any constitutional guarantee of access to dwellings of a particular quality"[117] casts serious doubt on arguments that make the quality of educational services a fundamental interest.

Proponents of the *Serrano*-type approach argue that education is different from other social welfare benefits because it affects the intellectual and political interests of the recipients.[118] But economic and social welfare benefits that would provide food for undernourished children or adequate shelter during the formative years seem just as important to intellectual and political development as formal schooling, yet are clearly precluded by cases like *Dandridge* and *Lindsey*. A recent case from the Second Circuit reflects the impact of these cases. In *Johnson v. New York State Education Department*,[119] children and parents who could not afford to purchase school textbooks confronted the court with the picture of "[i]ndigent children sitting bookless, side by side in the same classroom with other more wealthy children learning with purchase[d] textbooks"[120] The court found it realistic to describe the potential consequence as "a widespread feeling of inferiority and unfitness in poor children . . . psychologically, emotionally and educationally disastrous to their well being."[121] Although it perceived education as "an area of fundamental importance," the court, concluding that education is in the realm of social welfare, followed *Dandridge* in refusing to apply a strict standard of review.[122]

The relevance of the cases striking down classifications based on ability to pay is also uncertain.[123] Commentators have pointed out that such cases can be interpreted as securing not equality, but minimum protection in some areas—certain essential elements in a criminal defense and access to the vote.[124] Suits challenging resource distribution among schools and school districts, on the other hand, are directed at securing not a minimum, but equality. In a recent case the Supreme Court seemed to support the "minimum" interpretation of the ability-to-pay cases. Declining to invoke the equal protection clause, the Court struck down a filing fee prerequisite to an indigent's divorce application on the ground that some minimum access to divorce procedures is constitutionally essential under the due process clause.[125] Probably the severest blow to the whole idea that ability-to-pay classifications deserve special treatment, however, is a recent Supreme Court case involving public housing. In *James v. Valtierra*,[126] the Court dealt with a California statute requiring a local referendum before any public housing unit could be built for "persons of low income"—that is, "persons or families who lack the mount of income which is necessary . . . to enable them, without financial assistance, to live in decent, safe and sanitary dwellings, without overcrowding."[127] At the same time, public housing for the "aged, veterans, state employees, persons of moderate income, or any class of citizens other than the poor" required no such referendum.[128] As the dissent pointed out, these distinctions constituted a classification based on wealth.[129] Nevertheless, the Supreme Court specifically declined to apply its standards for "suspect" classifications.

Thus, there is no assurance that the attack on judicial restraint in the area of school finance will be successful. The strengths and weaknesses of the arguments have been debated at length elsewhere;[130] the Supreme Court will soon confront the issues, for it has noted probable jurisdiction in *San Antonio Independent School District v. Rodriguez*,[131] an inter-district financing case following the lead of *Serrano. Rodriguez* should settle the constitutional status of statutory distribution formulas that make the money available for education a function of the wealth of individual districts. Presumably in the process it will shed light on the relevance of "fundamental interests" and "suspect classifications" to school finance. But important characteristics that distinguish cases involving intra-district disparities suggest that *Rodriguez* should not for them be a determinative precedent.

First, for inter-district disparities, an explicit cause and effect relationship exists between district wealth and available educational funds: at a uniform tax rate, financing formulas in most states will condition a school district's resources on the district's assessed wealth. For intra-district disparities, where discretionary decisions concerning allocation are involved, however, a cause and effect relationship between available educational funds and the wealth of a family or school attendance area is not so easily proved. Even if schools in low-income neighborhoods within a school district are proved to receive less resources than other schools in the same district, only a correlation is shown. One may *suspect* that the neighborhood's status has something to do with the school's ability to attract funds, but the disparity alone will not provide the mathematical proof available in inter-district cases. Likewise, resolution of the inter-district questions will furnish no direct answer for intra-district disparities that break down either along lines of school racial composition or along line with no perceivable characteristics.

Second, inter-district redistribution raises concern for the integrity of local governmental units. There is fear that state-wide financial equalization would be achieved only at the expense of the fiscal and political independence of these smaller units.[132] Whatever the merits of this argument for resisting correction of inter-district disparities, in the case of intra-district distribution there are no subsidiary centers of governmental power to protect. Taxes are commonly levied for the education budget as a whole across the entire district. The distribution question is how the district shall administratively allocate the resources among its schools. As a consequence of these distinctions, a Supreme Court decision either for or against inter-district equalization will not automatically dispose of intra-district cases.

The Specific Issue of Intra-District Disparities

Two recent cases have addressed the constitutional issue of intra-district disparities.[133] In *Hobson v. Hansen*,[134] the plaintiffs proved that per pupil expenditures for teachers' salaries and benefits in Washington, D. C., were 36.7 percent greater in the wealthier and whiter areas than in the rest of the city and 40.0 percent greater than in Anacostia, one of the poorest and blackest sections. Because of these disparities, whiter and wealthier schools were favored with a 15.5 percent smaller pupil/teacher ratio and a 9.17 percent greater average teacher expenditure per pupil than the rest of the city. The whiter, wealthier schools enjoyed a 24.9 percent advantage in pupil/teacher ratio and a 12.5 percent advantage in average teacher expenditure over Anacostia. Significant disparities in sixth grade reading achievement test scores, according to the court, "strongly buttressed" the plaintiffs' case.[135] Judge Wright ordered the school board to bring its per pupil expenditures for teachers' salaries and benefits at each school to within five percent of the systemwide average.

In *Keyes v. School District Number One*,[136] the plaintiffs proved to the district court's satisfaction that for fifteen schools of seventy to seventy-five percent black or Hispano enrollment in the Denver system, disparities in achievement test levels varied up to one grade and twenty-two to twenty-nine percentile points from the district-wide average. In the segregated elementary schools, 23.9 percent of the teachers had no previous experience in Denver public schools; for twenty selected Anglo schools the percentage was 9.18. Almost fifty percent of the teachers in the segregated elementary schools were on probation compared to approximately twenty-five percent in the Anglo schools. Only 17.4 percent of the teachers in the segregated elementary schools had ten or more years of experience, whereas 47.1 percent in the Anglo schools had such experience. The plaintiffs submitted similar proof for the junior high and high schools and proved a higher teacher turnover rate, higher pupil dropout rate, and the existence of smaller and older physical plants for the segregated schools. The district court ordered desegregation of the system. In reversing this desegregation order, the Tenth Circuit found no unconstitutionality in the resource allocation. It accepted the plaintiffs' argument that the "quality of teachers" affects the quality of schooling, and agreed that the evidence showed that the segregated schools had less experienced teachers. But it refused to accept a cause and effect relationship between teacher experience and inferior education. The low student achievement and high dropout rates, it found from the school board's evidence, were caused by a curriculum "allegedly not tailored to [the children's] education and social needs," and for this deficiency the court ordered no relief.[137]

The divergent outcomes of no relief on the one hand and a stringent equalization requirement on the other are only partially reconcilable. The *Keyes* plaintiffs sought primarily the desegregation of the Denver System. The difficulties which the Tenth Circuit perceived in affording this relief submerged the resource distribution question. It is not clear that even the plaintiffs viewed resource equalization as satisfactory alternative relief. In *Hobson,* by contrast, plaintiffs focused specifically on a request for equalization, having had the school board under desegregation orders since 1967.[138] The *Keyes* plaintiffs directed much of their proof toward establishing that racial concentrations among the schools, however caused, created inequalities in the education afforded. This emphasis suggested that desegregation was the only viable remedy and resulted in somewhat less systematic proof of resource disparities than in *Hobson.* Finally, of course, the expert testimony may have differed in quantity, relevance, or persuasiveness in the two cases.

Such explanations, however, cannot dispel an ultimate divergence in the respective approaches of the two courts to the law and the educational data. The Tenth Circuit appears to have placed the burden of proof on the school children to show that items such as teacher experience caused a difference in student achievement.[139] In light of the educational data, it is not surprising that the plaintiffs failed in this proof. Apparently without it, the Tenth Circuit was not prepared to find a constitutional violation. In *Hobson,* on the other hand, once the plaintiffs had shown disparities in items such as teacher salaries and pupil/staff ratios between predominantly white and predominantly black schools, the court placed the burden on the school board either to rebut the inference of discrimination or to justify the disparities.[140] In this context, the nature of the educational data made it impossible to prove that the unequal resources had no impact on student performance. Without such proof, Judge Wright concluded that a constitutional violation had occurred.

Settling a difficult issue by concluding that one party failed to meet its burden of proof is, of course, a time-honored legal maneuver. But the state of knowledge concerning the significance of various school inputs effectively converts that maneuver into a substantive decision on the ultimate issue: whether inequality in the particular inputs is constitutionally permissible. Which conclusion does the equal protection clause, or its school-dressed counterpart, equal educational opportunity, demand? At least three general foci of equality are relevant for intra-district cases:[141] (1) resource equality—that students should have access to the same educational resources regardless of the differing results the latter may produce; (2) process equality—that students should have fair access to available programs, although the programs might differ in resources, per pupil expenditures, or effects; (3) outcome equality—that students, regardless of their initial endowment or backgrounds, should be made equal by the schools.

To conclude that one of these is the constitutional command to the exclusion of the others seems impossible. Even if consensus were attainable, we would still be far short of the precision needed to make the command intelligible.[142] If resource equality is the goal, the "educational resources" that must be equalized still are undefined. Is it expenditures? teacher experience? academic qualifications? ability to run an orderly class? ability to run a creative class? Equality in some of these resources may preclude equality in others. Is equality to be achieved despite differing preferences among students, their families or neighborhoods? If process equality is the goal, the elements of a "fair" choice still must be articulated. Criteria for assignment could be based on individual merit or ability to derive the most benefit from the program. If the goal is outcome equality, the student characteristics that are to be equalized (achievement? future earnings? respect for authority?) must be defined, ways to accomplish their equalization developed, and the cost of that equalization considered. Such problems effectively preclude for the present an abstract constitutional command of "equality" in education.[143]

That conclusion, however, does not resolve the issue of the *Hobson-Keyes* divergence. The plaintiffs in both those cases introduced proof that inequalities in some of the school inputs correlated with the schools' racial compositions. The long history of school desegregation provides a lesson for such disparities.

Even before *Brown v. Board of Education*[144] held that segregated education was unconstitutional, the constitutional command was that racially separate schools be "equal." Just prior to its decision in *Brown,* the Supreme Court had begun to give content to the requirement of equality. In *Sweatt v. Painter,*[145] for example, the state of Texas had established a law school for blacks in order to keep the University of Texas Law School segregated. In determining that the education offered at the black school was not equal to that at the University of Texas, the Court examined faculty, administration, curriculum, library, students, even alumni and the school's reputation. Perhaps the Court considered itself particularly competent to evaluate the characteristics of legal education, but the same year in *McLaurin v. Oklahoma State Regents,*[146] it did not hesitate to examine the "learning atmosphere" for graduate education students in determining that segregated conditions within a school produced unequal opportunities for black students.

A similar examination of the intangible learning environment produced the Court's judgment in *Brown* that segregated schools inherently could not be equal. Arguably, the Supreme Court should not have been so confident of its ability to pick those items where inequality mattered and to gauge their impact. But that argument implies that the constitutional concern is with outcomes and that achievement is the important focus. *Brown* and its progeny made clear that the evil to be remedied was not inequality in quantifiable impact, but discrimination.[147] Segregation in bathhouses, parks, buses, and courtrooms—areas where formal equality without desegregation seemed possible—soon fell under constitutional prohibition.[148] Similarly, without confronting the questions posed by the notion of "process equality," courts have prohibited the tracking of students into different programs when that process is used to separate the races.[149] In a very real sense, the doubts engendered by the Coleman Report are irrelevant to the constitutional arguments of discrimination. The cases following *Brown* demonstrate, moreover, that where purposeful discrimination is apparent, the importance of the items discriminatorily assigned is irrelevant; it is unnecessary to identify them as "fundamental interests" to secure a halt to the discrimination.

The same reasoning applies to a discriminatory allocation that favors schools identifiably white over schools identifiably black, even though outcome equality may not be affected and items which are truly educational resources may not be involved. Title I, for purposes of its comparability requirements, has identified various measures of pupil/staff ratios and per pupil expenditures as areas of concern.[150] During the years of the *Brown* mandate's enforcement, while freedom of choice was still an acceptable method of desegregation, several courts issued stringent equalization decrees for remaining black schools. These decrees applied to facilities and curricula, pupil/teacher ratios, and per pupil expenditures for operating and capital improvement costs.[151] *Hobson* identified per pupil expenditures for teachers' salaries and benefits (representing teacher experience and pupil/teacher ratio) and achievement test scores.[152] The plaintiffs' proof in *Keyes* related to achievement tests, teacher experience, teacher turnover rate, pupil dropout rate, and the size and age of physical plant.[153] Not all of these items are relevant to the constitutional issue of discrimination. Variations in student achievement and attendance habits, for example, appear to be beyond the direct control of a school board.[154] They would be more relevant if the equal protection clause were construed to demand that students achieve equally or exhibit the same propensity to attend school. Discrimination in any of the items that can be broadly characterized as inputs, or discrimination in provision of the opportunity to participate in a particular program,[155] on the other hand, constitutes the classic "invidious" discrimination outlawed by the equal protection clause,[156] regardless of whether education is deemed a fundamental interest or the items discriminatorily assigned measurably affect achievement.

The same conclusion should follow if school boards intentionally discriminate against schools serving low-income families in favor of schools serving wealthier families. This discrimination presents even a stronger case for constitutional prohibition than the state practices struck down by the Supreme Court for denying important services to those unable to afford them.[157] In the case of intra-district discrimination, no pricing system is involved. Since a family is not given the opportunity to purchase the school services it desires, it cannot be said that the state is treating all equally by making all pay the same price. Instead, students are administratively assigned to schools. This sort of wealth classification—matching low-income families with an inferior share of educational resources—is "suspect" in a fashion that a price system can never be. Like discrimination by race, no legitimate state purpose supports it.[158]

The practical question in intra-district distribution cases, however, is the proof of discrimination. In neither *Keyes* nor *Hobson,* for example, did plaintiffs prove purposeful discrimination against schools serving black or low-income students. Instead, they proved correlations between racial or wealth concentrations and resource disparities within a district. On occasion, such patterns justify a conclusion of purposeful discrimination. In *Yick Wo v. Hopkins,*[159] for example, the relevant evidence was, simply, that all of 200 Chinese applicants were denied laundry operating licences whereas all but one of the 80 non-Chinese applicants obtained them. The Supreme Court found that "the conclusion cannot be resisted, that no reason for it exists except hostility to the race and nationality."[160] Similarly, in *Gomillion v. Lightfoot,*[161] the plaintiffs' offer of proof showed that by statute Alabama had changed the shape of the municipality of Tuskegee "from a square to an uncouth twenty-eight-sided figure."[162] As a result no whites, but all except four or five of four hundred black voters, were removed from the city. Although this offer of proof showed only a correlation between race and those who had lost the municipal franchise, the Supreme Court found the conclusion "irresistible, tantamount for all practical purposes to a mathematical demonstration," that the legislation was designed to deprive black citizens of the municipal franchise.[163] When proof of a pattern of disparities leads to a conclusion of purposeful discrimination, arguments regarding the significance of its impact should be considered just as irrelevant as when proof of conscious discrimination is shown.

Yick Wo and *Gomillion* are particularly egregious examples of an almost perfect correlation between race and inferior treatment. In the case of schools, however, the correlation between race or wealth and unequal resources is likely to be less significant. In *Hobson*, for example, the school board contended that plaintiffs' proof did not justify a finding of discrimination because, even if disparities existed in favor of the traditionally white schools, those schools were no longer all-white, but twenty-six percent black.[164] Since the rest of the system was ninety-eight percent black,[165] however, the court properly found this proof inadequate to destroy the inference of discrimination; such differences were enough to confer racial identity upon the schools. Certainly, that some black students benefitted from the favored treatment of the predominantly white schools and that some white students suffered from the inferior resources of the predominantly black schools does not offset proof of a pattern of inequality among the schools.[166] Proof that the schools are racially identifiable ought to be sufficient. In a jury exclusion case just last Term, for example, the Supreme Court, unwilling to rely on statistical improbability alone, pointed to proof of the opportunity to discriminate in conjunction with a "striking" relationship between exclusion and race.[167] "Racial designation" of prospective jurors, providing a "clear and easy opportunity for racial discrimination," when combined with a correlation between exclusion and race, created a *prima facie* case of unconstitutionality.[168]

Although cases have not developed the subject, proof of correlation between inferior treatment and low income should be treated similarly to correlations with race in drawing an inference of discrimination.[169] In *Hobson*, the school board met the plaintiff's challenge of discrimination against schools serving low-income families by proving that no relationship existed district-wide between the median family income of a school and per pupil expenditures.[170] In the specific circumstances of the Washington case, the court found this proof unavailing because it left open the relationship between race and resources; the pattern of white children benefitting from superior resources remained.[171] Had the plaintiffs' case focused solely on income, however, the school board's proof would have nullified any attempt to show the existence of a discriminatory pattern relating to income and would have required plaintiffs to come forward with other evidence to sustain an inference of discrimination based on wealth. Similarly, if the school board could have shown that district-wide no statistical relationship existed between the racial composition of a school and its resources, the inference of discrimination on racial grounds would have failed.

Related to the issue of correlation between race or wealth and inferior treatment is the question of how disparate the treatment must be to raise the inference of discrimination. The Supreme Court has indicated that it must be substantial. In *Swain v. Alabama*,[172] the Court was unwilling to make an inference of discrimination from a ten percent underrepresentation of an identifiable group. In *Swain*, however, the Court spoke of *proof* of discrimination. Clearly a state might successfully prove that such a variation resulted from random selection or other legitimate criteria. But as Professor Ely has persuasively argued, such nonnegligible disparities ought at least to raise the inference that requires a state to offer its rebuttal.[173] Title I and *Hobson v. Hansen* together suggest that in the area of school resources variations under five percent ought to be considered negligible.

Once the inference of discrimination is raised, "the burden of proof shifts to the state to rebut the presumption of unconstitutional action by showing that permissible racially neutral selection criteria and procedures" produced the result.[174] The school board, after all, has the best knowledge of what procedures in fact produced the disparities. Failure to rebut this *prima facie* case requires a judgment that the conduct was purposefully discriminatory. The Supreme Court has emphasized that proof of systematic discriminatory impact is not rebutted by proof of individual instances of propriety: "The result bespeaks discrimination, whether or not it was a conscious decision on the part of any individual . . . ."[175] The strength of the *prima facie* case will determine the measure of the rebuttal: the more exact the correlation and the greater the disparity, the less convincing will be the assertion of neutral conduct. The extraordinary situations in *Yick Wo* and *Gomillion* make it difficult to conceive of any possible rebuttal, though even in *Yick Wo* the Supreme Court pointed out that the state had shown "no reason" for the disparate treatment[176] and in

Gomillion it said that no "countervailing municipal function" had been suggested.[177] In *Hobson* and *Keyes,* on the other hand, while the patterns certainly raise a suspicion of discrimination, a confident conclusion that only racial discrimination could explain them seems unwarranted. Conceivably, a school board in the posture of Washington or Denver could, in some instances, prove successfully what the District of Columbia school board failed to: that the alleged disparities were a wholly fortuitous consequence of a combination of such factors as a teacher assignment policy adopted without consideration of racial impact, the greater difficulty and expense of maintaining an adequate plant in a deteriorating geographical area, and unpredicted population movements.

Although a state must rebut the inference of discriminatory purpose arising from proof of disproportionate impact, courts and commentators have been divided on whether that rebuttal ends the constitutional inquiry. *Hawkins v. Town of Shaw*[178] exercised the Fifth Circuit over the proper analysis. In the little town of Shaw, Mississippi, residential segregation was "almost total." Ninety-seven percent of black residences were located in the sections of Shaw that were all black. Ninety-seven percent of the residences without sanitary sewer attachments were in these black neighborhoods. Of the houses that fronted on unpaved streets, only two percent were white. New mercury vapor street lights had been installed only in white neighborhoods. Water pressure, drainage, and traffic control were also poorer in black areas. Judge Tuttle for the majority argued that once the plaintiffs had established a *prima facie* case through proof of discriminatory effects, the next step was to consider whether the state had justified the pattern through a "compelling state interest."[179] Judge Bell, on the other hand, seemed to argue that the initial question was still the factual issue of whether or not a purposeful racial classification had been drawn. Only after the state's rebuttal on that issue had been considered would he proceed to the "compelling state interest" requirement.[180]

In *Chance v. Board of Examiners,*[181] the racial impact of competitive examinations for supervisory positions in the New York public school system was "significant and substantial." The Second Circuit found no suggestion of discriminatory purpose, however, and characterized the plaintiffs' proof as a *prima facie* case of "an invidious *de facto* classification."[182] Whether to apply the stringent equal protection analysis applied in cases of purposeful discrimination the court found "difficult . . . and . . . not to be resolved by facile reference to cases involving intentional racial classifications."[183] The court concluded that there was no need to decide that issue because the board's examinations were not even rationally related to its purpose of employee selection. But it reached this conclusion by holding the board to a "heavy burden of proof" in demonstrating the rationality of its classification—in this case, that the tests used were job-related.[184]

In *Castro v. Beecher*,[185] on the other hand, the First Circuit confronted the issue directly in a similar challenge to police recruiting examinations. The court found the "compelling interest" or "compelling necessity" requirements of a stringent equal protection analysis inappropriate "in their full rigor" for a "racial impact case" because of their inflexibility.[186] But the court required more than a rational relationship. The First Circuit constructed a new test: "The public employer must, we think, in order to justify the use of a means of selection shown to have a racially disproportionate impact, demonstrate that the means is in fact *substantially related* to job performance."[187]

Professor Ely has argued that once the inference of discriminatory purpose is rebutted, the constitutional inquiry should end.[188] To extend it, he contends, would be to constitutionally require a racially balanced impact. This end he finds dangerous because it might be used improperly and because it weakens the notion that in evaluation of people race is irrelevant to merit. But Professor Horowitz has argued that the presence of discriminatory purpose is not necessary to establish a constitutional violation.[189] Proof of disproportionate impact, he maintains, requires the state to justify the impact, under the strict standard of review, by the strength of its interests and the unavailability of alternative programs that would produce less disproportionate impact.

This important debate is basically the same as that over the constitutionality of defacto segregation: in the absence of prior discrimination, can a school board simply ignore race in drawing attendance zones, or must it be "race conscious" with a view toward avoiding disproportionate racial concentrations in a school? Resolution of the question depends ultimately on political and philosophical attitudes, and the Supreme Court has not explicitly faced the issue. But the Court has given implicit support to Professor Ely's position in another context last Term. In *Jefferson v. Hackney*,[190] the plaintiffs proved that a significantly larger percentage of blacks and Mexican-Americans in Texas participated in the Aid to Families with Dependent Children program than in other categorical assistance programs and that the AFDC program was funded at seventy-five percent of recognized need, while the other programs were funded at ninety-five and one hundred percent.[191] The Supreme Court affirmed the trial court's finding that no discriminatory purpose was present and concluded that the plaintiffs were "left with their naked statistical argument."[192] Applying the "traditional standard of review," the Court required proof that Texas' program was either "invidious" or "irrational." To apply the "compelling interest" standard, it concluded,

> would render suspect each difference in treatment among the grant classes, however lacking in racial motivation and however otherwise rational the treatment might be. Few legislative efforts to deal with the difficult problems posed by current welfare programs could survive such scrutiny, and we do not find it required by the Fourteenth Amendment.[193]

Thus, *Jefferson* implies that where discriminatory purpose is disproved, differences in treatment that parallel racial lines receive traditional equal protection analysis. In other words, any rational state objective will support them. Of course, *Jefferson* can be distinguished from cases involving school finance. First, *Jefferson* dealt with comparisons among four separate welfare programs with different objectives: aid to the elderly, aid to the blind, aid to the disabled, and aid to dependent children. Consequently, there was perhaps less reason to expect uniform treatment than in the case of different schools in the same community.[194] Second, *Jefferson* might be limited to the degree of inequality present in that case. Although the AFDC program at seventy-five percent funding was eighty-seven percent black and Mexican-American while the Old-Age Assistance program at full funding was only forty percent black and Mexican-American, the two programs which were funded at ninety-five percent were forty-seven percent and fifty-six percent black and Mexican-American.[195] Thus, viewed at their narrowest, the disparities were between two predominantly minority programs: seventy-five percent funding for a program eighty-seven percent minority in composition and ninety-five percent funding for a program fifty-six percent minority. The Court seemed to attach importance to the fact that "the number of minority members in all categories is substantial."[196] Arguably, more egregious situations, where the recipients of the favored treatment are more clearly identified as white, could escape the thrust of *Jefferson*. Moreover, welfare programs do not as obviously acquire racial identity as do schools[197] AFDC recipients are not brought together in one place, there to be treated inferior to old age recipients, all assembled at another location. That arrangement, of course, is precisely the situation with school inequalities. Where schools, long a focal point of discrimination, can be racially identified and differences in treatment are obvious, the case for correction is materially stronger than *Jefferson*.

All these distinctions, however, relate to the appearance of evil; they affect the inference of discrimination to be drawn from the context. Largely they are met by increasing the school board's burden of proving that discrimination is not the explanation. In that respect, the greater burden of justification required in *Castro* and *Chance* seems appropriate. Neither of those cases characterize the burden as a response to the inference of discrimination,[198] and they purport to apply different analyses—*Chance* a "rational relationship" test and *Castro* a "substantial relationship." But the requirement that a state must give more substantial justification for a program producing a racial effect that if no racial effect occurred can be viewed as necessary to dispel the inference discrimination. Otherwise, *Jefferson* seems to have rejected quite directly the claim that where discriminatory purpose is absent, the presence of inequalities rises to constitutional stature[199]—unless, indeed, the Supreme Court elevates school resources to the status of a fundamental interest and thus isolates them from the area of economics and social welfare involved in *Jefferson*.

CONCLUSION

The relationship between traditional school resources and student achievement is uncertain. But our current naïveté concerning the process of human learning argues for experimentation. Requiring school districts to equalize school inputs to concentrate a heavier allocation of resources on schools serving educationally disadvantaged students is consistent with that goal.[200] Articulation of educational objectives, together with proper monitoring of experiments, might produce effective programs. Although no abstract constitutional command of equality in education seems possible, discrimination on account of race or wealth in the provision of resources deserves prohibition under even a traditional reading of the equal protection clause. That conclusion implies that where discriminatory practices exist, they should be remedied.[201] In that respect *Hobson* is correct, and *Keyes* is wrong. But all we can confidently predict about a remedy like the *Hobson* equalization decree is that it will equalize those items which it orders equalized and remove some of the obvious indicia of discrimination.[202] Hopes for improved achievement among students previously discriminated against still have only shaky support. What is finally needed is the articulation of educational objectives and knowledge of how students learn and how they can be successfully taught. Then the access of individual students to appropriate resources within their schools will become the relevant consideration.

FOOTNOTES

[1] PRESIDENT'S COMM'N ON SCHOOL FINANCE, SCHOOLS, PEOPLE, AND MONEY (1972).

[2] NATIONAL EDUCATIONAL FINANCE PROJECT, FUTURE DIRECTIONS FOR SCHOOL FINANCING (1971).

[3] For purposes of this Article we shall use the term "resources" to refer to money and the services schools and school districts purchase with it such as teachers, supplies, and physical plant. We specify this definition because of the expansive reading sometimes given the term. For example, James Coleman, director of the survey that produced OFFICE OF EDUCATION, U.S. DEPT. OF HEALTH, EDUC. & WELFARE, EQUALITY OF EDUCATIONAL OPPORTUNITY (1966) [hereinafter cited as Coleman Report] maintains as a result of this and other studies that the educational resources available to each child in a school include as an important component the educational backgrounds of the other children in school—and any state which dictates the school or school district to which each child goes is unequally distributing those educational resources, however equally it is distributing finances.
Coleman, *Preface to* J. COONS, W. CLUNE & SUGARMAN, PRIVATE WEALTH & PUBLIC EDUCATION xiv (1970) [hereinafter cited as COONS, CLUNE & SUGARMAN].

[4] Serrano v. Priest, 5 Cal. 3d 584, 487 P.2d 1241, 96 Cal. Rptr. 601 (1971).

[5] Rodriguez v. San Antonio Independent School Dist., 337 F. Supp. 280 (W.D. Tex. 1971), *prob. juris noted,* 406 U.S. 966 (1972).

[6] Van Dusartz v. Hatfield, 334 F. Supp. 870 (D. Minn. 1971).

[7] Robinson v. Cahill, 118 N. J. Super. 223, 287, A.2d 187 (Hudson County Ct. 1972). *Cf.* Sweetwater County Planning Comm. v. Hinkle, 491 P.2d 1234 (Wyo. 1971). The only recent judicial resistance to this movement has come from Westchester County, New York. Spano v. Board of Educ., 68 Misc. 2d 804, 328 N.Y.S.2d 229 (Sup. Ct. Westchester County 1972). Hawaii effectively accepted the principle from the beginning by

inheriting one state-wide school administration unit from territorial government.

8 *See* note 5 *supra.*

9 *See, e.g.,* Berke & Callahan, *Inequities in School Finance,* in SELECT SENATE COMM. ON EQUAL EDUCATIONAL OPPORTUNITY, 92D CONG., 2D SESS., THE FINANCIAL ASPECTS OF EQUALITY OF EDUCATIONAL OPPORTUNITY AND INEQUITIES IN SCHOOL FINANCE 49 n.* (Comm. Print 1972) [hereinafter cited as Comm. Print]; COONS, CLUNE & SUGARMAN 24. Some of the literature treats the problem in passing. *See, e.g.,* Berke & Kelly, *The Financial Aspects of Equality of Educational Opportunity,* in Comm. Print 16. Professor Cohen observed this phenomenon in 1969:

> Since *Brown* there has been an almost complete lack of attention to the matter of *intra*-district resource inequality, something which might have been expected in view of the decision's emphasis on school outcomes . . . . [T]he increasing emphasis on school outcomes, and recent reports that few inequities still exist, have continued to distract attention from this subject.

Cohen, *Defining Equality in Education,* 16 U.C.L.A.L. REV. 255, 277-72 (1969). Only a few legal discussions deal directly with the problem. *See, e.g.,* Horowitz, *Unseparate but Unequal—The Emerging Fourteenth Amendment Issue in Public School Education,* 13 U.C.L.A.L. REV. 1147 (1966); Rousselot, *Achieving Equal Education Opportunity for Negroes in the Public Schools of the North & West: The Emerging Role for Private Constitutional Litigation,* 35 GEO. WASH. L. REV. 698, 714-17 (1967). *See also* Weitz, *Race & Equal Educational Opportunity in the Allocation of Public School Teachers,* 39 GEO. WASH. L. REV. 341, 373-77 (1971).

10 *See e.g.,* Berke & Kelly, *supra* note 9, at 16.

11 *See e.g.,* J. GUTHRIE, G. KLEINDORFER, H. LEVIN & R. STOUT, SCHOOLS & INEQUALITY 34-35 (1971) [hereinafter cited as GUTHRIE *et al.*], *citing* R. CRAIN, THE POLITICS OF SCHOOL DESEGREGATION (1968); J. DOLLARD, CASTE & CLASS IN A SOUTHERN TOWN (1937); R. STOUT & M. INGER, SCHOOL DESEGREGATIONS PROGRESS IN EIGHT CITIES (1966); and Coleman Report.

12 Federal funds under Title I of the Elementary and Secondary Education Act of 1965, 20 U.S.C. §§ 241a *et seq.* (1970) and state funds for the disadvantaged may have been responsible for such equalization, according to studies of Chicago, Rochester, Syracuse, and one decentralized district in New York City. Berke & Kelly, *supra* note 9, at 16. As pointed out in the text at note 70, *infra,* however, Title I funds are designed not to equalize, but to favor schools that service children from low-income families after state and local resources have already been equalized.

13 A 1969 review of current studies concluded that within districts "racial inequalities in the allocation of school resources persist." Cohen, *supra* note 9, at 272. *See also* sources cited in Hanushek & Kain, *On the Value of Equality of Educational Opportunity as a Guide to Public Policy,* in ON EQUALITY OF EDUCATIONAL OPPORTUNITY 142 n.10 (F. Mosteller & D. Moynihan eds. 1972) [hereinafter cited as ON EQUALITY OF EDUCATIONAL OPPORTUNITY].

14 Socio-economic status is a term used frequently in educational research. It refers to the "results of a complicated social rating process," GUTHRIE *et al.* 16, and is derived from the answers to a number of questions concerning a child's family, such as occupation, income, and educational background. For a more comprehensive discussion of the term and attempts to measure it, see *id.* at 16-25.

15 *Id.* at 33, *citing* C. E. Hansen, Central City & Suburb. A Study of Educational Opportunity (unpublished doctoral dissertation, University of California, Berkeley, 1969).

16 P. SEXTON, EDUCATION & INCOME 114-36, 211-23 (1961).

17 GUTHRIE, *et al., citing* E. Thornblad, The Fiscal Impact of a High Concentration of Low Income Families upon the Public Schools (unpublished doctoral dissertation, University of Illinois, Urbana, 1966).

18 Keyes v. School Dist. No. 1, 313 F. Supp. 61, 90 (D. Colo. 1970), *rev'd in part,* 445 F.2d 990 (10th Cir. 1971), *cert. granted,* 404 U.S. 1036 (1971).

[19] Hobson v. Hansen, 269 F. Supp. 401 (D.D.C. 1967), *aff'd sub nom.* Smuck v. Hobson, 408 F.2d 175 (D.C. Cir. 1969), *further relief granted*, 320 F. Supp. 409 (D.D.C. 1970), 327 F. Supp. 844, 848-49 (D.D.C. 1971).

[20] R. HAVIGHURST, F. SMITH & D. WILDER, A PROFILE OF THE LARGE-CITY HIGH SCHOOL 10:6 (1970), *quoted in* Mosteller & Moynihan, *A Path-breaking Report*, in ON EQUALITY OF EDUCATIONAL OPPORTUNITY 11 n.*. See Katzman, *Distribution & Production in a Big City Elementary School System*, 8 YALE ECON. ESSAYS 201 (1968) (no expenditure discrimination in Boston).

[21] Coleman Report 66-122. See discussion in Mosteller & Moynihan, *supra* note 20, at 8-11.

[22] In rural areas, insofar as school districts are consonant with county boundaries, limited inferences may be possible. Coleman Report 38.

[23] Elementary & Secondary Education Act of 1965, 20 U.S.C. § 241e(a)(3)(C) (1970).

[24] 45 C.F.R. § 116.26 (1972).

[25] Equal Educational Opportunities Act of 1972, S.3395, 92d Cong., 2d Sess. § 101(b)(3) (1972). Arthur Wise, Associate Dean of the Graduate School of Education, University of Chicago, has recommended in a report to the Citizens Commission on Maryland Government that a plan for school financing "require a school-by-school audit of funds in order to ensure that the effect of statewide equalization is not lost through misallocation within school districts." To that end he would allow no more than a five percent variation among schools in per pupil expenditure. Wise, *School Finance Equalization Lawsuits: A Model Legislative Response*, 2 YALE REV. OF L. & SOCIAL ACTION 123, 128 (1971).

[26] The bill further required:

> The board shall require reports from the superintendent of schools for such division as will enable the board to evaluate the program in each school and compare the educational program in the various schools in such division. The State Board of Education shall prescribe and enforce standards and tests within each school division to determine compliance herewith, and shall require such corrective measures as may be requisite by the school board of such division as will ensure uniformity therein of the education being provided.

Va. Gen'l Assembly, H.483, Reg. Sess. (1972).

[27] Lawsuits similar to those discussed in the text are reportedly pending in San Francisco and Chicago, Kirp & Youdof, *Serrano in the Political Arena*, 2 YALE REV. OF L. & SOCIAL ACTION 143, 147 n.10 (1971), and Detroit, Michelson, *Equal School Resource Allocation*, 7 J. HUMAN RESOURCES 283, 284 n.5 (1972).

[28] Currently, busing must be delayed during the appeals process. Education Amendments of 1972, Pub. L. No. 92-318, § 803, 41 U.S.L.W. 46 (June 23, 1972).

[29] *Cf.* GUTHRIE *et al.* 64.

[30] Hanushek & Kain, *supra* note 13, at 122-23.

[31] In vetoing the bill on December 9, 1971, President Nixon referred to the "family-weakening implications of the system it envisions," and described it as "the most radical piece of legislation to emerge from the 92nd Congress." Iglehart, *Welfare Report/Expensive Senate child-care package faces dim prospects in House*, 4 NAT'L J.1202 (1972).

[32] And such attempts have achieved only problematical measurable benefits. Lines, *Race & Learning: A Perspective on the Research*, 11 INEQUALITY IN EDUC. 26, 27 (1972).

[33] W. Mollenkopf & S. Melville, A Study of Secondary School Characteristics as Related to Test Scores, Research Bull. 56-6 (mimeographed, Educational Testing Service, 1956), *abstracted in* 10 AM. PSYCHOLOGIST 447-48 (1955).

[34] S. Goodman, The Assessment of School Quality (N. Y. State Educ. Dep't, March, 1969), *summarized in* Dyer, *School Factors and Equal Educational Opportunity*, in EQUAL EDUCATIONAL OPPORTUNITY 45-46 (Harvard Education Review, ed. 1969).

[35] "Classroom atmosphere," as measured by direct observations, also

had an independent relationship. Dyer, *supra* note 34 at 47. Other measures revealed that the correlations with these variations in school services could not be explained solely by the factor of socio-economic status. *Id.* at 46-47.

[36] M. Shaycroft, *The High School Years: Growth in Cognitive Skills* (American Institutes for Research and School of Education, University of Pittsburgh, 1967),*summarized in* Dyer, *supra* note 34, at 47-48.

[37] *Id.* at 48.

[38] J. Alan Thomas, Efficiency in Education: A Study of the Relationship Between Selected Inputs and Mean Test Scores in a Sample of Senior High Schools (unpublished Ph.D. dissertation, Stanford University, School of Education, 1962), *summarized in* GUTHRIE *et al.* 67.

[39] C. BENSON, STATE AND LOCAL FISCAL RELATIONSHIP IN PUBLIC EDUCATION IN CALIFORNIA. (Report of Fact Finding Committee on Revenue and Taxation of the Senate of the State of California, 1965), *summarized in* GUTHRIE *et al.* 67-68. In the same year Herbert J. Kiesling, using data collected in the Quality Measurement Project found a positive relationship between achievement and per pupil expenditures, although the relationship was strong only for large school districts. Kiesling, *Measuring a Local Government Service: A Study of School Districts in New York State*, 49 REV. OF ECON. & STATISTICS 356 (1967).

[40] Coleman Report 312.

[41] Coleman Report 312-16, 325.

[42] Mosteller & Moynihan, *supra* note 20, at 15. *See also* Coleman, *Equal Schools or Equal Students?*, 4 THE PUBLIC INTEREST 70, 73-74 (summer 1966).

[43] Coleman Report 325.

[44] Mosteller and Moynihan, *supra* note 20, at 28-30.

[45] Coleman Report 312-13.

[46] Bowles & Levin, *The Determinants of Scholastic Achievement—An Appraisal of Some Recent Evidence*, 3 J. HUMAN RESOURCES (1968).

[47] Hanushek & Kain, *supra* note 13, at 121.

[48] *Id.* at 120.

[49] Bowles, *Towards Equality of Education Opportunity*, in EQUAL EDUCATIONAL OPPORTUNITY 118 (Harvard Education Review, ed. 1969).

[50] Hanushek & Kain, *supra* note 13, at 129, 131-32.

[51] Bowles, *supra* note 49.

[52] Hanushek & Kain, *supra* note 13, at 120-21, 129-30, 131. The Report also noted a significant relationship between teacher characteristics and student achievement. Teachers who themselves scored high on verbal ability tests had students who performed better on achievement tests. The importance of instructor verbal ability, moreover, increased for students above the sixth grade and especially for black students. Some scholars have interpreted verbal ability as a representation of a teacher's general intelligence and suggested that the findings are therefore consistent with the intuitive judgment that a more intelligent instructor tends to make a better teacher. GUTHRIE *et al.* 70-71. The conclusion drawn by one scholar was that:

> the evidence of the Coleman Study itself, far from documenting the ineffectiveness of increased school resources, indicates that teacher quality is a major determinant of scholastic achievement among Negro students and that feasible changes in the level of quality of the teachers of Negro students would bring about significant changes in the achievement levels of these students.

Bowles, *supra* note 49, at 120.

[53] GUTHRIE *et al.* 79-84.

[54] *Id.* at 84-90.

[55] The authors interpreted this finding as suggesting that physical facilities affect student attitude and motivation and the avaliability of curriculum offerings. *Id.* at 88.

[56] *Id.* at 89-90.

[57] *See generally* ON EQUALITY OF EDUCATIONAL OPPORTUNITY.

[58] Armor, *School and Family Effects on Black and White Achieve-*

ment: A reexamination of the USOE Data, in ON EQUALITY OF EDUCA-
TIONAL OPPORTUNITY 168, 209-10 (1972).

[59] Smith, *Equality of Educational Opportunity: The Basic Findings
Reconsidered,* in *id.* at 230, 257-59.

[60] Jencks, *The Coleman Report and the Conventional Wisdom,* in *id.* at
69, 91, 99-100.

[61] *Id.* at 102. A similar ambiguity affects the weak relationship he
discovered between student achievement and teacher experience. *Id.* As
might be expected, the percentage of substitutes was negatively related to
achievement; here too, however, underachieving schools conceivably have
more trouble in retaining regular teachers. *Id.* The relationship between
teacher morale and student achievement was at best ambiguous. *Id.* at
103-104. Class size related to verbal achievement, but the relationship
almost disappeared when the comparison was among schools in the same
district, a factor that suggested to Jencks that the relationship might be
a function of differences among a few large cities. *Id.* at 97-99. Again
it is not clear in which direction a cause and effect relationship operates
(if it operates at all) between class size and achievement. Often, small
classes are established for advanced students.

[62] *Id.* at 93-94.

[63] *Id.* at 94-96.

[64] Mosteller & Moynihan, *supra* note 20, at 51. A more recent, government sponsored report on Title I, conducted by the American Institutes for Research, discovered gross mismanagement and no significant
achievement overall. Wash. Post, Apr. 10, 1972, at A3, col. 1

[65] BEHAVIOR TODAY, vol. 3, Apr. 10, 1972, at 1. For a recent debate on
the efficacy of compensatory programs, see Havemann, *Campaign '72
Report/Senate is key to busing moratorium, increased aid to inner city
schools,* 4 NAT'L J. 690, 698 (1972).

[66] Title I funds are supplied to local education agencies serving areas
with concentrations of children from low-income families to expand
and improve their educational programs by various means . . . which
contribute particularly to meeting the special educational needs for
educationally deprived children.
20 U.S.C. § 241a (1970).

[67] 20 U.S.C. § 241e(a)(3)(C) (1970).

[68] 45 C.F.R. § 116.26 (1972). The comparability requirements for the
school year 1972-73 are based on data from the school year 1970-71
("The second fiscal year preceding the fiscal year in which the project
. . . is to be carried out.") 45 C.F.R. § 116.26(b) (1972).

[69] 20 U.S.C. § 241e(a)(3)(B) (1970).

[70] Although state educational agencies have primary responsibility
for determining that local agencies meet comparability requirements, the
Commissioner of Education has promulgated specific regulations that
define the responsibility. 45 C.F.R. § 116.26 (1972).

[71] 45 C.F.R. §§ 116.26(b)-(c) (1972).

[72] *Id.*

[73] It is permissible, of course, for the district to treat its project
schools better than the nonproject school average.

[74] 45 C.F.R. § 116.26(c) (1972).

[75] 45 C.F.R. § 116.26(b) (1972).

[76] OFFICE OF EDUCATION, U.S. DEP'T OF HEALTH, EDUC. & WELFARE,
STATISTICS OF STATE SCHOOL SYSTEMS 1967-68, at 11 (1970). Salary expenses include indirect payroll expenses, such as medical and health
benefits and life insurance. The percentages cited include the annual costs
of these expenses.

[77] OFFICE OF EDUCATION, U.S. DEP'T OF HEALTH, EDUC. & WELFARE,
EDUCATION OF THE DISADVANTAGED: AN EVALUATIVE REPORT ON TITLE I
ELEMENTARY AND SECONDARY EDUCATION ACT OF 1965, FISCAL YEAR 1968,
at 8 (1970).

[78] It is probably realistic to expect problems in securing compliance
with the comparability requirements. The Commissioner of Education
has required some form of comparability since 1968, OFFICE OF EDUCATION,

U.S. DEP'T OF HEALTH, EDUC. & WELFARE, ESEA T*itle* I PROGRAM #44, § 7.1 (1968); 45 C.F.R. § 116.17(h) 1969), yet the Office of Education estimates that as many as ninety percent of the funded districts have used their Title I funds to supplant rather than supplement state and local funds. OFFICE OF EDUCATION, U.S. DEP'T OF HEALTH, EDUC. & WELFARE, THE COMMISSIONER'S ANNUAL REPORT TO CONGRESS 27 1970. *See also* NATIONAL ADVISORY COUNCIL ON THE EDUCATION OF DIS- ADVANTAGED CHILDREN, 1971 ANNUAL REPORT FOR THE PRESIDENT AND THE CONGRESS 2-3 (1971). If noncompliance continues, however, private law- suits may spring up to redress these illegalities. In an unreported opinion of October, 1970, a district court in Maine held that parents of poor and educationally disadvantaged children had standing to seek enforcement of Title I provisions, since they were the intended beneficiaries of the statute. Colpitts v. Richardson, C.A. No. 1838 (D. Me. Oct. 20, 1970), *noted in* 6 INEQUALITY IN EDUCATION 35 (1970). (Settled by stipulation in 1971, 10 INEQUALITY IN EDUCATION 35 (1971). The relief to be accorded under such a suit may be difficult, for enforcement of the comparability requirements could mean withholding of the federal funds rather than compelling the school district to equalize its non-federal funds.

[79] In *Hobson v. Hansen,* 327 F. Supp. 844 (D.D.C. 1971), for example, although the school board argued in court that differences in class size and teacher experience were unrelated to student performance, testimony was introduced that in requesting funds from the city council, the board had consistently maintained that such variables did affect the quality of education. *Id.* at 885, 857.

[80] What is clear is that when parents, with the means to do so, choose their children's schools, the ones they select, whether public or pri- vate, usually cost more to operate than the school they reject. PRESIDENT'S COMM. ON SCHOOL FINANCE, *supra* note 1, at x.

[81] Title I's stated purpose is to secure the expansion and improve- ment of educational programs "by various means . . . which contribute particularly to meeting the special educational needs of educationally de- prived children." 20 U.S.C. § 241a (1970).

[82] The requirements are tailored to the federal objective; expenditures and pupil/staff ratios need not be equalized among nonproject schools. School boards can continue to administer different programs of different costs in the nonproject schools so long as the Title I project schools are comparable to the district-wide mean.

Selection of Title I project schools is the responsibility of the local educational agency and is normally based on the percentage of children from low-income families living in a school attendance area. While there is no limit to the number of schools which may be selected, the goal is to provide comprehensive service to a limited number of children. The Title I investment per child should be equal to about one-half the expenditures per child for regular school programs. Only where the whole school dis- trict has a high concentration of children from low-income families and there is no wide variance in concentration of such children may funds be distributed to all schools in the district. OFFICE OF EDUCATION, U.S. DEP'T OF HEALTH, EDUC. & WELFARE, ESEA TITLE I PROGRAM GUIDE #44 (1968). "[Concentration] leaves two-thirds of Title I eligible students unserved and many more poor children whose parents gross more than $2,000-3,000 annually, ineligible." NATIONAL ADVISORY COUNCIL ON THE EDUCATION OF DISADVANTAGED CHILDREN, 1971 ANNUAL REPORT FOR THE PRESIDENT AND THE CONGRESS 1 (1971).

[83] NATIONAL EDUCATION FINANCE PROJECT, ALTERNATIVE PROGRAMS FOR FINANCING EDUCATION 16, 32 (1971).

[84] For example, achievement tests commonly do not measure the in- culcation of values, attitudes, and behavior. *Id.*

[85] The statute requires

that effective procedures including provision for appropriate objective measurements of educational achievement, will be adopted for evaluat- ing at least annually the effectiveness of the programs in meeting the special educational needs of educationally deprived children.

20 U.S.C. § 241e(a)(6) (1970).

[86] See note 63 *supra* and accompanying text.

[87] Mosteller & Moynihan, *supra* note 20, at 51 n.*.

[88] Performance contracting has not produced significant gains, according to a government-financed Rand Corporation study. Wash. Post, Dec. 11, 1971, at A3, col. 5. Adequate experiments with vouchers have still to be carried out.

[89] Mosteller & Moynihan, *supra* note 20, at 51-52.

[90] U.S. CONST. amend. XIV, § 1.

[91] Yick Wo v. Hopkins, 118 U.S. 356, 369 (1886).

[92] *See, e.g.,* Tussman & tenBrock, *The Equal Protection of the Laws,* 37 CALIF. L. REV. 341 (1949); Note, *Development in the Law—Equal Protection,* 82 HARV. L. REV. 1065 (1969). There are recent hints that the Supreme Court may be adopting a third approach. *See* Note, *New Tenets in Old Houses: Changing Concepts of Equal Protection in* Lindsey v. Normet, 58 VA. L. REV. 930 (1972).

[93] *See* Note, *Development in the Law—Equal Protection,* 82 HARV. L. REV. 1065, 1087 (1969). *But see* Note, *New Tenets in Old Houses: Changing Concepts of Equal Protection in* Lindsey v. Normet, 58 VA. L. REV. 930, 941 (1972).

[94] *See, e.g.,* Korematsu v. United States, 323 U.S. 214 (1944).

[95] Horowitz, *supra* note 9, at 1156-66.

[96] *Id.* at 1165.

[97] He relied on Carrington v. Rash, 380 U.S. 89 (1965); Douglas v. California, 372 U.S. 353 (1963); Griffin v. Illinois, 351 U.S. 12 (1956).

[98] *See* COONS, CLUNE & SUGARMAN, *supra* note 3.

[99] 5 Cal. 3d 584, 487 P.2d 1241, 96 Cal. Rptr. 601 (1971). For the other cases see notes 5-7 *supra.*

[100] 5 Cal. 3d at 604-10, 487 P.2d at 1255-59, 96 Cal. Rptr. at 615-19.

[101] *Id.* at 610-11, 487 P.2d at 1260, 96 Cal. Rptr. at 620.

[102] 351 U.S. 12 (1956).

[103] 372 U.S. 353 (1963).

[104] 383 U.S. 663 (1966).

[105] 5 Cal. 3d at 614-15, 487 P.2d at 1263, 96 Cal. Rptr. at 623.

[106] 5 Cal. 3d at 590, 487 P.2d at 1244, 96 Cal. Rptr. at 604 (emphasis supplied).

[107] *See, e.g.,* Katzenbach v. Morgan, 384 U.S. 641, 660-61 (1966) (dissenting opinion).

[108] *See, e.g.,* Shapiro v. Thompson, 394 U.S. 618 (1969); Harper v. Virginia Bd. of Elections, 383 U.S. 663 (1966).

[109] Weber v. Aetna Casualty & Surety Co., — U.S. — (1972) (dissenting opinion).

[110] *See, e.g.,* Brown v. Board of Educ., 347 U.S. 483, 493 (1954).

[111] *See* Comment, *Equality of Education:* Serrano v. Priest, 58 VA. L. REV. 161, 169 (1972).

[112] 397 U.S. 471 (1970).

[113] *Id.* at 485.

[114] *Id.* at 485-87.

[115] 405 U.S. 56, 74 (1972).

[116] *Id.*

[117] *Id.*

[118] *See, e.g.,* Coons, Clune & Sugarman, *Educational Opportunity: A Workable Constitutional Test for State Financial Structures,* 57 CAL. L. REV. 305, 387-89 (1969).

[119] 449 F.2d 871 (2nd Cir. 1971), *cert. granted,* 405 U.S. 916 (1972).

[120] *Id.* at 873, *quoting* Complaint, XII(6).

[121] 449 F.2d at 873.

[122] *Id.* at 876-77. In fact, the Second Circuit concluded that the plaintiffs' constitutional claim was sufficiently weak that it did not justify convening a three-judge court.

[123] *See* Comment, *supra* note 111, at 166-67.

[124] *See, e.g.,* Michelman, *The Supreme Court, 1968 Term, Foreword: On Protecting the Poor Through the Fourteenth Amendment,* 83 HARV. L.

REV. 7 (1969).
[125] Boddie v. Connecticut, 401 U.S. 371 (1971).
[126] 402 U.S. 137 (1971).
[127] *Id.* at 139 n.2.
[128] *Id.* at 144 (dissenting opinion).
[129] *Id.* at 145.
[130] *See, e.g.,* THE QUALITY OF INEQUALITY: URBAN & SUBURBAN PUBLIC SCHOOLS (C U. Daly ed. 1968); Goldstein, *Interdistrict Inequalities in School Financing:A Critical Analysis of* Serrano v. Priest *and its Progeny*, 120 U. PA. L. REV. 504 (1972); Comment, *supra* note 111.
[131] — U.S. — (1972).
[132] *See* Brief of Amici Curiae in Support of Jurisdictional Statement at 2-3, San Antonio Independent School Dist. v. Rodriguez, — U.S. — (1972) (noting probable jurisdiction).
[133] In an earlier case, a New York court held that parents could not be punished for failing to send their children to an all black and Puerto Rican school that had a disproportionately low quantity of licensed teachers. *In re* Skipwith, 180 N.Y.S. 852 (Dom. Rel. Ct. 1958).
[134] 327 F. Supp. 844 (D.D.C. 1971).
[135] *Id.* at 858.
[136] 313 F. Supp. 61, 90 (D. Colo. 1970), *rev'd in part*, 445 F.2d 990 (10th Cir. 1971), *cert. granted*, 404 U.S. 1036 (1972).
[137] 445 F.2d at 1004.
[138] Hobson v. Hansen, 269 F. Supp. 401 (D.D.C. 1967), *aff'd sub nom.* Smuck v. Hobson, 408 F.2d 175 (D.C. Cir. 1969) (en banc), *further relief granted*, 320 F. Supp. 409 (D.D.C. 1970).
[139] 445 F.2d at 1005.
[140] 327 F. Supp. at 860.
[141] This conceptual framework is taken from Michelson, *Equal Protection & School Resources*, 2 INEQUALITY IN EDUCATION 4, 10 (1969).
[142] The notion of minimum protection, sometimes advanced as a preferable substitute for equal protection, Michelman, *supra* note 124, faces the same difficulties. Michelson, *supra* note 141, at 15.
[143] *Cf.* Cooper, *State Takeover of Education Financing*, 24 NAT. TAX J. 337, 337-39 (1971).
[144] 347 U.S. 483 (1954).
[145] 339 U.S. 629 (1950).
[146] 339 U.S. 637 (1950).
[147] United States v. Jefferson County Bd. of Educ., 372 F.2d 836, 872 (5th Cir. 1966), *aff'd en banc*, 380 F.2d 385, *cert. denied*, 389 U.S. (1967); Rousselot, *supra* note 9, at 700. For an excellent analysis of the reasons supporting attention to discriminatory purpose, see Brest, Palmer v. Thompson: *An Approach to the Problem of Unconstitutional Legislative Motive*, 1971 SUP. CT. REV. 95, 116-31.
[148] Mayor of Baltimore v. Dawson, 350 U.S. 877 (1955) (public beaches and bathhouses); Holmes v. City of Atlanta, 350 U.S. 879 (1955) (golf courses); Gayle v. Browder, 352 U.S. 903 (1956) (buses); Johnson v. Virginia, 373 U.S. 61 (1963) (courtroom seating).
[149] *E.g., Hobson v. Hansen*, 269 F. Supp. 401 (D.D.C. 1967), *aff'd sub nom.* Smuck v. Hobson, 408 F.2d 175 (D.C. Cir. 1969).
[150] *See* text at note 71 *supra*.
[151] *See, e.g.,* Kelley v. Altheimer, 378 F.2d 483 (8th Cir. 1967); United States v. Jefferson County Bd. of Educ., 372 F.2d 836 (5th Cir. 1966), *aff'd en banc*, 380 F.2d 385, *cert. denied*, 389 U.S. 840 (1967). Other cases are cited in *Hobson*, 327 F. Supp. at 863.
[152] 327 F. Supp. at 848-49.
[153] 313 F. Supp. at 77.
[154] In *Hobson v. Hansen*, the court's use of tested reading skills was apparently objected to by both plaintiffs and defendants. Dimond, *School Segregation in the North: There is But One Constitution*, 7 HARV. CIV. RIGHTS—CIV. LIB. L. REV. 1, 17 n.82 (1972). The court did exclude building expenditures related to vandalism, age, and economies of scale because they were beyond the school board's control, 327 F. Supp. at 847-48

nn.3-4.

[155] *Cf.* Rogers v. Paul, 382 U.S. 198, 199 (1965) (unavailability to blacks of courses offered at white high school).

[156] Both black and white students at the disfavored school should be entitled to challenge the discrimination. *Cf.* Loving v. Virginia, 388 U.S. 1 (1967); McLaughlin v. Florida, 379 U.S. 184 (1964).

[157] *See, e.g.*, Griffin v. Illinois, 351 U.S. 12 (1956); Douglas v. California, 372 U.S. 353 (1963).

[158] Admittedly, the *Valtierra* case, presents a significant challenge to this argument. But *Valtierra* was concerned with defacto wealth discrimination, and the majority opinion was swayed by the fact that a referendum, a democratic procedure, was the only obstacle placed in the way of low-income housing.

[159] 118 U.S. 356 (1886).

[160] *Id.* at 374.

[161] 364 U.S. 339 (1960).

[162] *Id.* at 340.

[163] *Id.* at 341.

[164] 327 F. Supp. at 850.

[165] *Id.*

[166] The District of Columbia school board also attempted, by showing substantial differences in expenditures among all schools, black or white, to establish that disparities did not correlate with the racial identity of the schools. 327 F. Supp. at 850. But again, presence of other variations in a system does not effectively meet proof that among variations, white schools consistently receive the superior resources.

[167] Alexander v. Louisiana, 405 U.S. 625 (1972). The accused had offered no proof of conscious discrimination, but showed that the parish population eligible for jury service was twenty-one percent black, that a questionnaire administered by an all-white jury commission created a pool only fourteen percent black, that further selection procedures during which prospective jurors were identified by race produced a pool seven percent black, a venire for the defendant five percent black and a grand jury that was all-white. *Id.* at 629-30.

[168]*Id.* at 630-31.

[169] Greater reluctance to draw the inference might be supported on the ground that racial discrimination is more prevalent than wealth discrimination. Empirical evidence would be necessary to sustain that hypothesis; intuitively it seems unlikely.

[170] 327 F. Supp. at 851.

[171] *Id.* Actually, evidence on the statistical correlation between per pupil expenditures and median family income conflicted, but the court found it unnecessary to resolve that factual issue because even the school board's figures did not meet the proof of racial correlations.

[172] 389 U.S. 202 (1965).

[173] Ely, *Legislative & Administrative Motivation in Constitutional Law*, 79 YALE L. J. 1205, 1264-65 (1970). *But cf.* Whitcomb v. Chavis, 403 U. S. 124 (1971).

[174] Alexander v. Louisiana, 405 U.S. 625, 632; *See* Larry P. v. Riles, no. xxxx (N.D. Cal. filed June 21, 1972) (where I.Q. tests produce an Educable Mentally Retarded Program 66 percent black while the school population is 28.5 percent black, burden shifts to school district to justify tests).

[175] 405 U.S. at 632.

[176] 118 U.S. at 374.

[177]364 U. S. at 342.

[178] 437 F.2d 1286 (5th Cir. 1971), *aff'd en banc*, no. 29013 (5th Cir., filed Mar. 27, 1972).

[179] *Id.* at 1288.

[180] *Id.* at 1293 (concurring opinion).

[181] 458 F.2d 1167 (2d Cir. 1972).

[182] *Id.* at 1176.

[183] *Id.* at 1177.

[184] *Id.*
[185] 459 F.2d 725 (1st Cir. 1972).
[186] *Id.* at 733.
[187] *Id.* at 732 (emphasis supplied).
[188] Ely, *supra* note 165, at 1255-61.
[189] *See* Note 9 *supra.*
[190] 92 S. Ct. 1724 (1972).
[191] *Id.* at 1732. In 1969, the Old Age Assistance Program was forty percent black and Mexican-American, Aid for the Permanently and Totally Disabled was forty-seven percent, Aid to the Blind was fifty-six percent, and Aid to Families with Dependent Children was eighty-seven percent.
[192] *Id.*
[193] *Id.* at 1732-33.
[194] That distinction may disappear, however, if the disparities among schools result from the offering of different programs from school to school, and all students have access to the program of their choice.
[195] These are the 1969 figures. There were no substantial differences in 1967 and 1968. *Id.* at 1732 n.17.
[196] *Id.* at 1732.
[197] In fact, there was testimony in *Jefferson* that even welfare officials were unaware of the racial composition of the programs in Texas. *Id.*
[198] In *Chance,* no contention of purposeful discrimination seems to have been made, 458 F.2d at 1175. After *Jefferson,* plaintiffs in racial impact cases are unlikely to concede the nonexistence of purposeful discrimination.
[199] The Court emphasized this by quoting from *James v. Valtierra:* "But of course a law-making procedure that 'disadvantages' a particular group does not always deny equal protection." 92 S. Ct. at 1733 n.18.
[200] The program expires at the end of fiscal year 1973 unless Congress extends it. 20 U.S.C. § 241b (1970). The current administration's preference for revenue-sharing suggests some difficulties in extending the program, but predictions are untimely in an election year. *See* Havemann, note 65 *supra.*
[201] A remedy for proved intra-district discrimination should not present the difficulties perceived in early challenges to inter-district disparities. Courts were reluctant to accept the measurable standard of equal dollar expenditure per pupil because it would ignore variations in a dollar's purchasing power (somewhat less likely intra-district), the objective of preserving experimentation, and the existence of varying needs among students. McInnis v. Shapiro, 293 F. Supp. 327 (N.D. Ill. 1968), *aff'd mem. sub nom.* McInnis v. Ogilvie, 394 U.S. 322 (1969). Where intra-district discrimination has been proved, a court can give the school district opportunity to produce a different allocation without the discrimination, or order equalization of the offending disparities pending development of a new program.
    Clearly we lack any firm idea of the cost of such remedies in terms of items like school administration costs, court administration costs, and legal fees. Conceivably, such costs could exceed measurable gains. O'Neill, Gray, & Horowitz, *Educational Equality & Expenditure Equalization Orders,* 7 J. HUMAN RESOURCES, 307, 308 (1972). But to some extent it can be said that the equal protection clause has ruled such costs irrelevant where discrimination occurs.
[202] The skeptic might question even this statement. At the beginning of 1972, only 67 of 136 schools were in compliance with the order. The other schools ranged from thirty percent above the district-wide average to twenty percent below. The geographic pattern of disparities, however, had disappeared. Wash. Post, Feb. 29, 1972, p. at A1, col. 4. More reshuffling has now taken place. Wash. Post, May 2, 1972, at C1, col. 4.
    It should be noted that equalization of monetary resources among schools could have particular importance for districts that move to community control if individual schools are given authority to determine expenditures. *See* NATIONAL EDUCATIONAL FINANCE PROJECT, *supra* note 83, at 38-39.

CHAPTER 5

An Overextension of Equal Protection

Jo Desha Lucas

During World War II the writer was enrolled for a brief period of time in an army program in the social sciences operated by one of the eastern universities. One morning the instructor was explaining to the class that the solution to the world's problems is largely dependent upon the instruction of the population in liberal modes of thought. "A liberal," he said, "is the kind of person who votes for school bonds and does not quibble about the cost." At this juncture I raised my hand and upon being recognized, I suggested that some particular community might not need a new school, or might need a new sewer more desperately. He did not actually call me a fascist, but indicated in no uncertain terms that it was just my type of unenlightenment that holds back progress.

The plaintiffs in the first wave of school tax cases, and to an extent the second wave, adopt this view that somehow or another education is a thing apart from other activities of government, and argue that there is some constitutional requirement, derived from the geist, if not the words, of the Equal Protection Clause, that the state act to achieve what is referred to as equal educational opportunity.

The first wave, the so-called *McInnis* type cases, after *McInnis v. Ogilvie*,[1] would read equal protection to require that funds be distributed according to need, a sort of "substantive equal protection." These cases were largely unsuc-

The author is Professor of Law, University of Chicago.

cessful, and small wonder. While no doubt in our system it is a usual and worthwhile objective of government to ameliorate the disadvantages of sub-groups in the community, the number of differences in advantage that exists among various sub-groups is very large. Of course some are ignorant and some learned, but so are some blind and some sighted, some strong and some weak, some sick and some well, some poor and some rich, some disturbed and some well adjusted, and so forth ad infinitum. Since the cornerstone of the American Revolution was the fundamental proposition that taxation is based upon the political consent of the people through their representatives, the choice of areas in which disadvantages are to be attacked through the expenditure of public funds in our system is made through political consensus. For that reason, there can be no substantive equality. Further, while it is a legitimate activity of government to tax and spend to achieve equality, and while this is the objective of many programs, equality is only one objective of government spending. Education is a perfect example. The public is often faced with choices as to whether the community benefits more by bringing up the lowest in the group, or advancing the most able. If equality were the objective, of course this would be perverse. The general public advantage is a factor, however, and in every state and many localities we spend vast sums on subsidizing the most able through the provision of higher education facilities which cannot be used directly by those who in one sense of the word "need" education most. So, too, do we spend money on the development of competitive athletic teams, money that might have been spent on development of the bodies of the puniest children in the school.

There is no need to multiply examples. The determination of "public purpose" is surely largely a matter of democratic decision, and surely the mere fact that one group or another benefits in varying degree from the expenditure of public funds in one program or another, or that there is no precise balance between burden, need, and benefit, is not the predicate for a claim of constitutional deprivation.

The second wave of cases, the so-called *Serrano* type, after *Serrano v. Priest*,[2] represents a somewhat more sophisticated attempt to tie the Equal Protection Clause to de facto differences in support for public schools in different areas of the state. These cases proceed on a number of assumptions. The first is that the Equal Protection Clause applies, at least as it relates to education in the public schools, to the state as an entity. The second is that equal protection is denied to the taxpayer when a given millage per dollar of taxable property "buys" less education per school child in one district than it does in another. Third, it is argued that the school children in the districts with the lower tax yield per child from a constant millage are denied equal protection. Fourth, the assumption is indulged that "poor" children live in districts with low totals of taxable property, and consequently it is argued that the local property tax system of school financing is, de facto, a wealth classification, to be viewed with particular suspicion.

In dealing with the long term implications of these cases, it is to be noted that while they drop the "need" implication of the *McInnis* type cases, they still depend to a large extent on the "holy cow" designation of public education. This is so because the general application of the Equal Protection Clause in the manner suggested would eliminate all important functions of local government in the United States. In this connection it should be borne in mind that the arguments advanced in these cases, though they arise in the context of the asserted unfairness of the local property tax, and their flames are fed by homeowners in districts with high property tax rates, really have nothing to do with high property tax as distinct from other taxes locally imposed, for they are all bottomed on alleged inequalities that proceed from differences between districts in the rate-yield ratio per school child. Thus, if the local taxes were imposed upon sales, or upon income, the differences between total income in the district, or total sales in the district, and those in some other district would be just as inevitable as the present differences in the total of taxable property.

With this preface I should like to talk briefly about the relationship of the Equal Protection Clause to the five underlying premises of the *Serrano* type cases: (1) the Equal Protection Clause and local government generally; (2) the Equal Protection Clause and geographical classifications for tax purposes; (3) the Equal Protection Clause and geographical classifications of services or benefits; (4) the Equal Protection Clause and classifications as to wealth; and (5) the Equal Protection Clause and education.

THE EQUAL PROTECTION CLAUSE AND
LOCAL GOVERNMENT GENERALLY

The Constitution of the United States nowhere mentions local government. This reflects, no doubt, the view that the task of the draftsmen was limited to the distribution of powers between nation and state and that the internal distribution of power was a matter of local concern only. This view is buttressed by the terms of the Tenth Amendment, which reserves the powers not conferred upon the national government to "the States" and to "the People," leaving the people of the states free to design "republican" government that limited the exercise of the reserved powers by the state. Over the years, the people of the states have taken frequent advantage of the power to change their state-local power distribution, a number adopting home rule provisions of one sort or another, and nearly all limiting the power of the legislature to interfere selectively with the management of local concerns.

Independent of these constitutional provisions allocating authority between units of government, of course legislative delegation of governmental powers to counties, cities, towns, and a variety of special function districts has been common throughout the history of the Republic. Judge Cooley spoke of this decentralization principle as "one which almost seems a part of the very nature of the race to which we belong."[3] One does not have to go so far to recognize that decentralization of decision making has played an important role in American democratic government. This is true partly because state legislatures have always been ill equipped to make decisions as to what regulations or what expenditures will benefit individual communities throughout the state, and partly because it permits local consensus to develop where state-wide consensus would be difficult or impossible, indeed, in some early cases predating the home rule movement it was suggested that the right to manage local affairs without legislative interference was an inherent one.[4]

Prior to the adoption of the post civil war amendments, the Constitution contained no peg on which to hang an attack upon the power of the state to delegate authority to local subdivisions. It is to be noted, however, that both the Due Process and Equal Protection clauses of the Fourteenth Amendment prohibit the *state* from depriving any person of life, liberty or property without due process, and from denying to any person within *its* jurisdiction the equal protection of the laws. If emphasis is put upon the word "state" and upon "its," and "jurisdiction" is read to mean geographical jurisdiction, it is possible to suggest that different subdivisions of the state must be within whatever standard of equality was envisiond by the Amendment.

Since equality under the Equal Protection Clause has been measured by the standard of reasonable classification, of course this would leave considerable room for difference of treatment. There could be geographical classification when the classification was justified by geographical differences, such as density of population, geological characteristics, and the like. Presumably, however, the difference must be justified by some rational connection to a legitimate end of government action. Geographical classifications of this sort have been before the Supreme Court on a number of occasions. Thus in *Missouri v. Lewis*,[5] in 1879, residents of St. Louis offered challenge to a statute enacted by the Missouri legislature creating a special court of appeals in the city and county of St. Louis and three other counties and limiting appeals from its decisions to the supreme court of the state, while permitting right of appeal to the supreme court in all other counties of the state. The plaintiffs contended that limitation of appeal to the supreme court could result in conflicting decisions, one binding on the residents of some parts of the state and the other on residents of other parts. The Court noted that no conflicting decisions had been shown to exist, but added that there is no federal constitutional principle requiring the state to provide a single hierarchical court system to assure the absence of conflicting decisions. It saved the case of race or class discrimination affected by creating separate jurisdictions. Similarly, in *Salzburg v. Maryland*,[6] in 1954, the Court upheld a statute which in effect adopted the then "federal" rule on exclusion of illegally obtained evidence, but provided that the common law rule should obtain in gambling cases in Anne Arundel County. And it has been held that the state may impose a tax upon the inhabitants of a single county for the improvement of a harbor,[7] and may create a park district with power to levy taxes upon the community, though its members are appointed by the local probate judge.[8]

As to the creation of local government units, the determination of their boundaries, and the disposition of their property, the Court has recognized that in the nature of things there can be no precise equality and consistently has refused to interfere, though particular persons have been disadvantaged, or units treated differently. Thus in *Hunter v. Pittsburgh*,[9] annexation of a satellite community to the city of Pittsburgh was challenged on the ground that the residents had already been taxed for the provision of facilities that were yet to be provided in the city, thus subjecting the residents to double taxation. The Court held that this contention stated no constitutional claim since it could not be said that the residents of the smaller community would not receive some benefit from inclusion and they had no right to be in any particular subdivision of the state. The fixing of municipal boundaries was characterized as a political act, not subject to review by the court. And in *Texas, ex rel Panama Production Co. v. Texas City*,[10] the Court refused to intervene to prevent annexation of a body of water to the city, over the contention that it could not possibly benefit.

There have been three sets of cases in which the Court has departed from the rule in *Hunter*. The first of these include the cases in which the state has manipulated local boundaries for the purpose of infringing constitutional rights. Typical is *Graham v. Folsom*[11] in which the state extinguished a township and the argument was made that the debts of the township died with it. The Court held that since there were county officers who could levy taxes in the area, mandamus would lie to require a levy to discharge the obligations, thus making it plain that while the power of the state to create and abolish its own political subdivisions, and to determine their boundaries, is very broad, this power may not be used to defeat the application of the Contracts Clause of the Constitution.

In *Gomillion v. Lightfoot*,[12] the Alabama legislature passed an Act changing the boundaries of the city of Tuskeegee from square to a twenty-seven sided shape achieved by excising from the city limits practically every one of its Negro residents. In an opinion by Mr. Justice Frankfurter and joined by seven other justices, the Supreme Court held the Act unconstitutional. Mr. Justice Frankfurter reasoned that the purpose and effect of the Act being to eliminate the Negro vote in the city, it was a violation of the Fifteenth Amendment. The defendants in the case had relied strongly on the decision in *Hunter v. Pittsburgh*, in which the Court had made a sweeping statement about the

unfettered power of the state over its subdivisions. In reject-
ing the application of *Hunter* to the facts of the case, Mr.
Justice Frankfurter pointed out that the statement in that
case must be read in the light of the particular constitutional
deprivation alleged, the right not to have the boundaries altered in a way that would raise the plaintiff's taxes, a right not
guaranteed by the Constitution. With *Hunter,* he compared
Graham v. Folsom, involving a contractual right protected by
the Contracts Clause. Since the state could not use the power of
controlling the boundaries of its municipalities to defeat a right
protected by one clause in the Constitution, he reasoned, it could
not use that power to defeat a right protected by another.
Thus the rights of the plaintiffs under the Fifteenth Amendment
could not be denied by the ingenious method of carving up a city.
Mr. Justice Whittaker concurred in an opinion in which he
placed the violation on the Equal Protection Clause. To him
the Act was an arbitrary denial of the city's services to persons of a particular race. He could not see how there was a
denial of the right to vote, as a person has a right to vote only
in the jurisdiction in which he finds himself. Viewed either
way, however, the *Gomillion* case dealt with a thinly disguised
racial discrimination. Since the *Hunter* case was argued under
the Due Process Clause, the Court's opinion cannot be read as
suggesting that boundary determinations may not be disguised
discriminations in violation of the Equal Protection Clause,
and certainly later cases hold flatly that they can. In *Whitcomb
v. Chavis,*[13] for example, it was held that the design of multi-
member representation districts so as to minimize or cancel
out the voting strength of racial or political elements of the
voting population is a denial of equal protection, and the deliberate drawing of school attendance boundaries along racial
lines was held to be a violation of the Equal Protection Clause
in *Keyes v. Denver School District.*[14] While the *Keyes* case
dealt with the fixing of boundaries for attendance within a
single district, no doubt the principle is applicable to the
creation of gerrymandered districts as well.[15]

Aside from these decisions identifying purposeful discrimination guised in the form of geography, the Supreme Court has
maintained a rigid hands off position on the creation and design
of political subdivisions exercising the power to levy taxes
and spend money for public purposes. To date it has not seen
fit to interfere even in cases in which the result of boundaries

neutrally drawn have resulted in so-called de facto segregation.[16] This issue in all likelihood will be before the Court again this term. In the Richmond, Virginia, desegregation case, the district court ordered consolidation of the Richmond system with those of the two contiguous counties to achieve a greater measure of desegregation in the area despite the fact that the three systems have existed as separate for many years and were not drawn for purposes of segregation.[17] The case was recently argued in the Fourth Circuit.

Twice the Court has affirmed three judge district court decisions declining to declare the local property tax system for support of schools in violation of the Equal Protection Clause as discriminating against the residents of property poor districts.[18]

The second set of cases in which there has been judicial intervention in the creation of local taxing units and the fixing of their boundaries deals with the creation of special tax districts designed to effect local improvements to real property. In such cases the Court has made it plain that the requirement that special assessments, as distinct from general taxes, be equated to benefit, cannot be avoided by manipulation of the boundaries of the districts subject to assessment. The problem is illustrated by a comparison between *Davidson v. New Orleans*,[19] in 1877, and *Myles Salt Co. v. Iberia Drainage District*[20] in 1916. In the *Davidson* case, the Court upheld the levy of a tax for the drainage of swamp lands in two Louisiana parishes, disposing of the benefit argument by observing that it is impossible to say who benefits from the drainage of swamp lands. In *Myles Salt*, however, the record showed that the plaintiff's land was situated on a hill and was affected by rapid run-off, and the Court took it as established that the land could in no way benefit from drainage and held that accordingly it could not be included in the taxing district. The decision made it clear that the land was included for the purpose of imposing a tax for special benefit under circumstances precluding any such benefit.

The third set of cases are those involving representative districts. In these cases, beginning with *Baker v. Carr*,[21] in 1962, the Supreme Court has held that the Equal Protection Clause requires equal representation in the state's deliberative assemblies, and therefore, if representatives are elected from geographical districts, the ratio of representatives to population must be substantially the same in each district. It is to be noted that these cases deal with statewide decision making. They do not deal with the power to delegate governmental powers to local governments, or differences that stem from the exercise of that power. While the general principle of equal representation has been held to apply to the internal affairs of local government in a somewhat more relaxed fashion,[22] it has no application to interjurisdictional differences.

In summary, the state has an undoubted power to create geographical subdivisions and to delegate to them the power to tax and spend for public purposes. While this power may not be used as a subterfuge to hide an unconstitutional discrimination, or to avoid a statewide constitutional duty, it is only in the plainest cases that the Supreme Court has interfered with its exercise. It remains to examine the cases in which differences in treatment stem from the action of local government.

It is clear that the acts of a municipal corporation are state action for the purposes of the Fourteenth Amendment. That is to say that within its jurisdiction a municipal corporation may no more deny due process or equal protection than the state can. It goes without saying, however, that if it is not a denial of due process to delegate the police power to local subdivisions, no denial of equal protection can stem from the mere fact that two such subdivisions exercise their delegated power differently. When the same authority treats persons or classes of persons differently without reason, there is a denial of equal protection, though either rule would be otherwise proper. The unconstitutionality in such a case lies in the unjustified difference in treatment rather than in the illegality of the treatment of either. When one jurisdiction acts in one way, and another in another way, the difference is not the product of irrational classification, but simply of difference of opinion as expressed in local democratic decision. Thus the fact that different regulations, different taxes, and different services are in force simultaneously in different communities cannot be looked upon as a denial of equal protection without destroying local government altogether. This accounts for the fact that all of the boundary cases have proceeded as attacks upon initial inclusion as a denial of due process, or upon local action after inclusion as a denial of equal protection.

THE EQUAL PROTECTION CLAUSE
AND LOCAL TAXATION

These principles have been applied repeatedly in the area of local taxation. Indeed the logic underlying the decisions has peculiar force in the taxing area. The cases have held (1) that it is within the power of the legislature to delegate to municipal corporations the authority to tax for any public purpose, and (2) that there is no constitutional right to be taxed in the same way or in the same amount independent of the unit in which one finds himself. In a sense this is to say the same thing in different ways, for if the local unit of government can be delegated the power to tax within its geographical limits, of necessity its residents will bear a tax not borne in other units that have not imposed such a tax. The Supreme Court has regularly upheld the imposition of local taxes. In *Gundling v. City of Chicago*,[23] in 1909, the plaintiff challenged the imposition of a license tax of $100 on vendors of cigarettes within the city. The tax was upheld. In *Bradley v. City of Richmond*,[24] challenge was made to a city ordinance imposing a classified privilege tax varying from $10 to $800 depending upon the type of business. The Court noted that of course the city, as well as the state, is regulated by the Fourteenth Amendment, and therefore the classification of businesses must be reasonable, but finding nothing arbitrary in the scheme at issue it held that no constitutional inhibition existed that would prevent the state from delegating to the city the authority to impose such a tax or make such a classification.

It should be noted that the taxes involved in the *Gundling* and *Bradley* cases were for general revenue purposes, to be spent in the discharge of whatever powers were delegated to the cities involved. Therefore the question of public purpose was not at issue. Since real estate tax levies are more often earmarked, this question has arisen most frequently in cases dealing with such exactions. In *Kelly v. Pittsburgh*,[25] in 1881, the plaintiff resisted the payment of local property taxes after the annexation of his undivided 80 acres of farm land to the city of Pittsburgh. He contended that taxation for municipal services was limited to property that could benefit from the expenditures. The taxes that were at issue were for general city purposes, for the building of municipal buildings, for streets within the city, for schools, and for water and fire protection. In upholding the taxes, the Court observed.

It may be true that he does not receive the same amount of benefit from some or any of these taxes as do citizens living in the heart of the city. It probably is true, from evidence found in the record, that his tax bears a very unjust relation to the benefits received as compared with its amount. But who can adjust with precise accuracy the amount which each individual in an organized civil community shall contribute to sustain it, or can insure in this respect absolute equality of burdens, and fairness in their distribution among those who must bear them?

We cannot say judicially that Kelly received no benefit from the city organization. These streets, if they do not penetrate his farm, lead to it. The waterworks will probably reach him some day, and may be near enough to him now to serve him on some occasion. The schools may receive his children, and in this regard he can be in no worse condition than those living in the city who have no children, and yet who pay for the support of the schools. Every man in a county, a town, a city, or a State is deeply interested in the education of the children of the community, because his peace and quiet, his happiness and prosperity, are largely dependent upon the intelligence and moral training which it is the object of the public schools to supply to the children of his neighbors and associates, if he has none himself.

The officers whose duty it is to punish and prevent crime are paid out of the taxes. Has he no interest in maintaining them, because he lives further from the court-house and police station than some others?

There is some old state court authority for the proposition that local taxes must be imposed for purposes that are municipal, as well as public. It was held, for example, that a municipal expenditure for supplements to the pay of soldiers who had defended the town during the War of 1812 was ultra vires, since it is no purpose of a town to raise armies and pay their compensation,[26] and it has been held that a city could not expend its funds to offer a reward for the apprehension and conviction of the person who had murdered the chief of police, since the prosecution of felons is the business of the state.[27] Other cases have been less restrictive.[28] In any case, however, what is a municipal purpose depends upon state law, subject to any limitations imposed by the Fourteenth Amendment upon what functions may be delegated, and it has been held that the delegation of the unlimited power to levy local taxes for special purposes (in the particular cases for the county farm and pauper relief) raises no substantial federal question. No one ever seems to have argued the bald proposition that public schools are not a municipal as well as a state purpose and therefore, municipal corporations may not be given the authority to raise and spend money for public schools. It is to be noted in this connection that in *Kelly,* the Court made specific reference to local interest in education such as will support local taxes, and upheld the imposition of the local taxes partly on this very ground.

The principle that a person may not object to being placed in a particular subdivision of the state merely on the ground that his taxes will be higher than they were prior to the change in boundaries, or would be if he were in some different subdivision, was stated squarely in *Hunter v. Pittsburg,* already adverted to, and reiterated in *Gomillion v. Lightfoot.*

It is suggested in the *Rodriguez* case that the unfairness involved in the local property tax system lies in the fact that the imposition of a given millage in the "property poor" district produces less money per school child than the same millage would produce in the "property rich" district. This is true, of course, but it does not follow that the taxpayer has been discriminated against in the constitutional sense. The tax has been democratically imposed, and the money has been spent for a public purpose. The community has received a dollar's worth of education for a dollar in taxes. In the sense suggested in the *Kelly* case, the taxpayers have received a dollar's worth of benefit. If all municipal corporations in the state were reapportioned every year according to the total amount of taxable property located within them, and they were all made equal in this regard, the school taxes, or else the expenditure per pupil, would still vary, for different communities would still contain different numbers of school children. The different amount raised *per child,* therefore, has nothing to do with differences in the levy of the tax, but with the level of educational need in the community. In this connection it should be noted that while school taxes are often separately stated, the total property tax bill is the product of a division of projected expenditures for *all* public purposes into the total assessed value of property in the community. Thus, as to the taxpayer, at least, there is nothing unique about the school tax, for his tax rate varies with perceived need in all service categories. One community may have more school age children per dollar of assessed value of property. Another may have more crime, more mosquitoes, more aged, more poor, more pollution, water in need of more expensive purification, or may have levees to maintain to protect against flood, or snow to remove from the streets. Thus to spread the school taxes according to need, and not similarly to adjust other taxes would worsen the position of the resident of a community with a small educational problem and large problems of other sorts. Take the city of Chicago, for example. The ratio of taxable property to the number of school children is slightly more favorable than the general average throughout the state. On the other hand, the need for other urban services in Chicago is such that the *total* tax rate in the city is relatively high compared with many communities with fewer non-educational problems. Were school expenditures to be equalized throughout the state and the costs spread upon property statewide with no attention to other community needs, it is quite obvious that the taxpayer in the dormitory community with minimal general services but a high number of school children would benefit partly at the expense of urban residents whose property must bear the burden of solving many problems other than public education.

Thus, while it is undoubtedly true that communities vary greatly in total resources, and in total demands on those resources, there is no reason to believe that viz-a-viz the local taxpayer the equalization of burden statewide as to the cost of a single function would result in a greater level of equality or a fairer system of distributing costs of government than we now have. But be this as it may, to date the Supreme Court decisions indicate that the Due Process Clause interdicts simple robbery of one for the private benefit of another, but permits an organized community, state or local, to levy taxes for public purposes, independent of any direct and provable benefit to a particular taxpayer, and the Equal Protection Clause requires only that within the community levying the tax the distribution of burdens be based on some rational basis. Surely public schools are a public purpose, and several times the Court has held that property taxes may be levied for the purpose of operating them.

THE EQUAL PROTECTION CLAUSE AND LOCAL EXPENDITURES

The problem of expenditure classifications is closely con-

nected, of course, with the problem of taxation, for taxes may
be levied only for a public purpose, that is to say with an eye
to some expenditure. It has been seen, however, that there
need be no very direct connection between burden and benefit.
Of course there cannot be any such close connection, for often
the very purpose of taxing and spending is to correct some felt
inequality. That the Equal Protection Clause requires reasonable classification in expenditures there is no doubt. So it was
held in *Brown v. Board of Education* as to public schools. More
recently, it has been held that distribution of welfare payments
is governed by equal protection principles.[30] As in the case of
taxation, however, great latitude is permitted. It has already
been pointed out that it is impossible to have every program
benefit all persons and all classes alike. Education is a perfect
example. Even within the same jurisdiction, every school building cannot be built at the same time, and even if they were,
some would deteriorate faster than others. Unless books are to
be thrown away after each using, some must get old books while
others get new ones. Since teachers differ in ability, some students get experienced ones and others get beginners. Since
seniority is a factor in compensation, the students whose teachers have been in the system a long time have more spent upon
them per pupil than those who are taught by other teachers,
and so forth ad infinitum. Since no precise equality is possible,
and since measures of overall equality of treatment are want-
ing, courts have been very reluctant to interfere. The problem
was put this way by Mr. Justice Harlan in 1899 in *Cumming
v. Board of Educations*:[31]

> We may add, that while all admit that benefits and
> burdens of public taxation must be shared by citizens
> without discrimination against any class on account of
> their race, the education of the people in schools main-
> tained by state taxation is a matter belonging to the
> respective States, and any interference on the part of
> the federal authority with the management of such
> schools cannot be justified except in the case of the rights
> secured by the supreme law of the land.

It is to be noted that he speaks of "benefits and burdens" of
public taxation, and sharing by citizens. The principle is that
while public policy may dictate that government take from
some for the benefit of others, both the formula for taking and
the formula for giving must be grounded upon a rational basis.

It has been seen that in the case of taxation, a member of the organized community cannot object to being taxed, though no similar amount is exacted from members of other communities, because it cannot be said that he derives no benefit from public expenditures. By parity of reasoning, the members of an organized community cannot complain if some other community provides services to its members not provided in his own, for his community is not subject to taxation to pay for them. Again, the very purpose of the creation of the organized community is to permit the residents to *tax themselves* for services not provided by the state, or to supplement the amounts provided by the larger community.

The utility of this arrangement is apparent. In a country founded on the cry that taxation without representation is tyranny, the imposition of taxes and the expenditure of public funds must await political consensus. This may take place in the state legislature, of course, and the state may assume the function of providing services statewide. To require that it *must* take place in the legislature, however, is to assure that until it does the population must provide such services out of private funds, or do without. The local government system permits consensus to take place in local communities when it cannot be reached statewide. Thus in the case of school taxes, the levy of taxes in one community for the purpose of providing better schools than can be agreed upon in the legislature deprives the residents of some other community of nothing to which they are entitled, for to prohibit the local levy would in no way improve the schools in the second community, and they are in no way called upon to pay for the better schools in the first.

Differences in expenditures for services vary for a number of reasons. Failure of consensus has been mentioned. Of course the relative resources in the community are a factor. Where the ratio of property to school children is low, and sustaining a given level of expenditure per child will result in a correspondingly high millage, there is a pressure against expenditure greater than there is where less tax effort will raise more money per child. It is to be recognized, however, that if we take the child to be the person within the jurisdiction, and the state to be the jurisdiction, the difference in treatment between children in different communities would be identical whether the local vote was predicated upon the necessity to raise taxes one mill or two, and whether it was caused by variations in local resources or by differences in local preferences for education against some other service. Surely if equal treatment is required by the constitution, it cannot be voted away by the school board.

When differences in local expenditures are the result of local preferences, the community which spends the least is usually happy with its lower services because it has lower taxes. At least the taxpayers are happy. As pointed out, however, the parents of school children, who may be a minority, will not be happy, and will continue their efforts to shift the decision to the state legislature where they may be a majority. When the differences are attributable to lack of resources, they may be joined by the non-parent taxpayers who are burdened with high taxes that yield a small amount per child. In this connection it should be noted that while there are "rich" school districts and "poor" districts within every state, there are also "rich" states and "poor" states. Since the citizen of the local community is represented in all three levels of government, he will turn in the direction in which he believes there is the highest probability of achieving a political consensus.

No doubt this hierarchical political maneuvering has not achieved absolute equality in public expenditures, tax burdens, or public services. It cannot be said, however, that it does not work. School finance is an excellent example. In 1928-29, local funds provided 82.7% of support for elementary and secondary schools, the states providing 16.9%, and the federal government less than half of one percent. By 1967-1968, local tax support had dropped to 52.7%. State funds constituted 38.5%, and federal support had risen to 8.8%. Taking a longer span of years, between 1902 and 1969, state aid grew from 45 million dollars to 15 billion, and federal aid from one million to over 4 billion.

What has been said of school finance can be said as well of welfare payments. As it became apparent that the county farm and the city poor house could not deal with the volume, the funds for welfare have come increasingly from state and federal taxes. From 1902 to 1969, state expenditures went from nothing to nearly 4 billion dollars, and federal expenditures from one million to nearly six and a half billion.

Federal programs in support of urban housing and police and court functions bespeak the same process. State subsidies to local governments for general purposes reached 2 billion dollars in 1969, ranging from nothing in four states to half a billion dollars in New York. The federal government, through the model cities program, is also involved, and there is persistent talk of general revenue sharing. Special disadvantaged areas, such as the Appalachian region, have been singled out for assistance, and federal aid is disbursed to school districts having high concentrations of "disadvantaged pupils."

In the public school area, the state has in effect placed a floor under the amounts spent for education. In 1967-1968, the amounts spent from state funds for each student ranged from $369 in Mississippi to $1077 in New York. The direction of the school tax cases is to require that all school spending decisions be made by the state legislature and by Congress, and at least with respect to state expenditures, to require that any differences among communities be justified by the process of rational classification of recipients statewide. This would be accomplished, of course, by a simple decision to the effect that the power to levy school taxes cannot be delegated to municipal corporations. Unless the court would be prepared to determine the level of expenditures, however, it is well to remember that expenditures per child would be limited to the amount that could be agreed upon statewide, and there would be nothing to prevent the legislature from providing $369 to public schools, leaving the people with incomes high enough to support it to seek education for their children on the free market. Thus, ultimately such a decision might not achieve equality of educational opportunity at all. Further, since all public services are provided from the resources of the community, even if the courts were prepared to enforce equal and quality education for all, it would mechanically reduce amounts available for other expenditures. Therefore, unless they were prepared to adjust the boundaries of all local government units to equate tax resources to needs, or to prohibit local taxes altogether, they would be simply relieving one inequality to create another, for the community with more than average resources per school child, but higher than average non-educational problems, would be called upon to contribute an increased amount toward the education of the children in other communities, and left to solve its other problems with diminished resources. Lest this be thought of as inconsiderable, it should be noted that in 1969, the per capita local expenditures of cities over a million for education averaged $85.45 compared with a figure of $11.80 in cities of less than 50,000, or seven times as much. Expenditures for public welfare in cities over a million averaged $88.48, compared with $1.24 per capita in cities under 50,000, or twenty-nine times as much. Similarly cities over a million spent twenty times as much for health, and fifteen times as much for housing and urban renewal, and roughly twice as much for most other services. This is the crux of the whole home rule movement. Urban centers represent large concentrations of property and wealth, but they also represent large concentrations of problems. They are union ridden and suffer from other causes of high cost. While the representation cases have made them less subject to rural dominated legislatures, as it turns out suburban areas were probably more under-represented than they were and it seems unlikely that forcing them to plead with state legislatures by limiting their power to impose local taxes for local purposes will improve their position. In any event, any statewide agreement that they can achieve by their increased representation is open to them without limiting their powers in the absence of such an agreement.

THE EQUAL PROTECTION CLAUSE AND "WEALTH" CLASSIFICATIONS.

It is suggested in the *Serrano* and *Rodriguez* cases that the local property tax system for financing schools is a classification based on wealth, and therefore to be closely scrutinized. The standard to be applied to such a classification, it is said, is not mere rationality, but reasonable necessity to the accomplishment of some legitimate end. The authority for this special treatment of classifications based upon wealth lies in two lines of cases. The first is the line dealing with wealth classifications and the right to vote. The other is the line of cases dealing with the rights of indigent litigants in courts of law.

The voting cases hold that payment of a poll tax may not be made a condition to exercise of the franchise,[32] and that the right to vote may not be made dependent upon ownership of property.[33] These cases deal with a political right quite simple of definition,[34] and the classification found invalid was imposed by a single jurisdiction and related directly to the wealth of the persons classified.

The cases dealing with equal access to the courts hold that an indigent defendant appealing from his conviction must be provided with a transcript of the proceedings in the trial court,[35] and with counsel on appeal,[36] and that even in civil cases the state may not in effect deny access to the courts by indigents by imposing high filing fees,[37] or onerous security requirements that are not necessary for the protection of adverse parties.[38] As in the voting cases, the relationship between wealth of the class affected and the right asserted is direct. If the litigant is indigent, he must try his appeal without a transcript or attorney to represent him, or in the case of the filing fee or security requirement, must forego the appeal altogether. It is to be noted that all these cases are limited in their effect to the case of indigents. They do not purport to require that the state adjust financial inequalities along the entire income range. While the indigent must be provided with counsel, there has been no suggestion that counsel be paid the highest figure paid by any litigant in the courts, nor that counsel assigned to indigents generally receive as much on the average as all counsel privately retained. Nor is there any suggestion that because lawyers in a given community are paid less for their services than they may be in some other, or may be less competent on the average that the indigent is entitled to legal services as good as any obtainable anywhere.

Thus the counsel and transcript cases do not purport to hold that all differences attributable to the vicissitudes of location be adjusted with precision.

In the area of taxing and spending, there has never been any requirement that any precise distribution of either burden or benefit to be made according to wealth. Indeed the community abounds with programs that preclude participation by persons who do not have enough income to pay the $1.50 poll tax involved in *Harper v. Virginia Board of Elections*,[39] or the $15 to $50 charge for service involved in *Boddie v. Connecticut*.[40] Most state operated facilities for higher education are financed to some extent by tuition payments. Every state, and national park that is approachable only by automobile or commercial transportation is beyond the reach of distant indigents. Those who cannot afford the tolls on toll roads and bridges must bear the inconvenience of travel on the back roads. Those who cannot afford a subway token walk.

Thus, while the general impact of taxing and spending

is balanced to some extent to the advantage of lower income groups, it has never been suggested that every program benefit the poor at the expense of the rich, or that every program be equal in its impact regardless of the income of the user.

Unlike higher education, it is usual today that elementary and secondary education is provided from general tax revenues and made available free to all members of the taxing district. This has not always been so, of course, and in *Cumming v. Board of Education,*[41] in 1889, Mr. Justice Harlan saw no constitutional deprivation in the abolition of the local Negro high school when there were in the vicinity private schools that charged no higher tuition than the public school had been charging. It is not necessary to ponder over the question whether the Equal Protection Clause has expanded to the point at which tuition charges in public schools would fall within the *Griffin* rationale as a classification that puts schooling beyond the purse of the poor. The fact of the matter is that the local property tax financing system is not such a classification. Indeed it is not a classification of rich and poor within the jurisdiction levying the tax, since the service is made available to all within the jurisdiction without regard to wealth. Viewed statewide, it is not a classification according to wealth. Thus, the poor person in the district with large gross resources receives benefits greater than the rich person in the poor district. If one talks of the tax impact, the person in the poorer district who owns much property may be the loser, for the local community has recourse to his purse and he must pay a larger amount for the education of other people's children than is paid to sustain the same level of educational expenditure provided in districts with a more favorable ratio of property to school children.

Further, since commercial and industrial property bear the same tax imposed upon residential property, there is no necessary connection between the wealth, or even the property, of persons living within a school district and the total tax resources of the district. In suburbs of similar income level, the movement of a factory, or the building of a shopping center, will alter the property/pupil ratio in a way that will affect the tax rate or the level of services locally supportable.

In this connection it is interesting to note that schemes of state-wide school support might result in a more direct shift in benefits and burdens to the disadvantage of lower income groups than one can recognize in the present system. If the state taxes were raised by increases in sales taxes and business taxes, for example, causing a shift to consumers, it is entirely possible that while geographical differences in available expenditures per child would be eliminated, the benefit/burden position of the poor would not be improved, and in many instances it would be worsened.

Of course it is within the power of the Congress to spend money with the objective of eliminating geographical pockets of poverty, witness the programs in the Tennessee Valley, the programs in Appalachia, and various school support programs in districts with a large percentage of low income families. Equally, it is within the power of the state to do so, witness the universal state aid programs. But as Mr. Justice Harlan observed in his dissenting opinion in *Douglas v. California*,[42] "[S]urely, there would be no basis for attacking a state law which provided benefits for the needy simply because those benefits fell short of the goods or services that others could purchase for themselves." Just as surely, legislation permitting the poor in each community to tax the rich to provide more equal educational services is not unconstitutional simply because in some communities there happen to be fewer rich or more school children than there are in others. This view of equal protection as a duty to eliminate substantive differences between rich and poor, or to see that the precise degree to which such differences are eliminated must be equal, independent of locality, resources, and democratic choice would spell the death of all local government in the United States, and the Court has shown no disposition to push the equal access to justice cases so far. In *Palmer v. Thompson*,[43] for example, it was held that the closing of public swimming pools does not violate any constitutional provision. Mr. Justice Douglas dissented, noting in passing that the closing of the public pools probably affected the poor more than the rich, but placing his disagreement on the ground that the action had the effect of perpetuating segregation. Justices White, Brennan, and Marshall also dissented. They did not mention the poor, but were of the opinion that the city had acted to avoid a desegregation order. And in *James v. Valtierra*,[44] the Court upheld a provision requiring that no public housing be built in the community unless approved by the voters in a referendum. Mr. Justice Marshall, joined by Justices Brennan and Blackman, dissented on the ground that the provision applied in terms only to housing for people of low income and therefore the referendum provision was a direct classification discriminating against the poor. He noted the distinction that had been drawn by Mr. Justice Harlan in his *Douglas* dissent between such classifications and statutes that merely happen to weigh most heavily on the poor.

Thus while the Court has held that a citizen's political right to vote may not be sold to him, even for so small a price as a dollar and a half, and has held that even handed justice requires that a person convicted of a crime or ordinance violation and encarcerated or fined may not be denied an effective appeal because he can't pay for it, and further, that an effective appeal cannot be had without a transcript of the proceedings below, and in the case of the first appeal, at least, without the assistance of counsel, it has shown no disposition whatever generally to monitor either state or local expenditures or regulations or taxes to determine whether statistically it can be determined that as a practical matter they have a differential effect on various income groups.

THE EQUAL PROTECTION CLAUSE AND PUBLIC SCHOOLS

It has been noted that such a monitoring of local taxation and expenditures would be the death of all local government, for the very purpose of leaving the decisions on local taxes and expenditures to local voting publics is to permit variations as between units, and political communities cannot be redistricted every ten years to achieve dollar equality in tax resources as representative districts can be redesigned to achieve equal population. It remains to inquire whether the public school function is somehow special and not subject to delegation.

It is argued that the right to equality of educational opportunity is a fundamental right that cannot be made to depend upon the whimsical circumstance of residence. Comparisons are sometimes drawn between the decisions in *Griffin v. County School Board of Prince Edward County*[45] and *Bush v. Orleans Parish School Board*,[46] on the one hand, and *Palmer v. Thompson*,[47] on the other. In *Griffin* and *Bush*, it was held that local government units could not abolish public schools in the face of desegregation orders, while in *Palmer* it was held that the city of Jackson, Mississippi, was not prevented by the Fourteenth Amendment from closing its public swimming pools when it was found that it could not operate them without financial loss if required to operate them on a desegregated basis. It must be admitted that in these cases there is some talk about the importance of education as compared with recreational services such as swimming pools. The importance of public education is also adverted to in *Brown v. Board of Education,* where it is referred to as "perhaps the most important function of state and local governments."

It is to be noted, however, that the *Brown* decision refers to education as the most important function of state *and* local governments. It does not suggest in any way that it is not a proper function of local governments, nor cast doubt on the venerable principle, decided in *Kelly v. Pittsburgh* in 1881, that the resident of a local subdivision of the state has sufficient interest in the education of the children of his neighbors to justify the requirement that he contribute ratably to cover its cost.

The term education derives from the Latin educare, to bring up a child. Obviously the duty of child rearing, absent public intervention, devolves upon the parents. The cost varies, of course, with the number of children the parents happen to have, and the excellence of the education may vary with the talents of particular parents, or if the function is farmed out, with the income of particular parents divided by the number of children he has. As far as the child is concerned, this is all in the luck of the draw, for he has no control over either his parents' income or the number of children his parents may have. This fact engenders a certain level of sympathy in the voting population. Like other matters of democratic decision, however, sympathy for the position in which the many children of the poor may find themselves is attenuated somewhat by loyaties to one's own, and thus the willingness to contribute to the education of other people's children is conditioned to some extent by one's appraisal of the needs of one's own. Thus, democratic government is bottomed on the principle that some people are better off than others and the principle that they are not to be deprived of their advantages absent consent through their elected representatives. The suggestion that a group of appointed wise men will distribute equally among the population the "goodies" of this world is wholly antithetical to our principles.

To return to the subject of this paper, the long term implications of the state and lower federal court school tax cases, local government in this country stands at Armagedon. If the Supreme Court adopts the reasoning of these cases, which allocates to courts of law, manned by judges appointed for life, the function of determining what are "important" functions of government, and in such areas the function of determining who shall pay taxes and who shall benefit, all local government is at an end. Indeed, democratic government, local or state, is in great jeopardy, for once we begin to think that the task of courts of law is to achieve social levelling despite the absence of political consensus, it seems unlikely that the process can stop at the requirement that decision be made at the state level.

It has already been suggested that the decision that local governments may not levy taxes for the purposes of educating the children within the geographical limits of the unit, thus limiting expenditures to those that can be agreed upon statewide, may as easily result in a marked reduction in the total amount appropriated for public schools and the growth of private educational facilities, as it might in the increase in expenditure that would be necessary to bring the poorest district up to the expenditure level of the richest. If this is the result, what is to be the next step? Reversal of *Pierce v. The Society of Sisters?*[48] Mandamus to the state legislature to provide enough money to make public schools the equivalent of private?

It has already been mentioned that geographical discrepancies in resources are as plain between states as they are between school districts. Since the principles of the Equal Protection Clause have been read through the Fifth to apply to federal government activities as well as state,[49] is the next step an order to Congress to submit to the courts a plan for eliminating the state to state inequalities?

All this is a rather doleful prediction. But then it is not really a prediction, but rather a parade of horribles. The present writer reads the cases decided by the Supreme Court as in no way justifying the decisions in the *Serrano* and *Rodriguez* cases, and predicts that when the latter reaches the Court, it will be reversed.

This is not to suggest that people of good will should not lend their political support to measures that will assure to the nation's children the opportunity to receive a quality education. It is to suggest, however, that the achievement of this worthwhile end is a normal problem of democratic government and that it is unlikely that courts of law have very much to contribute toward its solution. The reason for this lies in the fact that quality education for all is probably not attainable by application of a simple formula for equality of per pupil expenditure, and because equal educational opportunity is not the only objective of government. Thus application of the equal protection principle to the balance of tax burdens and service benefits in education would either introduce an unfortunate rigidity into what should be an area of fluid experimentation, or else it would elevate federal judges into provincial governors empowered to order the spending priorities of their subjects.

FOOTNOTES

1. 394 U.S. 322 (1969).
2. 96 Cal. Rptr. 601 (1971).
3. Cooley, Constitutional Limitations, 189 (1868).
4. See, e.g., People ex rel LeRoy v. Hurlbut, 24 Mich. 44 (1871). It should be noted, however, that education has not been looked upon as of purely local concern under the "inherent right" doctrine or under the home rule provisions. See 1 Antieau, Municipal Corporation Law, § 3.28 (1955).
5. 101 U.S. 22 (1879).
6. 346 U.S. 545 (1954).
7. County of Mobile v. Kimball, 102 U.S. 691 (1880). In the *County of Mobile* case, Mr. Justice Field observed:

> "The objection to the act here raised is different from that taken in the State court. Here the objection urged is that it fastens upon one county the expense of an improvement for the benefit of the whole State. Assuming this to be so, it is not an objection which destroys its validity. When any public work is authorized, it rests with the legislature, unless restrained by constitutional provisions, to determine in what manner the means to defray its costs shall be raised. It may apportion the burden ratably among all the counties, or other particular subdivisions, or lay the greater share or the whole upon that county or portion of the State specifically and immediately benefited by the expenditure."

8. Ohio v. Akron Park District, 281 U.S. 74 (1930).
9. 207 U.S. 161 (1907).
10. 335 U.S. 603 (1958).
11. 200 U.S. 248 (1906).
12. 364 U.S. 339 (1960).
13. 403 U.S. 124 (1971).
14. 445 F.2d 990 (CA10th, 1971), cert. granted, 92 S. Ct. 707 (1972).
15. Cf. Gomillion v. Lightfoot, 364 U.S. 339 (1960).
16. See Spencer v. Kugler, 92 S. Ct. 707 (1972).
17. Bradley v. School Bd. of City of Richmond, Civ. Act. No. 3353 (E.D. Va., 1972). The *Bradley* case is now on appeal to the Court of Appeals for the Fourth Circuit.
18. McInnis v. Ogilvie, 394 U.S. 322 (1969); Burruss v. Wilkerson, 397 U.S. 44 (1970).
19. 96 U.S. 97 (1877).
20. 239 U.S. 478 (1916).
21. 369 U.S. 186 (   ).

22. See, e.g., Sailors v. Bd. of Ed., 387 U.S. 105; Abate v. Mundt, 403 U.S. 183 (1971).

23. 177 U.S. 183 (1909).

24. 227 U.S. 477 (1912).

25. 104 U.S. 78 (1881).

26. Stetson v. Kehpton, 13 Mass. 272 (1816).

27. Madry v. Town of Scotland Neck, 214 N.C. 461 (1938); see also Winchester v. Richmond, 93 Va. 711 (1896). It is to be noted that such cases proceed upon the theory that absent specific delegation of authority, municipal corporations may exercise a very limited range of authority. They do not gainsay that the legislature has the authority to confer the power by specific authorizations.

28. See, e.g., Albritton v. City of Winona, 181 Miss. 75 (1938).

29. Nashville, C. & St. L. Ry. v. Benton County, 161 Tenn. 588 (1930), appeal dismissed for want of a federal question, 283 U.S. 786 (1930).

30. See, e.g., Shapiro v. Thompson, 394 U.S. 618 (1969).

31. 175 U.S. 528 (1899).

32. Harper v. Bd. of Elections, 383 U.S. 663 (1966).

33. Cipriano v. City of Houma, 395 U.S. 701 (1969).

34. At least it was made simple by definition with the adoption of the "one man - one vote" standard. See Reynolds v. Sims, 377 U.S. 533 (1964).

35. Griffin v. Illinois, 351 U.S. 12 (1956).

36. Douglas v. California, 372 U.S. 353 (1963).

37. Boddie v. Connecticut, 401 U.S. 371 (1971).

38. Lindsey v. Normet, 92 S. Ct. 862 (1972).

39. See Note 32, *supra.*

40. See Note 37, *supra.*

41. See Note 31, *supra.*

42. See Note 36, *supra.*

43. 403 U.S. 217 (1971).

44. 402 U.S. 137 (1971).

45. 377 U.S. 218 (1961).

46. 365 U.S. 569 (1961).

47. See Note 43, *supra.*

48. 268 U.S. 510 (1925).

49. See Bolling v. Sharpe, 347 U.S. 497 (1954).

CHAPTER 6

Some Critical Issues in School Financing

ROE L. JOHNS

State school finance policies are determined by legislative bodies and by the courts. Although the legislative bodies make the laws, the courts declare the meaning of the laws. The courts, in interpreting the meaning of the laws, tend to reflect the morals and ethics of the time although they may deny doing so. The Supreme Court of the United States, in explaining its ruling on the Social Security Act in 1937 stated the following:

> "Nor is the concept of general welfare static. Needs that were narrow or parochial a century ago may be interwoven in our day with the well-being of the nation. What is critical or urgent changes with the times."[1]

I take an optimistic view of the times. As I shall show in this chapter, there is considerable evidence which indicates that in general we are developing a higher sense of morality and ethics than our ancestors had. It is beyond the scope of this chapter to treat that subject in detail, but even a casual survey of high court decisions will show that our courts have evolved from a legalistic determination of Shylock's "pound of flesh" to Portia's humanistic "quality of mercy."

Let us consider the concept of equality held by the founding fathers. Our ship of state was launched with the stirring

The author is Professor Emeritus, Department of Educational Administration, College of Education, University of Florida and Director, Technical Assistance, National Educational Finance Project.

declaration, "We hold these truths to be self-evident, that all men are created equal, that they are endowed by their Creator with certain unalienable Rights, that among these are Life, Liberty and the pursuit of Happiness." Who were these men that were created equal? It did not include blacks, women or children.

On a recent television program, a black comedian discussed his impressions of some of the heroes in the white history of the United States. He said his history book told him what great men George Washington and Thomas Jefferson were and he said they must have been great men. However, he could not help thinking that "them cats had slaves." Although the Fifteenth Amendment was adopted 100 years ago, the right of blacks to vote was not assured in all states until after 1960. Women were not given the right to vote until 1919. Although young men 18 to 20 years of age inclusive have been drafted for the armed services for more than 100 years, they were not given the right to vote until 1971. Although we declared all men were created equal in 1776, in many states they are not equal, with respect to voting, unless they were John Galworthy's "men of property" described in his book *The Forsythe Saga*. Even at the present time, the constitutions of some states permit only property owners to vote on bond issues and referenda on property tax levies.

Education was considered important by the founding fathers. However, education was not considered the constitutional right of a child, but rather a privilege which could be given to him by the state or withheld. Although public education was established in the New England colonies in the 17th century, it was not established for humanistic or altruistic reasons. The primary purpose or reason for establishing education in the New England colonies was to defeat "ye olde deluder Satan." Prior to 1800 in all states except the New England states, education was considered primarily a church or family responsibility except for the children of paupers. Public education was extended very gradually during the first quarter of the 19th century. However, during the period of 1830 to 1860, tax support for public schools was authorized also in the middle and western states. This period has been frequently referred to as a period in which the public school system of the United States developed. However, legal authorization for the levy of taxes to support schools is not always accompanied by the levy of taxes.

The Seventh Census of the United States in 1850 shows that only about 1/2 of the children of the New England states were provided free education, 1/6 of the Western states and 1/7 of the Middle states by 1850. In the Southern states almost no free tax supported schools were available at that time except for paupers.

It is interesting to examine the arguments used for the establishment of public schools. I have not been able to find any authentic documents published between 1830 and 1860 in which it is argued that children have a right to a free public education. Thaddeus Stevens, in his plea to the Pennsylvania House of Representatives in 1835 for the continuance of tax supported public schools, stated the following:

> "If an elective republic is to endure for any great length of time, *every* elector must have sufficient information, not only to accumulate wealth, and take care of his pecuniary concerns, but to direct wisely the legislatures, the ambassadors, and the executive of the nation—for *some* part of all these things, *some* agency in approving or disapproving of them, falls to every freeman. If then, the permanency of our government depends upon such knowledge, it is the duty of government to see that the means of information be diffused to every citizen. This is a sufficient answer to those who deem education a private and not a public duty—who argue that they are willing to educate their *own* children, but not their neighbor's children."[2]

This is typical of the arguments advanced for the establishment of tax supported schools prior to 1860. As a matter of fact, those arguments are still being advanced. Furthermore, in recent years, books written on school finance, including those written by me, give great importance to the contribution that education makes to the economy of the nation. Until fairly recently, tax supported public schools were established primarily because they benefited and protected the adult society, not because children had a right to tax supported public education. There is evidence, however, that our morals and ethical ideas concerning the rights of children have been changing. In the famous *Brown v. Board of Education* in Topeka, Kansas case the court said:

> "Today, education is perhaps the most important function of state and local government. . . . In these days, it is

doubtful that any child may reasonably be expected to succeed in life if he is denied the opportunity of an education. Such an opportunity, where the state has undertaken to provide it, is a right which must be made available to all on equal terms."[3]

It is strange that although the Fourteenth Amendment was adopted 100 years ago and although we declared that all men were created equal almost 200 years ago, that we are just now beginning to apply these great concepts to the education of children. There is no doubt, whatsoever, that *Serrano v. Priest, Rodriguez v. San Antonio School District, Van Dusartz v. Hatfield* and *Robinson v. Cahil* reflect an evolution in the moral and ethical concepts of the people with respect to the rights of children. At the present time, we do not know whether these cases will be upheld by the Supreme Court of the United States. However, regardless of whether these cases are upheld, the moral and ethical ideals of the people of this nation have advanced to the point that they will force our Congress and our state legislatures to provide equality of educational opportunity in this land. That is why I am optimistic as I contemplate the future of education.

The growth of the moral and ethical ideals of the people of this nation with respect to education has been favorably influenced by a host of educational leaders and philosophers, the greatest of which was probably John Dewey. It would require volumes to record the contributions of these men. Let us look for a moment at a few of these leaders who have had particular influence on school finance policies. All of these men were theorists, all made their contributions in the 20th century and all were university professors.

The first of these early theorists was Ellwood P. Cubberley. He wrote his doctor's dissertation at Teachers College, Columbia University in 1905. He proposed the following theory of state support:

"Theoretically all the children of the state are equally important and are entitled to have the same advantages; practically this can never be quite true. The duty of the state is to secure for all as high a minimum of good instruction as is possible, but not to reduce all to this minimum; to equalize the advantages to all as nearly as can be done with the resources at hand; to place a premium on those local efforts which will enable communities to rise above the legal minimum as far as possible; and to encourage communities to extend their educational energies to new and desirable undertakings."[4]

Among his recommendations were the following:

1. That due to the unequal distribution of wealth, the demands set by the states for maintaining minimum standards cause very unequal burdens. What one community can do with ease is often an excessive burden for another.

2. That the excessive burden of communities borne in large part for the common good should be equalized by the state.

3. That a state school tax best equalizes the burdens.

4. That any form of state taxation for schools fails to accomplish the ends for which it was created unless a wise system of distribution is provided.

Cubberley's concepts on school finance had great influence on the leaders in school finance during the first quarter of the twentieth century.

The next contribution to the theory of school financing was proposed by Harlan Updegraff of the University of Pennsylvania in a survey he made of the rural schools of New York state in 1921.[5] He was the first theorist who proposed that wealth of the local school district be entirely eliminated as a factor affecting the quality of a child's education. In lieu thereof, he proposed that the quality of a child's education be made dependent upon local effort but that the state should equalize educational opportunity with state funds so that the total amount of revenue per teacher unit would be the same in all districts making the same effort regardless of variations in wealth. This concept was rediscovered by Coons, a distinguished attorney, 50 years later and named "district power equalizing."[6]

Beginning with the report of the Educational Finance Inquiry Commission published in 1923, George D. Strayer, Sr. began to exercise major influence on the direction of school financing. He was a classmate of Cubberley's at Teachers College. He also graduated from Teachers College in 1905. Cubberley went to Stanford University and Strayer remained at Teachers College.

There were thirteen volumes in the report of the Educational Finance Inquiry Commission. Only one of them is remembered today. It was Volume 1 written by Strayer and Haig and entitled *The Financing of Education in the State of New*

York. Only four pages of that volume were devoted to the theory of school financing and those four pages have had more influence on the development of school finance policies than the remainder of the thirteen volumes. In that volume, Strayer and Haig stated the following:

"There exists today and has existed for many years a movement which has come to be known as the 'equalization of education opportunity' or the 'equalization of school support.' These phrases are interpreted in various ways. In its most extreme form the interpretation is somewhat as follows: The state should insure equal education facilities to every child within its borders at a uniform effort throughout the state in terms of the burden of taxation; the tax burden of education should throughout the state be uniform in relation to taxpaying ability, and the provision for schools should be uniform in relation to the educable population desiring education. Most of the supporters of this proposition, however, would not preclude any particular community from offering at its own expense a particularly rich and costly educational program. They would insist that there be an adequate minimum offered everywhere, the expense of which should be considered a prior claim on the state's economic resurces."[7]

They then presented the following conceptual model of state support which incorporated the principles they advocated:

1. A local school tax in support of the satisfactory minimum offering would be levied in each district at a rate which would provide the necessary funds for that purpose in the richest district.

2. The richest district then might raise all of its school money by means of the local tax, assuming that a satisfactory tax, capable of being locally administered, could be devised.

3. Every other district could be permitted to levy a local tax at the same rate and apply the proceeds toward the cost of schools but

4. Since the rate is uniform, this tax would be sufficient to meet the costs only in the richest district and the deficiencies would be made up by the state subventions.[8]

They presented the following arguments against the reward for local tax effort advocated by Cubberley and Updegraff:

"Any formula which attempts to accomplish the double purpose of equalizing resources and rewarding effort must contain elements which are mutually inconsistent. It would appear to be more rational to seek to achieve local adherence to proper educational standards by methods which do not tend to destroy the very uniformity of effort called for by the doctrine of equality of educational opportunity."[9]

Paul Mort, one of Strayer's students, developed the technology for implementing the concepts proposed by Strayer and Haig. However, he was more than a technologist. He was also a theorist and disseminator. He proposed the following elements to be included in a state's guaranteed minimum program:

1. An educational activity found in most or all communities throughout the state is acceptable as an element of an equalization program.

2. Unusual expenditures for meeting the general requirements due to causes over which a local community has little or no control may be recognized as required by the equalization program. If they arise from causes reasonably within the control of the community they cannot be considered as demanded by the equalization program.

3. Some communities offer more years of schooling or a more costly type of education than is common. If it can be established that unusual conditions require any such additional offerings, they may be recognized as a part of the equalization program.[10]

Mort, his students and students of his students have been great disseminators of the concepts of equalization. I was one of Mort's students. He was my major professor. By 1971-72, forty-two states used some type of an equalization formula which allocated some state funds in inverse relationship to wealth per unit of need.

The last of the early theorists was Henry C. Morrison. In his book, *School Revenue*[11] written in 1930, he recommended full state funding for the public schools. He argued that local school support disequalized educational opportunity and that the equalization formulas proposed by Cubberley, Strayer and Mort had failed to equalize educational opportunity and never would do so. His arguments fell on deaf ears at that time, but they sound loud and clear today. One state, Hawaii, has already adopted the Morrison model.

Despite the pleas of our philosophers and our theorists in school finance, the progress toward equalization of educational opportunity has been slow. Equalization of education opportunity involves much more than financial equalization. We have given much lip service to equality and freedom in this country but our policies have not always been consistent with our verbalized values and beliefs. For example, I was a student at "ultra liberal" Teachers College 1926-28 and was a member of Phi Delta Kappa. Prior to 1927, Blacks and Jews were not admitted to the Teachers College chapter of Phi Delta Kappa. It required the threatened resignation of a large group of us to force a change in policy at that time. It was not until 1954 that the courts abolished enforced segregation of blacks in the public schools of seventeen states.

The movement toward financial equalization of educational opportunity during the first half of this century has frequently been actively opposed by some of the school superintendents in wealthy school districts. I have personal knowledge of this because during the past forty years I have provided consultant services at one time or another in half the states in this nation. It was during the period 1920 to 1960 that most of the states initiated state plans for financial equalization of school support. I have had the pleasure of participating in the development of many of those plans. During the first half of this century, it was the large core cities that usually had the best financed schools and the most developed educational programs. The city school districts were the wealthiest districts and they had less problems in financing their schools than any other type of school district. Therefore, school superintendents, state senators, and state representatives from many of these wealthy districts actively opposed not only state aid for education but also federal aid. They considered state and federal financial equalization of educational opportunity as the Robin Hood Philosophy. The National School Boards Association has been dominated largely by urban boards of education. Only recently has that organization withdrawn its opposition to federal aid.

Now the situation has changed. The large core cities are facing critical problems in school financing. While these cities are still wealthy, they face an enormous burden of municipal costs that they did not have to carry in the first quarter of this century. These costs include welfare, transportation, pollution control, public safety, urban renewal and other costs associated with a concentration of population. In addition to municipal costs, school costs have increased enormously in the core cities. Part of this increase has been due to the concentration of culturally disadvantaged high cost pupils in the great cities. The core cities have lost their privileged financial position and they have changed their political philosophy! The great cities are now among the most ardent advocates of state and federal aid for education. Welcome aboard! That is another reason why I am optimistic of the future. There is no longer a significant split between school districts in their support of state and federal aid.

However, as we move into the future, I would not have you believe that we will face no problems in equalizing educational opportunity. The desire for an elite society is still strong in America despite our pretentions of belief in an equalitarian society. This desire for an elite society is expressing itself in two main directions as follows: (1) efforts on the part of wealthy school systems to retain their privileged position under the light house theory and (2) advocacy of the use of public funds to support non-public schools. I shall discuss briefly both of these threats to equalization of educational opportunity.

Some of the wealthiest districts are now suburban districts. However, some of our great cities are still among our wealthiest school districts. Following are some of the arguments being advanced for maintaining higher per pupil expenditures in these districts:

1. We need light house districts to advance educational practice. In my judgment the value of light house districts has been grossly exaggerated. Light house districts have almost invariably been wealthy school districts and about the only innovative practices that they have ever demonstrated is what any well managed district could do if it only had the money.

2. The great cities should be given additional funds because of municipal overburden. These municipal overburden costs are real costs and they must be funded. It is the position of the National Educational Finance Project that costs of municipal overburden cannot be adequately funded by manipulating the state aid formula for schools. The cities should receive state and federal aid directly in accordance with need in order to meet legitimate municipal costs.

3.   There is a concentration of disadvantaged high cost pupils in the great cities. That is true but there are also concentrations of disadvantaged pupils in some rural, small city and suburban districts. These extra costs of high cost pupils should be funded in any district in which they live. One cannot control the flooding of the Mississippi River by leveeing the delta. The control of floods must start at the head waters.

4.   The cost of living is higher in the urban districts. This may be true. However, the research in this area is very limited. It is yet to be demonstrated that the cost of living for the same quality of living varies significantly from district to district within a state. Much research is needed on this subject.

It is argued by some that tax support for non-public schools will improve education by giving parents a choice of the schools to which they send their children. This is only an excuse to establish an elitist system of privately controlled schools segregated by race, religion or socio-economic class. If court decisions or legislation prohibited the allocation of public funds to parochial schools or to non-public schools which have a lower percentage of Blacks, Puerto Ricans and Chicanos enrolled than the public school of the district in which they are located, 99 percent of the support of tax funds for non-public schools would vanish.

Equality of educational opportunity in the United States will require substantially full state and federal funding of public education. A fiscal policy of making a child's education a function of the wealth of the district in which he resides is an obsolete concept, inconsistent with the ideals and principles upon which this nation was founded. A number of courts have recently ruled that this policy is unconstitutional because it violates the equal protection clause of the Fourteenth Amendment. Following are some major policy issues with respect to financing public schools that must be faced by every state legislature.

1.   What educational programs and services will be funded in the state's school finance plan and for whom will these programs be provided?

2.   Will state funds be apportioned on the flat grant basis which ignores differences in the wealth of local school districts, or on the equalization basis which provides more state funds per unit of educational need to districts of less wealth than to districts of greater wealth?

3. Will necessary variations in unit costs of different educational programs and services be recognized or ignored in allocating state funds on either the flat grant or equalization basis?

4. What proportion of school revenue will be provided by the state and what proportion from local sources?

5. How progressive (or regressive) will be the state's tax structure?

6. To what extent will the state provide for financial equalization of educational opportunity among school districts of the state?

7. As the state moves toward the equalization of educational opportunity, will it "level up" or "level down?"

8. As a state moves toward full state funding, will appropriate local control of the public schools be preserved?

9. Will tax funds be appropriated to non-public schools in such a manner as to promote the segregation of pupils by race, religion or social class?

10. What are the financial needs of the public schools and how nearly can those needs be met taking into consideration needs for other governmental services and the financial ability of the state?[12]

Space does not permit me to discuss these issues adequately. They will be resolved by our state legislators in accordance with our values and beliefs. Following are some options suggested by the National Education Finance Project.

1. If one believes that educational opportunities should be substantially equalized financially among the districts of a state, but that districts should be left with some local tax leeway for enrichment of the foundation program, an equalization model is the best model. However, the higher the priority one gives to equalization, the more he will prefer the equalization model that provides the most equalization.

2. If one believes that educational opportunities should be completely equalized financially, among the districts of a state, the complete state support model is the preferred model. If the *Serrano v. Priest* decision of the Supreme Court of California in August, 1971 is upheld by the United States Supreme Court, complete state and federal support of the public schools or complete equalization of local ability by an equalization model may be the only legal alternatives.

3. If one believes that all children regardless of variations

in ability, talent, health, physical condition, cultural background, or other conditions which cause variations in educational needs, have a right to the kind of education that meets their individual needs, he will select school finance models which incorporate the programs needed and which provide for necessary cost differentials per unit of need.

4. If one believes that educational opportunity should be substantially equalized among the states he will support a revenue model which provides a substantial percent of school revenue in general federal aid apportioned in such a manner as to tend to equalize educational opportunities among the states.

5. If one believes that the taxes for the support of the public schools should be relatively progressive rather than regressive, he will prefer revenue models which provide a high percent of school revenue from federal and state sources.

6. If one believes that publicly financed education should tend to remove the barriers between caste and class, and provide social mobility, he will oppose any plan of school financing which promotes the segregation of pupils by wealth, race, religion or social class.

7. If one believes that all essential functions of state and local government should be equitably financed in relation to each other, he will oppose any finance model for any function of government, including education, under which either federal or state funds are allocated to local governments on the basis of "the more you spend locally, the more you get from the central government" rather than on the basis of need.

8. If one believes that the educational output per dollar of investment in education should be maximized, he will support finance models that will promote efficient district organization and efficient organizations of school centers within districts.

9. If one believes in a federal system of government, he will support finance models which will not require a decision governing public education to be made at the federal level when it can be made efficiently at the state level, and will not require a decision to be made at the state level when it can be made efficiently at the local level, regardless of the percent of revenue provided by each level of government.

10. If one believes that education is essential to the successful operation of the democratic form of government in a free enterprise society and if he believes that education is es-

sential to the economic growth of the nation and to the ful-fillment of the legitimate aspirations of all persons in our society, he will support revenue models sufficiently financed to meet educational needs adequately.[13]

As I stated in the Horace Mann lecture that I delivered in April of this year at the University of Pittsburgh:

"The struggle for freedom and equality has been as long as the history of civilization. Will we have an elitist society dominated by the privileged few or will we have an equalitarian society where every human being has an equal chance for 'life, liberty and the pursuit of happiness?' Will we have an elitist public school system promoting an elitist society or will we have an equalitarian school system promoting an equalitarian society? Equality is a necessary condition precedent to freedom. There can be no freedom without equality. Equality of educational opportunity, equality of protection under the law, equality of economic opportunity and equality in receiving the benefits of the Bill of Rights of the Constitution are all conditions necessary for freedom. Let us press on toward realizing the American dream of an equal chance in life and liberty and justice for all by equalizing educational opportunity throughout this land."

FOOTNOTES

1. Helvering v. Davis, 301 Cr. S619, 57 Sup. Ct. 904 (1937).
2. Hazards Register of Pennsylvania, Vol. 15, Number 18, May 2, 1835.
3. Brown v. Topeka Board of Education, 347 U.S. 483 (1954).
4. Ellwood P. Cubberley. *School Funds and Their Apportionment.* New York: Teachers College, Columbia University, 1905, P. 16.
5. Harlan Updegraff, *Rural School Survey of New York State: Financial Support.* Ithaca: by the author, 1922, p. 117-118.
6. See John E. Coons, William H. Clune III and Stephen D. Sugarman, *Private Wealth and Public Education.* Cambridge, Mass.: The Belknap Press of Harvard University, 1970, Chapter 6.
7. George D. Strayer and Robert Murray Haig, *The Financing of Education in the State of New York.* Report of the Educational Finance Inquiry Commission. Vol. 1, New York: McMillan Co., 1923, P. 173.
8. *Ibid.,* P. 174-175.
9. *Ibid.,* P. 175.
10. Paul R. Mort, *The Measurement of Educational Need.* New York: Teachers College, Columbia University, 1924, PP. 6-7.
11. Henry C. Morrison, *School Revenue,* Ccicago: University of Chicago Press, 1930.
12. Adapted from Roe L. Johns, Director; Kern Alexander, Associate Director, *Alternative Programs for Financing Education,* Vol. 5, Gainesville, Fla.: The National Educational Finance Project, 1971.
13. *Ibid.,* PP. 348-349.

CHAPTER 7

Future Financing of Nonpublic Schools

BISHOP WILLIAM E. MCMANUS

On April 21, 1970, the President of the United States appointed a four member Panel on Nonpublic Education to undertake an unprecedented, government-financed study of the nation's nonpublic elementary and secondary schools. President Nixon asked the Panel:

—to study and evaluate the problems concerning nonpublic schools;
—to report the nature of the crisis confronting these schools;
—to make specific recommendations for action which would be in the interest of the entire national education system.

For two years, the Panel, whose members were Clarence Walton, President of Catholic University of America, Chairman, William Saltonstall, Principal Emeritus, Philips Exeter Academy, Ivan Zylstra, Administrator of Government Relations, National Union of Christian Schools, and I, reviewed voluminous research on nonpublic education, dialogued with experts in school administration and finance, consulted authorities on constitutional law, debated the issues both within the President's Commission on School Finance and within the Panel, and finally completed a unanimous Final Report which was formally presented to President Nixon on April 20, 1972.

The author is Director of Catholic Education, Archdiocese of Chicago.

Though a full summary of the Panel's Final Report might be only remotely relevant to the assigned topic, its financial recommendations to the nonpublic schools themselves and to government are both pertinent and timely.

The Report advises nonpublic schools to intensify their efforts for the expansion and improvement of all private income sources. The Panel proposes specifically that (1) church-related schools encourage increased donations to the churches which support them, at least in proportion to inflationary trends; (2) tuition rates be regularly raised so tuition income will not lag behind higher prices charged for the schools' normal purchase of goods and services; (3) professionally prepared budgets be developed in consultation with the school's patrons and benefactors to avoid hand-to-mouth financing in an atmosphere of constant crisis; (4) full public accounting be made of all revenues and expenses with a view to publicizing both the generosity and the needs of those supporting and operating nonpublic schools.

The Panel also recommended that nonpublic schools exercise firm control over operating costs. Again its advice was specific and pointed:

> *Operate at full capacity.* Staff, alumni and sponsors must engage in "aggressive recruitment" in a school buyers' market where children of school age are in short supply.
>
> *Achieve payroll savings.* Differential staffing, part-time teachers in special fields and use of volunteer paraprofessionals will reduce payroll costs.
>
> *Purchase equipment and supplies through cooperative agencies at wholesale prices.*
>
> *Take steps to give full-time employment to teachers by means of the year-round school and/or assignment to summer school.* Supplemental employment, e.g., adult education classes, may be one way to guarantee teachers an annual wage commensurate with their professional status and performance.

To recapture some of the lost trade in a highy competitive educational market the Panel advised each nonpublic school (1) to clarify its unique identity as a voluntary enterprise by setting forth its particular goals and objectives within the context of its resources and commitments; (2) to follow a policy of broad based fiscal, professional, academic and civic accountability; (3) to take risks with the expectation that exceptionally good nonpublic schools surely will survive; (4) to break out of the "problem-psychosis web" which has created an utterly negative image that every nonpublic school is in hopeless difficulties; (5) to pool resources with other nonpublic schools in a united effort for publicizing nonpublic education's vital role in American education.

In its report the Panel applauds the recent organization of the nation's outstanding nonpublic school leaders into a new group called the Council for American Private Education which in its initial activities has exhibited remarkable cooperation and vision, including its resolution to relate as closely as possible to major public school organizations.

After a study of the research on the critical financial condition of the nation's nonpublic schools a majority of the Commission on School Finance and the full Panel concluded that ways to provide some kind of substantial government help should receive at least "prompt and serious consideration." The Panel, however, called not only for "consideration" but also for action by the Congress and by the Administration.

Assessing the financial problem, the Panel noted that funding from churches, philanthropies, foundations and individual donors was not keeping pace with the nonpublic schools' escalating expenses with the result that additional costs were being passed along to consumers. "Many parents," the Panel Report says, "already hard-pressed by pleas for more donations to nonpublic schools (notably church-related ones), by higher tuition and fees, and by rising taxes (property, income, sales and other) for public education feel that the limit has been reached. . . . For the inner-city poor the weight is crushing; for middle Americans in the $7,500 - $15,000 levels (and especially for those at the low end) the load is significant; for young suburbanites with new homes, new mortgages, and possibly new value orientations, the encumbrance is more marginal. Consequently, "there are nonpublic schools in the central city which go unused by many who want and need them, but cannot afford them; there are nonpublic schools in metropolitan areas" (where public schools now are in serious fiscal trouble) "which are under utilized because parents are unsure of their ability to meet expected tuition increases and are uncertain of the school's ability to survive financially. . . ."

In light of ample and well documented evidence that govern-

ment aid, notably federal aid, for the benefit of nonpublic school
pupils and their parents would be sound public policy for the
public welfare, the Panel proposed four major recommendations to the President. They are:

1.   Federal assistance to the urban poor through (a) sup-
plemental income allowances for nonpublic school tuitions for
welfare recipients and the working poor; (b) experiments with
vouchers; (c) full enforcement of ESEA provisions entitling
nonpublic school pupils to certain benefits and (d) an urban
assistance program for public and nonpublic schools.

2.   Federal income tax credit for part of nonpublic school
tuition.

3.   Federal construction loan program analogous to the
FHA instrumentality for home buyers.

4.   Tuition reimbursements to insure equity for nonpublic
school children in anticipated long-range programs of Federal
aid to education.

Nonpublic schools most in need and those most needed are in
the nation's inner-city areas.

Inner-city church-related schools, says the Panel Report,
"face difficult financial problems" because their revenues are
derived from low-income clientele in parishes with very few
contributors besides those who have children in school; their
ancient school buildings are costly to maintain and to repair;
payroll expenses are mounting to cover the cost of additional
lay teachers. Yet these are the schools whose pupils, like those
in public schools, need experienced and devoted teachers, a
curriculum designed for inner-city conditions, compensatory
and remedial programs, health and nutritional services, counsel-
ing for their parents, safe and clean school buildings, and
many extracurricular projects.

The Panel has refused to presume that the inner-city poor
are a "nondescript mass of culturally, socially, intellectually,
and economically disadvantaged people." On the contrary,
"these people are individuals, each with talents and aptitudes,
hopes and dreams, determinations and drives to make life
worthwhile despite job discrimination and other prejudice."
The Panel, therefore, favored welfare reform plans which would
give welfare recipients and the low income working poor (those
with family income under $5,000) incentive allowances in
their welfare budgets to pay the cost of education, training, or

rehabilitation designed in due time to render them economically self sufficient.

From its review of school conditions in the inner city and from personal experience, the Panel concluded that an incentive allowance for tuition paid to a nonpublic school would encourage some welfare recipients to give their children the unique advantages of nonpublic education. There is evidence that inner-city nonpublic school pupils stand a better than even chance of breaking out of the dread cycle of poverty which all too often starts with enrollment in a crowded, demoralized inner-city public school and ends with dropping out into the ranks of the idle, unwanted, and unemployable. Children who depend on public welfare for their food, on public housing for their homes and on public clinics for their health care find that a nonpublic school, by the very fact that it is nonpublic, motivates them to strive for self dependence outside the ghetto of poverty.

Parents of about 375,000 inner-city, nonpublic school pupils now would be eligible for the proposed incentive allowances for tuition at an annual cost to the federal government of about $30 million. This estimate presumes that the maximum allowance per child would be slightly less than $100 a year. In terms of the total outlay for welfare, the proposal has an extraordinarily modest price tag.

Wealthy parents generally have a real choice of either an excellent public or an excellent nonpublic school for their children's education. Because they have considerable control over tax expenditures for public schools and because they have private resources to pay high nonpublic school tuition rates, the wealthy can command high quality education. Most of the poor have no such choice. Like it or not, they have to send their children to a public school. The Panel therefore has recommended immediate experimentation with the long delayed voucher plan under study for many months in the Office of Economic Opportunity. There is, the Panel's Report notes, "a pressing need to determine whether inner-city parents with vouchers in hand could bring about improvements in both public and nonpublic schools."

With no little regret and disappointment, I recently have heard that the OEO, allegedly bowing to public school pressures, has excluded nonpublic schools from the San Jose, California, experiment with vouchers. I understand, however, that the real difficulty may not be public school pressure against nonpublic school participation but rather the need for legislation in California which would permit the San Jose Board of Education to distribute vouchers to parents of prospective nonpublic school pupils.

The Panel has given its unqualified support to the School Finance Commission's recommendations for a Federal Urban Education Assistance Program to help large central city public and nonpublic schools finance such programs as experimental and demonstration projects on urban educational problems; replacement and renovation of unsafe, unsanitary and antiquated school buildings and equipment; addition of remedial, bilingual and special teachers and professional personnel; addition of teacher aides and other supporting personnel; and provision of instructional materials and services.

This recommendation was one of few which had the unanimous approval of all 18 members of the Commission on School Finance. That seems to say that the needs of all schools and their pupils in the nation's inner-city areas are so compelling that deep differences of opinion on church and state were set aside in the hope that the federal government would act promptly to give every inner-city child an opportunity for adequate education in a school of its parents' choice.

The Panel, well aware of court-ordered restrictions against direct aid to church-related elementary and secondary schools, is of the opinion that the Courts will have to face "the real-world situation where nonpublic schools provide sound education, generally across sectarian lines, in areas where public schools are often overcrowded and understaffed. Presently the poor have little or no choice, and this poverty factor could make a difference in judicial reasoning regarding aid to a church-related school. In the Panel's judgment it should make a difference."

Perhaps constitutional considerations will require inner-city nonpublic schools to change their corporate structure as a condition for receiving federal funds. Though this requirement could be regarded as an intolerable intrusion, virtually any adjustment is to be preferred to closing down inner-city nonpublic schools. There is no price too great to pay for the survival of the nation's inner-city nonpublic schools.

During the early stages of its deliberations on constitutional methods of government aid to nonpublic schools the Panel was inclined to recommend purchase of secular educational services as an effective method which would meet the constitutional criteria in the U. S. Supreme Court's New York textbook decision. In that decision the Court, upholding the legality of loaning textbooks to nonpublic school students, said a statute is constitutional if it has a secular purpose, a secular effect, and neither advances nor inhibits religious practice. In June of 1971, however, the Panel had to reconsider its position in light of the Lemon-DiCenso decision which ruled a Pennsylvania secular services law and a Rhode Island secular teacher salary supplement law to be unconstitutional because, though they had a secular purpose and a secular effect, they nevertheless involved "excessive entanglement" of government and the church-related schools in violation of the Court's interpretation of the First and Fourteenth Amendments. This reconsideration led to the Panel's recommendation of legislation authorizing federal income tax credits to parents for part of tuition payments to nonpublic elementary and secondary schools.

A bill introduced by Congressman Wilbur Mills, Chairman of the House Ways and Means Committee, is a good illustration of the tax credit program recommended by the Panel. Mr. Mills' measure would authorize parents of nonpublic school pupils to deduct from their final total federal income tax liability an amount equal to half of the tuition paid to a nonpublic school which is in full compliance with civil rights laws. The maximum credit would be $400 per child. Parents with a gross adjusted family income in excess of $25,000 a year would have their credit reduced at the rate of one dollar for every $20 of income in excess of $25,000. So a family in the $35,000 bracket would have their aggregate credit reduced by $500.

The Panel is confident that tax credit legislation will meet constitutional criteria, sustain the current private investment in education, gain widespread public support, and bolster the morale of parents of nonpublic school pupils.

Constitutional criteria by which to judge the legality of an untested program like tax credits are far from being perfectly clear. Indeed, my review of church-state decisions from 1947 until the present strongly suggests that the Court actually develops its criteria in the very process of passing judgment on a particular law. Furthermore, the U. S. Supreme Court candidly has acknowledged that it can only "dimly perceive the lines of demarcation" which separate government and religious establishments. Consequently, the Court said, judicial caveats against entanglement of church and state "must recognize that the line of separation, far from being a 'wall,' is a blurred, indistinct and variable barrier depending on all the circumstances of a particular relationship."

In the Panel's judgment, tax credit legislation for tuition paid to church-related schools meets all presently proclaimed constitutional criteria.

Tax credit legislation does not require any appropriation of tax funds; it simply exempts parents from part of their tax liability in an amount related to their investment of personal funds in a nonpublic school. In that sense, tax credit legislation differs substantially from tuition reimbursement programs which presuppose an appropriation of public funds.

Tax credit, like tax exemption, has a secular purpose. In the U.S. Supreme Court's *Waly* decision, upholding tax exemption for real property owned by religious organizations, Mr. Justice Brennan in a concurring opinion, said: "Government has two basic purposes for granting real property tax exemptions to religious organizations. First, these organizations are exempted because they, among a range of other private, non-profit organizations, contribute to the well being of the community in a variety of non-religious ways and thereby bear burdens that otherwise would have to be met by general taxation, or be left undone, to the detriment of the community. . . . Second, government grants exemptions to religious organizations because they uniquely contribute to the pluralism of American society by their religious activities."

In terms of secular purpose, what was said about tax exemption would have equal validity for tax credits.

Mr. Justice Brennan also ruled that tax exemption does not "serve the essentially religious activities of religious institutions" and the principal effect is "to carry out secular purposes — the encouragement of public service activities and of a pluralistic society."

Apropos is Mr. Justice White's majority opinion in the New York textbook decision: "Americans have considered high quality education to be an indispensable ingredient for achieving the kind of nation and kind of citizenry that they have desired to create. Considering this attitude, the continued willingness to rely on private school systems, including parochial systems, strongly suggests that a wide segment of informed opinion, legislative and otherwise, has found that those schools do an acceptable job of providing secular education to their students. This judgment is further evidence that parochial schools are performing, in addition to their sectarian function, the task of secular education."

Tax credit legislation would not violate the Court's latest standard of "no excessive entanglement." Under the tax credit plan, the Panel has observed, the taxpayer, not the school, is subject to audit and the prime beneficiary is the parent who exercises a constitutionally guaranteed option of enrolling his children in a nonpublic school. No administrative burden is placed upon public school agencies; no public school system **need share its resources** with nonpublic schools; there need be no competition between public and nonpublic school interests for funds appropriated for the benefit of all school children. Finally, tax credit legislation as presently drafted is simple, clear and enforceable, and thus meets the criteria of sound tax legislation.

Tax credit legislation, the Panel's Report says, will encourage continuation and possibly the expansion of the present investment of at least $2 billion a year for the operation of nonpublic schools. As such, the legislation is compatible with other laws granting exemptions and deductions for private expenditures in activities which serve the public good. "Every dollar of tax credit allowed for nonpublic school tuition," the Panel has said, "will be matched by a dollar or more of private money invested in American education. The alternative to no credit could be a diminution of private investment to the point where virtually all American education would have to be publicly financed."

The Panel hopes that tax credit proposals will merit widespread public support. Testimony from several sectors suggests that the Panel's hope is well founded. It may be anticipated that from the nonpublic school sector, now organized in a nonsectarian group appropriately named CREDIT (Citizens Relief for Education by Income Tax) there will be considerable enthusiasm.

This enthusiasm will be well worth generating if it serves to renew parents' confidence in the future of nonpublic education. One great parental fear at the moment, and it's understandable, is that financial difficulties may prompt school authorities to cut corners in the academic program with resultant harm to the pupils' academic progress. "Tolerance of mediocrity," says the Panel's Report, "has sharp limits among those able to make a choice." In the public eye, a tax break can be a powerful stimulant to invest money in a worthwhile private enterprise. That, the Panel believes, will be the outcome of tax credit legislation.

Tax credit legislation in its present form would mean a tax saving of approximately $500 million a year. About 85% of the parents with children in nonpublic schools would benefit. Those excluded would be mainly welfare mothers and the working poor whose tuition payments far exceed their minimal or non-existent federal tax liability. For these parents, as I have said before, the Panel has recommended tuition allowances in lieu of tax credits. Very wealthy parents would derive no benefit.

This $500 million estimate is calculated at present rates of tuition and enrollment. If one or the other or both increase, the total savings will, of course, increase proportionately. The fact remains, however, that parents will have to pay at least half of all tuition charges plus the full price of all fees and supplies, and pleas for donations to churches providing most of the support for parish schools will continue undiminished. What at first may be a bonanza to parents will in a short time be primarily an incentive for increased private investment in nonpublic education.

One reason for the recent decline in nonpublic school enrollment is the movement of families from areas with nonpublic schools to areas where there are none. Construction of nonpublic school facilities in new suburban communities is virtually nonexistent. This situation would seem to contradict the wishes of the American public which in a Gallup survey indicated that when a completely new community is established (a development which soon may be quite frequent), both public and nonpublic schools should be included in the community plan. The Panel, therefore, has recommended a federal school construction loan program analogous to the Federal Housing Administration's program for home buyers. Availability of such loans might initiate construction of new nonpublic schools in areas heavily populated by former nonpublic school pupils who have moved away from the city.

General federal aid to education long has been a desire and hope on the part of educational leaders who see such aid as the only effective way to bring about a reasonable degree of equality of educational opportunity for all American children regardless of their place of residence. A long-standing obstacle to the enactment of general aid legislation has been the nonpublic school problem. Most observers of the Washington scene now would agree that a general federal aid bill without some kind of provision for nonpublic school pupils will not pass the Congress.

The Panel has recommended that formulas for allocating federal funds to the states include the total school population and that the vehicle for delivering aid to nonpublic school pupils be parental reimbursement programs like those enacted by Ohio and Pennsylvania. This recommendation envisioned parents of nonpublic school children being reimbursed either for all school expenses, as in Ohio, or only for tuition, as in Pennsylvania, in an amount not to exceed the per capita allocation of federal funds to a State.

Since the Panel filed its Final Report, Federal District Courts in Pennsylvania and Ohio have rendered opinions which declare State financed parental reimbursement programs to be unconstitutional. The Pennsylvania opinion was announced in connection with a decision to deny plaintiff's petition for a dismissal of a complaint against the Pennsylvania law. The full force of this opinion will not become clear until the Pennsylvania litigation is further processed. The Ohio decision, however, is a definite opinion on the part of a District Court and is, of course, subject to appeal to the U. S. Supreme Court.

The Ohio decision concedes that the Ohio parental reimbursement law has a secular purpose but it questions whether the law's effect is secular, not because that is not its intent, but because in effect the law mainly benefits parents of Roman Catholic school children and through the parents, the schools to which they choose to send their children. In so many words, the Court seems to say that even though a law may authorize benefits for all parents who choose to enroll their children in any church-related or non church-related nonpublic school of their choice, the law will not pass a constitutional test if it happens to give most benefits to Roman Catholic schools. Admitting that parental reimbursement does not "excessively entangle" the state administratively in the affairs of a church-related school, the Court opines that its ban on excessive entanglement also outlaws any program of aid in which a particular religious group might take an active political interest because of actual or potential benefits to the particular group. The Court's decision forbids both administrative and political entanglement. Concluding its rationale, the Ohio Court asserts that any kind of help, direct or otherwise, to a Roman Catholic parochial school is aid to the Church itself and as such is forbidden by the First Amendment.

As U. S. Supreme Court Justice White said in his dissenting opinion in the Lemon-DiCenso decision, the Court has created "an insoluble paradox for the state and the parochial schools. The state cannot finance secular instruction if it permits religion to be taught in the same classroom; but if it exacts a promise that religion not be so taught . . . and enforces it, it is then entangled in the 'no entanglement aspect' of the Court's Establishment Clause jurisprudence."

The Pennsylvania and Ohio District Courts' decisions have impaled state aid programs on the horns of the Supreme Court's impossible dilemma: aid for secular services was struck down because enforcement would entail entanglement; tuition payments were struck down because the state could not entangle itself to see if any of the funds somehow helped religion.

If the Court, whose function hardly is the creation of insoluble paradoxes and dilemmas, does not clear a way for nonpublic schools to meet its own established criteria in programs of state and federal aid, it justifiably will merit the criticism that, all its language aside, it simply wants to ban forever any prospect of substantial government help to Roman Catholic elementary and secondary schools in this nation. With distress and sorrow I have noted the Court's attempt to silence the spokesmen in favor of government aid for parochial schools by threatening to invalidate their success on the score that their action of itself created an entanglement of church and state in violation of the First Amendment. I cannot accept this restriction on my freedom of speech and freedom of religion, both of which I regard as constitutionally guaranteed freedoms. Hopefully the Court soon will realize that not a few citizens of this nation are looking for an oasis of freedom of religion in the Court established desert of no establishment.

In its most recent decision on the church-state issue, the U. S. Supreme Court in a summary docket action has affirmed a lower court's opinion that parents do not have a constitutional right to government aid for nonpublic schools to which they send their children. This decision, rendered in connection with ill advised litigation in Missouri, should come as no surprise to anybody who had read the Everson decree of 1947 in which the Court, while upholding the right of New Jersey to provide a public service for all school children, explicitly said that a law initially restricting service to public school pupils would be constitutional. A state may not, however, deny a child a benefit solely because of his faith or lack of it. The real question at this time, therefore, is not a parent's constitutional right to aid but the government's constitutional right to enact legislation for the benefit of the nation's nonpublic school pupils.

The last word on the constitutional issue has not been pronounced. Perhaps tomorrow, or some Monday very soon, the U. S. Supreme Court will render its verdict on the celebrated Amish law testing the constitutionality of Wisconsin's effort to force Amish children into high schools against their parents' wishes and conscientious religious convictions. Tutition reimbursement and tax credit laws probably will wind up in the Supreme Court for final adjudication.

Whatever may be the Court's decision in the future, it is comforting and reassuring to recall that in 1925 the U. S. Supreme Court laid down a constitutional principle which, though far from being fully implemented in this nation's legislatures and courts, still is fundamental law. It reads: "The fundamental theory of liberty upon which all governments in this Union repose excludes any general power of the state to standardize its children by forcing them to accept instruction from public school teachers only. The child is not the mere creature of the state; those who nurture him and direct his destiny have the right, coupled with the high duty, to recognize and prepare him for additional obligations."

CHAPTER 8

Implications of Supreme Court Decisions for Public Aid to Parochial Schools

EDD DOERR

INTRODUCTION

Should public funds be used to aid or support parochial and private education? Controversies over this question have raged in many countries, including the United States, for generations. How this question is answered has an important bearing on all education, on religious liberty and church-state relations, on intercreedal, interracial, and other social relations, and upon educational economics and levels of taxation.

In recent years more than half of our state legislatures have experienced vigorous debates over the issue. Several of them — New York, Rhode Island, Connecticut, Vermont, New Hampshire, New Jersey, Pennsylvania, Maryland, Ohio, Michigan, Illinois, and Minnesota — have passed bills since 1968 to provide more than merely peripheral aids to nonpublic education. Most of these programs have been struck down by the courts, or may reasonably expect to be struck down. In one state, Michigan, a constitutional amendment referendum in 1970 eliminated a major aid program.

In 1972 President Nixon and most Democratic presidential

The author is Educational Relations Director, Americans United for Separation of Church and State and Managing Editor, *Church & State Review.*

aspirants have expressed themselves as favorably disposed toward some form of public aid to parochial and private schools. President Nixon's Commission on School Finance recommended on March 3, 1972, that federal, state, and local tax sources be used to provide aid to nonpublic education through such means as tax credits, tax deductions for tuition, tuition reimbursements, scholarships for needy children, and such "child benefit" services as transportation, nutritional services, health services and examinations, loans of textbooks, and psychological testing, therapeutic and remedial services.[1] The commission also recommended experiments with voucher systems for full public funding of parochial and private education. The U. S. Office of Economic Opportunity has subsidized studies of voucher systems by the Center for the Study of Public Policy, Cambridge, Mass., and has provided grants for voucher plan feasibility studies to pulic school districts in California, Washington, Indiana, and New York. Despite considerable OEO pressure, however, no school district has agreed to a public-nonpublic voucher demonstration. This would require enabling legislation that has nowhere been passed. The Seattle, Washington, school board voted 5-2 on April 12, 1972, to withdraw from any voucher plan demonstration.

On April 20, 1972, a four-man panel on nonpublic education, a segment of the President's Commission on School Finance, urged passage of a $500 million per year program of federal income tax credits to aid parochial and private schools, together with school construction loans and tuition allowances for poor children.[2] These recommendations were to have been expected, of course, since 100% of the members of the panel are or have been intimately associated with parochial or private education. Bills have been introduced in the U.S. House of Representatives to provide parochiaid by means of tax credits. Identical bills sponsored by Reps. Wilbur Mills and Gerald R. Ford would provide tax credits up to the lesser of (a) 50% of the tuition for each child, or (b) $400 per child. Two lobby groups have been formed to press for passage of such bills: the Committee for Parental Rights and Public Assistance in Education, and Citizens Relief for Education by Income Tax (CREDIT).[3] The first group was established by the U.S. Catholic Conference, while the second represents the U.S. Catholic Conference, the National Catholic Educational Association, the National Union of Christian Schools, the Lutheran Church —

Missouri Synod, Agudath Israel of America, and the National Association of Independent Schools.

Less well publicized, unfortunately, than the President's Commission's recommendations are those of the National Educational Finance Project (funded under Public Law 89-10), which oppose tax paid aid for nonpublic education.[4]

Vast amounts of effort and money have been and are being spent by the advocates and opponents of public aid for parochial schools to influence public opinion and lawmaking bodies and to test the constitutionality of parochiaid measures in the courts.

(Since nonpublic education in this country is overwhelmingly church-related, this paper will use the convenient shorthand term "parochiaid" in a strictly non-pejorative sense to refer to any form of direct or indirect public aid to nonpublic education.)

Both advocates and opponents of parochiaid regard the issue as being of crucial importance, involving, as it does, religion, politics, personal and public finance, race, educational theory, and conflicting views as to how society should be organized.

The controversy may continue to swirl for a while about the host of public policy and political considerations, but a series of court decisions, beginning with *Everson* in 1947, peaking with *Lemon* in 1971, and continuing through the present, may well have settled the matter for all practical purposes. It would seem, as we shall see, that parochiaid is all but dead, except, possibly, for such peripheral services as transportation, textbook loans, and certain auxiliary services.

SCOPE AND PROBLEMS OF NONPUBLIC EDUCATION

According to the Census Bureau,[5] approximately 52 million children attended schools in grades K-12 in the United States in October 1971. Of these, 5.4 million (10.4%) attended parochial and private schools. Of the nonpublic school children, about 4 million (75%) attended Roman Catholic schools, with the remainder in an assortment of Lutheran, Seventh-day Adventist, Christian Reformed, Episcopal, Friends, other Protestant, Jewish, Black Muslim, and secular private schools.

Nonpublic school enrollment, particularly Catholic school enrollment, has been declining since about 1965. According to a University of Notre Dame study, *Economic Problems of Non-*

public Schools, conducted under the auspices of the President's Commission on School Finance, total nonpublic enrollment is expected to drop 46% between 1970 and 1980. Catholic school enrollment decline is estimated to total about 52% for the decade, while non-Catholic nonpublic enrollment should not slide by more than 16.5%.[6] It is commonly claimed that financial factors are chiefly responsible for the decline of nonpublic enrollment, but this view does not square with the facts. The projected Catholic school decline by 1980 is more pronounced at the elementary level (58%) than at the secondary level (32%),[7] though elementary tuition averages only about $50 per year,[8] considerably lower than the secondary average. Catholic school enrollment decline is also much more pronounced than that of other parochial and private schools which charge much higher tuition.

The Notre Dame study concludes that "it would be wrong to say that recent declines in Catholic school enrollment were caused, to any significant extent, by tuition increases,"[9] and that "state aid *in the amounts likely to be forthcoming* [emphasis added] would not have any significant impact upon enrollment."[10] Rather, the study says, "the causes seem to be geographic movement by families and changes in tastes."[11] A Boston College study, *Issues of Aid to Nonpublic Schools,* also prepared for the President's Commission, concludes that "church-related schools have existed to assist their clients with problematic societal relationships, religious persecution, social exclusion, and ethnic adaptation and survival. When these problems disappeared, the schools were largely abandoned."[12] This study also concludes that parochial schools have been and are operated chiefly by very conservative and non-ecumenical religious bodies and that enrollment problems could be expected to affect the school-sponsoring church experiencing the most profound shift in social and religious orentation.[13] The authors add that

> . . . the Americanization process has deflated the necessity of the Catholic school system as the primary agency for religious education, particularly in the minds of the younger, better-educated members of the Church. . . .
> In light of these realities, one must be naive, uninformed or dishonest to depict the current enrollment decline in nonpublic schools as fundamentally a consequence of cost increase . . . . [14]

THE NATURE OF NONPUBLIC EDUCATION

At least 90% of nonpublic education is parochial or church-related education. Parochial schools resemble public schools in many ways, or they could neither function nor be allowed to function, but they differ from public schools radically in many ways.

While public schools are required by law, by common sense, and by the pluralistic nature of our society to be religiously and politically neutral institutions, parochial schools, of whatever tradition, are markedly different.

The Rev. John L. McKenzie, professor of theology at the University of Notre Dame, handily sums up the principal distinctives of Catholic education:

> The Roman Catholic schools have always placed religious education as the primary purpose of the schools with no attempt to mask this under some other purpose. With the growth of the educational system, the elementary school has become the major agent of religious instruction rather than the home or the parish.
>
> The principle on which church education is conducted goes far beyond formal religious instruction. Children also learn the way of worship; they are taught respect and reverence for prelates, clergy, and religious. They are daily reminded of their identity as Catholics. They grow up in an atmosphere of Roman Catholic traditions and attitudes which are communicated not so much by instruction as by prolonged close association under the direction of professional religious persons.[15]

The Rev. Neil G. McCluskey, currently dean of teacher education at Lehman College of City College of New York, rounds out the picture of parochial education. He points out that religion pervades the parochial curriculum, particularly in literature, history, and the social studies. He adds that "The function of the Catholic school is not merely to teach the formulas of the Catholic religion but . . . 'to impart in a thousand ways, which defy formularization, the Catholic attitude toward life as a whole.' "[16]

Missouri Synod Lutheran schools are similarly denominational in operation. Professor Harry C. Coiner of Concordia Theological Seminary explains:

> The Church-related school, which does not face the problem of religious pluralism and is free to teach Bibli-

cal doctrines, can do much more specific work in Christian education.

The [Lutheran] school enables the child to experience a totally Christ-centered program, a program which focuses the application of God's word on him and on all areas of his life.

The relationship of science, social studies, language, arithmetic, and other subjects to Biblical truth may be taught without limitation.

Daily social contact between teachers and pupils of the same Christian faith reinforces learning by attitude and example. The absence of any formal educational influence that is strange, foreign, or antagonistic in any way to the positive Christian educational process permits the building of one stone on another without destructive influence.[17]

Other church-related schools are similar in being scarcely neutral religiously.

Another prominent feature of parochial education is its sectarian separatism or segregation. A child is seldom barred from a parochial school for religious reasons, but the pervasively denominational nature of the schools attracts clients who are members of the sponsoring church and has very little attraction for non-members. According to the National Catholic Education Association, 97.3% of all students in Catholic schools are Catholic.[18] The Notre Dame study *supra* indicates that "An applicant must be Jewish to be admitted to a Jewish Day School."[19] Lutheran and Adventist school enrollment is reliably estimated to be at least 90% Lutheran and Adventist, respectively.

Significant also is the fact that parochial and private schools enroll a much smaller percentage of racial minority children than do the public schools. According to the National Catholic Educational Association study *supra,* only 4.8% of Catholic school enrollment is black,[20] while public school enrollment is 14.5% black.[21] The Notre Dame study shows that in the nation's largest city, only 7.3% of total nonpublic enrollment is black (7.4% in Catholic schools), while public school enrollment is 33.8% black.[22] The situation is similar in most major cities, such as Baltimore and Philadelphia. In 1967 the U.S. Commission on Civil Rights concluded that "private and parochial school enrollment also is a major factor in the increasing concentration of Negroes in city school systems."[23]

PRO AND CON

It would be useful at this point to summarize briefly the more common arguments for and against parochiaid.

Advocates generally insist that fairness and justice require tax support for all schools; that school finance policy must support "freedom of choice"; that parents choosing non-public education for their children have a right to some educational benefit for their taxes; that without tax aid parochial schools will close and impose serious burdens on public schools; that parochiaid is necessary to promote pluralism, diversity, and experimentation in education; that tax support for parochial education is necessary since public schools teach "secular humanism."

These arguments are not persuasive. The courts have just held the "fairness" or "justice" argument untenable. Freedom of choice now exists and, in any case, may not be used to override more important considerations. All parents are presently free to enjoy the benefits of the public schools which they support and which they control through elected boards. Pluralism and diversity are found more in our public schools, with their rich mix of students and teachers of every faith, outlook, race, and background, than in the more homogeneous and generally ideology oriented nonpublic schools. And it is utter nonsense to mistake the public schools' respectful neutrality toward all faiths for the religious position of secular humanists. More experimentation and innovation is taking place in public schools than parochial schools, and, in any case, there is no reason why public schools cannot be as experimental and innovative as nonpublic schools.

Opponents of parochiaid are on surer ground. They point out that once the principle of tax aid for nonpublic schools is accepted, such aid will eventually escalate to a level approximating full support, as it has in Great Britain, the Netherlands, and parts of Canada. This, in turn, would destroy public education as we know it and make all education much less efficient and more costly than at present. A Gallup survey in 1969 showed that 59% of respondents in major population centers would send their children to parochial or private schools if they had the money or if their children could get free tuition.[24] This development, probably stemming from a "greener grass on the other side of the hill" psychology, would surely

mean a splintering or balkanizing of education, with disastrous
effects for educational economy and quality. Since secondary
schools should have graduating classes of at least 100 students
and elementary schools should have 60-100 students per grade,
the splintering of education under any massive parochiaid
plan would leave nearly all schools below optimal size except
some public schools and some Catholic schools.²⁵

Parochiaid opponents, observing the separatist and segregated nature of most nonpublic education, recognize that a
massive aid program could only greatly add to the creedal,
racial, class, ideological and other centrifugal forces threatening to rend the fabric of our society. Sectarian segregation in
education is an important factor in the genesis of the tragic
situation in Northern Ireland.

Opponents also hold that tax aid for religious institutions
is government action establishing or tending to establish religion, that it is preferential treatment by government toward
certain sects, and that it conflicts with every citizen's right to
support only the religious institutions of his free choice.

Other objections commonly cited are that opinion polls and
referenda consistently show substantial opposition to parochiaid; that parochiaid would cost parochial and private schools
their independence, even compelling them to sacrifice every
vestige of denominational religion in line with the U.S. Supreme
Court's 1962 and 1963 rulings striking down school sponsored
devotional activities; that such aid would constitute government interference in the internal affairs and controversies of
churches operating private schools.

THE COURTS: CLOSING THE DOORS

In our times, at least, the courts seem to be having the last
word or words about tax aid for nonpublic schools. Indeed,
the past year has seen a rapid-fire series of decisions which
have probably closed the doors against all but the most peripheral and minor forms of parochiaid.

In 1947 the Supreme Court ruled in *Everson v. Board of
Education* (330 U.S. 1) that a state may, though it is not required to, provide transportation for children attending parochial schools as part of a general safety program. (Since 1947
several state courts have upheld bussing laws, several have
ruled them to be in violation of state constitutional provisions,

and the Supreme Court has declined to review any of these state court rulings.) In *Everson* the Supreme Court held that New Jersey's bussing program approached the verge of state power, stating that "New Jersey cannot consistently with the 'establishment of religion' clause of the First Amendment contribute tax-paid funds to the support of an institution which teaches the tenets and faith of any church."

In *Everson* the Court also spelled out an interpretation of the First Amendment that has stood as a beacon for all defenders of public education and religious liberty:

> The "establishment of religion" clause of the First Amendment means at least this: Neither a State nor the Federal Government can set up a church. Neither can pass laws which aid one religion, aid all religions, or prefer one religion over another. Neither can force nor influence a person to go to or to remain away from church against his will or force him to profess a belief or disbelief in any religion. No person can be punished for entertaining or professing religious beliefs or disbeliefs, for church attendance or non-attendance. No tax in any amount, large or small, can be levied to support any religious activities or institutions, whatever they may be called, or whatever form they may adopt to teach or practice religion. Neither a State nor the Federal Government can, openly or secretly, participate in the affairs of any religious organizations or groups and vice versa. In the words of Jefferson, the clause against establishment of religion by law was intended to erect "a wall of separation between church and state."

The Court did not deal again with parochiaid *directly* for 21 years. In the meantime, the Court ruled in 1948, in *McCollum* (333 U.S. 203), that religious instruction, even on a voluntary and "released time" basis, could not be held on public school property. In 1962, in *Engel* (370 U.S. 421), and in 1963, in *Schempp* (374 U.S. 203), the Court ruled against government prescribed, sponsored, or mandated religious exercises. These rulings would seem to require the secularization of any schools receiving public support. Were parochial schools to be secularized their basic reason for existing as separate institutions would disappear.

In 1968 the Court, in *Flast v. Cohen* (392 U.S. 83), ruled for the first time that individual taxpayers have standing to sue in federal courts in cases involving possible First Amendment violations. This ruling made possible subsequent federal court challenges to parochiaid laws and programs.

On the same day that it ruled in *Flast* the Supreme Court upheld the constitutionality of a New York statute which requires school boards to lend nonreligious textbooks to students attending parochial and private schools. The decision in *Allen* (392 U.S. 236), which was argued solely on motions, noted that no evidence had been presented to show that the books were being used as instruments of religious indoctrination. (Abundant evidence now exists, that many of the text books approved by public school boards for lending to parochial students in New York are sectarian books which could never be tolerated in public schools. A court test of the implementation of the New York textbook loan law is being considered.)

In 1970 the Supreme Court in *Walz v. Tax Commission* (397 U.S. 664) enunciated a new test of the constitutionality of laws claimed to violate the First Amendment's "no establishment" clause: "We must also be sure that the end result — the effect — is not an excessive government entanglement with religion. . . . the questions are whether the involvement is excessive, and whether it is a continuing one calling for official and continuing surveillance leading to an impermissible degree of entanglement." Thus did the Burger Court set the stage for the historic *Lemon* decision.

The U.S. Sixth Circuit Court of Appeals, in *Protestants and Other Americans United v. United States,* ruled on December 16, 1970, that the lending of library facilities to parochial schools under Title II of Public Law 89-10, the 1965 Elementary and Secondary Education Act, might possibly run afoul of the "excessive entanglement" test laid down in *Walz.* The court distinguished this practice from *Allen* and remanded the case to a federal district court in Ohio for further proceedings.

On June 28, 1971, finally, the U.S. Supreme Court handed down its watershed decision in *Lemon v. Kurtzman* (403 U.S. 602).[26] In *Lemon* the Court had to construe the constitutionality of two state laws, Rhode Island's 1969 Salary Supplement Act and Pennsylvania's 1968 "purchase of services" act. Under the Rhode Island statute the state was to supplement, by up to 15%, the salaries of teachers of only secular subjects in nonpublic schools. All of the teachers who qualified for salary supplements under this act taught in Catholic parochial schools.

Under the Pennsylvania statute the state was authorized to reimburse parochial and private schools for their actual expenditures for teachers' salaries, textbooks, and educational materials in certain secular subjects.

The Court concluded that both the Rhode Island and Pennsylvania acts fostered an impermissible degree of entanglement between government and religion. The Court affirmed a Rhode Island federal district court ruling that parochial schools constitute "an integral part of the religious mission of the Catholic Church" and that the schools are "a powerful vehicle for transmitting the Catholic faith to the next generation." Both state legislatures, the Court agreed, had recognized that church-related elementary and secondary schools have a significant religious mission and that a substantial portion of their activities are religiously oriented." While the legislatures "sought to create statutory restrictions designed to guarantee the separation between secular and religious educational functions and to insure that State financial aid supports only the former," the Court concluded that "the cumulative impact of the entire relationship arising under the statutes in each state involves excessive entanglement between government and religion."

The Court held that a "comprehensive, discriminating, and continuing state surveillance" would be required to restrict state aid to purely secular functions, and concluded that "these prophylactic contacts will involve excessive and enduring entanglement between church and state."

The "divisive political potential" of parochiaid programs was also cited by the Court as another base for excessive entanglement.

In a community where such a large number of pupils are served by church-related schools, it can be assumed that state assistance will entail considerable political activity. Partisans of parochial schools, understandably concerned with rising costs and sincerely dedicated to both the religious and secular educational missions of their schools, will inevitably champion this cause and promote political action to achieve their goals. Those who oppose state aid, whether for constitutional, religious, or fiscal reasons, will inevitably respond and employ all of the usual political campaign techniques to prevail. Candidates will be forced to declare and voters to choose. It would be unrealistic to ignore the fact that many people confronted with issues of this kind will find their votes aligned with their faith.

Ordinarily political debate and division, however vigorous or even partisan, are normal and healthy manifestations of our democratic system of government, but political division along religious lines was one of the principal evils against which the First Amendment was intended to protect. . . . It conflicts with our whole history and tradition to permit questions of the Religion Clauses to assume such importance in our legislatures and in our elections that they could divert attention from the myriad issues and problems which confront every level of government . . . . The history of many countries attests to the hazards of religion intruding into the political arena or of political power instruding into the legitimate and free exercise of religious belief . . . . Political fragmentation and divisiveness on religious lines is thus likely to be intensified.

The *Lemon* ruling, as expected, triggered a continuing chain reaction. Two days after *Lemon,* the Court affirmed the 1970 decision of a three-judge federal district court in Connecticut that that state's Pennsylvania-like "purchase of services" parochiaid law violated the First Amendment's "no establishment" clause *(Johnson, et al. v. Sanders, et al.).* On January 11, 1972, a three-judge federal court in New York ruled in a one-page decision that New York's 1971 "purchase of services" law did not differ in any significant respect from statutes invalidated in *Lemon* and was therefore unconstitutional *(Committee for Public Education and Religious Liberty, et al. v. Levitt, et al.).*

On March 6, 1972, a three-judge federal district court in Vermont, in *Americans United, et al. v. Oakey, et al.* (No. 6393, 40 U.S.L.W. 2597, D. Vt.), struck down that state's 1971 parochiaid statute. That act was designed to permit local school boards to lend teachers, textbooks, and other services to parochial schools and receive up to 50% reimbursement from the state.

The Vermont court, following *Lemon,* held that "In order that any funds, goods, or services granted by the state do not have the impermissible effect of advancing religion, the state must see that the effects of any such grant will not permit of their being put to religious uses." But, the court added, in order to avoid the Scylla of advancing religion, the state may find "that the supervision required to police the grant causes it to become so deeply 'entangled' in religious matters as to find its plan shipwrecked on the Charybdis of over-involvement in parochial matters."

Noting that "All the church schools are vehicles for transmitting the faith of the sponsoring church to the next generation," the court found that

> . . . involvement with this vital and valuable religious activity results in an involvement with the religion itself. The Vermont Act will thrust the state not only directly into the physical plants of the schools but also into their operation and control. As such it surely involves excessive entanglement between government and religion. . . . Through the state control of teachers in the church schools, government control would become entangled with the existing religious control, and the day - to - day instructional administration would of necessity be the result of close cooperation between the school's administration and the public school district's administration . . . . Thus, it becomes highly probable that parochial school policy would, under the Vermont enactment, become the product of an interaction between the religious and the secular authorities, an interaction which in this case obviously would result in an excessive entanglement of the state in religious matters.

The Vermont court also found that the act in question created a "potential for church involvement in the political process" and an "explosive potential for citizen friction and political subdivision along religious lines." It further pointed out that

> . . . in the operation of this statute a potential exists for the impermissible fostering of religion. We are not convinced that the statute as written guarantees that the parochial school utilization of school district teachers would not have the primary effect of the advancement of religion.

The Vermont decision was followed on April 17 by the unanimous ruling of a three-judge federal district court in Ohio, in *Wolman, et al. v. Essex, et al.*, striking down that portion of Ohio's 1971 income tax law which was designed to provide state aid to parochial and private schools through the device of reimbursements to parents for moneys spent on nonpublic education. (The statute in question also provides certain auxiliary services to parochial schools. These services were upheld by the Ohio Supreme Court on November 24, 1971, in *P.O.A.U. v. Essex.* They were not challenged in *Wolman,* but might be in a future federal court test.) The Ohio statute provided parental grants at $90 per year per student, for the school years 1971-72 and 1972-73, with the size of grants for future years to be "determined by the State Board of Education."

The Ohio federal court found that "On the basis of the stipulated evidence before us, the Court concludes that non-public sectarian schools in Ohio retain a substantial religious purpose and denominational character as well, and that the grants of state aid to such schools therefore raise substantial questions under the First Amendment. . . ."

The reimbursement aspects of the Ohio statute, the court found, "are directed only towards the parents of children who attend non-public schools. The limited nature of the class affected by the legislation and the fact that one religious group so predominates within the class, makes suspect the constitutional validity of the statute." The court noted that the transportation and textbook loans approved in *Everson* and *Allen* applied to all students, not just those in a narrow class:

> In each of these cases religiously affiliated institutions were among a broad class of beneficiaries deriving benefits of a general, broad-based, public policy. These cases are truly analogous to situations in which the state provides police and fire protection generally to all people and property within its jurisdiction, regardless of religious affiliation.

Further, the class benefitting from the Ohio statute "is overwhelmingly sectarian in character."

The Ohio court concluded that, whereas the "Ohio statute contains none of the restrictions that hedged the Rhode Island and Pennsylvania schemes in *Lemon,*" the "absence of these restrictions on use . . . must of necessity tend to increase vastly the possibility that public funds will be used for sectarian, non-secular ends. No such general purpose statute has ever been held valid against Establishment Clause challenge."

The court also held that

> . . . payment to the parent for transmittal to the denominational school does not have a cleansing effect and some-

how cause the funds to lose their identity as public funds . . . . (T)he Court has held with unvarying regularity that one may not do by indirection what is forbidden directly; one may not by form alone contradict the substance of a transaction.

The Ohio federal court found that "the substance and direction" of the Ohio reimbursement program

. . . is simply to transfer public moneys to denominational schools. Its operation concerns itself with a simple relationship among three parties: The State of Ohio, a parent who enrolls a child in a non-public school, and the school itself. At the outset of the transaction, the State of Ohio has a fund of money accumulated by the imposition of a tax upon all of its citizens. The parent has voluntarily undertaken an obligation to pay tuition to a non-public school and the school in return has agreed to educate that child in an atmosphere oriented, if not dominated, by the teachings of that specific religion. At the end of the transaction, the parent has applied for and received reimbursement from the State of Ohio in the sum of $90.00 solely and specifically because he has paid that sum to the denominational school. There is $90.00 less in the public treasury and $90.00 more in that of the denominational school. Since the parents in this scheme serve as mere conduits of public funds, the State retains a responsibility of insuring that public moneys thus provided and which retain their public character throughout the transaction, are used for constitutionally permissible ends and continue to be so used. . . . We conclude that it is of no constitutional significance that state aid goes indirectly to denominational schools . . . through the medium of parental grants. Since the potential ultimate effect of the scheme is to aid religious enterprises, the Establishment Clause forbids its implementation regardless of the form adopted in the statute for achieving that purpose.

A final infirmity of the Ohio plan, the court held, was that it provided for direct money grants, thereby containing "the seeds for increased political involvement along religious lines at every level of government, from the local school boards to the General Assembly. This, of course, is the ultimate evil to be protected against by the Religion Clauses" of the First Amendment. "To uphold this statute would be to introduce the religious issue to the very center of state politics."

Summing up, the Ohio court said that

. . . the principle of the First Amendment is to prohibit
the State from providing *any* funds which directly support or sponsor *any* church-related institution. This constitutional policy does not turn on the amount of aid a
statute provides in any particular school year. Nor does
it matter that the aid goes to some or all religions. . . .
Section 3317,062 O.R.C., as it permits reimbursements
for tuition, will transfer public funds to religiously oriented private schools. These provisions do, therefore, violate
the Establishment Clause of the First Amendment to the
United States Constitution and therefore should be permanently enjoined.

April 1972 also saw three other important federal court
rulings. On April 6 a three-judge federal court in Philadelphia
unanimously denied a motion to dismiss a challenge, *Lemon v.
Sloan,* to the constitutionality of Pennsylvania's Parent Reimbursement Act for Non-public Education, a statute similar
to the Ohio statute *supra.* In its ruling the Philadelphia court
concluded

. . . that the effect of the Act is to aid the schools and
therefore the failure of the state to insure that the funds
are restricted to secular education or general welfare
services renders the Act unconstitutional. . . . (W)e do
not perceive any constitutional significance in the fact
that payments are made in the form of reimbursements
to the parents, a conduit plan or directly to the school.
The economic consequences are the same for the church-
related school whether it receives funds through a direct
grant, a conduit plan or because the state increases
family incomes through a reimbursement program which
enables the parents to continue to pay tuition. In each
case, tax-raised funds are being used to subsidize religious education.

"Finally," the court said, "even if we held that the Act
does not aid sectarian schools, we must still conclude that the
Act supports religion because it aids parents in providing a
religious education for their children."

While the Pennsylvania challenge may yet require a summary judgment, the newest Pennsylvania parochiaid plan,
rammed through the state legislature without hearings less
than two months after the *Lemon* ruling, would seem to be
dead.

On April 27, a three-judge federal district court for the

Southern District of New York ruled the state's 1970 Mandated Services Act unconstitutional in *PEARL*,[27] *et al. v. Rockefeller, et al.* The law had been designed to provide state funds to parochial and private schools to cover expenses connected with the administration, grading and reporting of examinations, the maintenance of enrollment and health records, the recording of personnel information, and the preparation of other reports required by law. The act was evidently drafted to take advantage and distort the meaning of a clause in the New York State Constitution which bars all public aid to denominational schools "other than for examination or inspection."[28]

The New York court held the Mandated Services plan to closely resemble the Pennsylvania purchase of services plan ruled unconstitutional by the Supreme Court in *Lemon v. Kurtzman*. "The dilemma . . . is insoluble. Either the statute falls because a system of surveillance and control would create excessive entanglement, or, without such a system, the schools would be free to use funds for religious purposes. The constitution is breached whichever route is chosen."

Finally, on April 17, the U.S. Supreme Court affirmed a September 28, 1971, ruling of a three-judge federal court in Missouri, in *Brusca, et al. v. State of Missouri,* which held that the First Amendment does not require states to assist parents in providing religiously oriented education for their children. The Missouri court had dismissed the suit by parochial parents who claimed the state's failure to aid parochial schools abridged their right to freely exercise their religion, denied them equal protection and due process of law, and failed to extend the benefits of state laws concerning education to all citizens.

TOWARD THE FUTURE

After reviewing the relevant Supreme Court and other federal court rulings from *Everson* through *Lemon* to the 1972 decisions, a reasonable person would have difficulty visualizing how any public aid could constitutionally be provided for parochial or private education except for rather peripheral and minor aids. Governor William T. Cahill of New Jersey seemed to recognize this when he announced on April 20 that he was abandoning support for all but peripheral aids for parochial schools.[29] Gov. Cahill, a strong supporter of parochiaid, reluctantly said, "I am not going to force anything on the legislature that is patently unconstitutional."

Battles over various parochiaid plans will continue, however futile they might be. Maryland citizens will vote in a November 7, 1972, referendum on a 1971 statute which provides $75 to $200 tuition grants to parochial and private school students.[30] The New York legislature is considering a package of bills to aid parochial schools through such devices as tax credits for tuition payments, state assistance for building maintenance, and tuition reimbursements for low-income parochial students. New York Senate Majority Leader Earl W. Brydges has even sponsored a resolution calling for a federal constitutional convention to amend the U.S. Constitution to permit some form of parochiaid.[31] However, with public opinion nationally opposing parochiaid by about a 60-40 margin, there is little likelihood that such an amendment would ever gather sufficient support for passage.[32]

Tax credit plans may still be debated in Congress, in state legislatures, and in public forums, and the OEO may continue to promote its voucher plan, but the logic of the federal district court rulings in Pennsylvania and Ohio in April should persuade most lawmakers that both tax credits and vouchers have insuperable constitutional defects. Both plans would involve the transfer of money from the public treasury to parochial and private schools. They would either aid religious institutions without safeguards against use for advancing religion or require safeguards certain to involve "excessive entanglement" between religion and government.

Nonpublic enrollment declined from a high of 7 million students in 1965 to 5.4 million in 1971, a drop of 23%. During the same period public school enrollment grew from 41.5 million to 46.6 million, an increase of 12.3%. According to the Notre Dame study, nonpublic enrollment will probably slide to about 3.2 million by 1980, with most of the decline taking place in Catholic schools. Census Bureau statistics[33] indicate that total school enrollment will decline by about 1.6 million students between October 1971 and October 1975. Public schools should be able, then, to absorb additional students without undue strain. The ability of public school systems to expand rapidly has been amply demonstrated. The Prince Georges County, Maryland, district, with 161,405 students enrolled for the 1971-72 school year, grew by an average rate of 8.7% per year between 1957-58 and 1969-70.[34] The Fairfax County, Virginia, district, with 135,948 students in ADM in 1971, grew by an average rate of an even 10% per year between 1954 and 1971.[35] Both school districts are functioning reasonably well. Contrast these growth rates with the national average public school increase of 2.05% per year from 1965 through 1971.[36]

Martin A. Larson, in a major study of parochial enrollment decline, to be published late in 1972 by the Americans United Research Foundation, found upon investigating 16 communities from California to Michigan during 1971 that transfers from parochial and private schools have caused only slight problems, that support for public education is weakest in communities with large percentages of children in parochial schools, and that the shift of students from parochial to public schools draws communities closer together and increases support for public education.

Absorbing parochial school transfers into public schools in some areas might result in increased educational costs, but in the long run these will be far less than the economic, educational, and social costs of dividing public support among public schools and a proliferation of less than optimal size nonpublic schools.

Catholic schools can survive without public aid if they meet the felt needs of Catholic parents, just as Protestant, Jewish, and private schools seem to be meeting such needs. Catholic schools could help themselves by emulating the consolidation process which has aided public education so much. In any case, however, whether church schools survive or decline is essentially not a public problem but a private one.

Beyond the scope of this paper are the public problems of providing adequate support for public education and of making educational opportunity for all children in public schools more nearly equal. Surely our country has the material and intellectual resources to do the job. All we need is a little more determination.

A suitable conclusion to this discussion has been supplied by the New York Commission on the Quality, Cost and Financing of Elementary and Secondary Education in its report to Governor Rockefeller in February 1972:[37]

> The principle of separation of church and state should not be abrogated: public funds or tax revenues ought not to be used in support of the attendance of students at sectarian schools. . . . We . . . recommend against public support of nonsectarian nonpublic schools. . . . As . . .

transfers [from nonpublic to public schools] take place, special grants [influx aid] should be made to those public school districts where unusual expenses are encountered because of rapid increases in enrollment. . . . Also, a policy of state purchase or lease of nonpublic school facilities should be adopted in preference to construction of new public school facilities wherever this is possible.

As the courts dissolve the controversy over parochiaid, educators, lawmakers, parents, and citizens generally should be able to devote more attention to solving the remaining problems of that great instrument of American democracy and progress, the public school.

FOOTNOTES

1. The President's Commission on School Finance, *Schools, People, and Money: The Need for Educational Reform,* Washington, D.C., 1972, pp. xvi-xvii, 53-57.
2. *Washington Post,* April 21, 1972.
3. *Church & State,* Silver Spring, Md., May 1972.
4. National Educational Finance Project, *Alternative Programs for Financing Education,* Gainesville, Florida, 1971, pp. 2-3, 41, 343-344.
5. Bureau of the Census, U.S. Department of Commerce, *Population Characteristics,* March 1972.
6. Office for Educational Research, University of Notre Dame, *Economic Problems of Nonpublic Schools,* Notre Dame, Ind., 1971.
7. *Ibid.* pp. 193 and 195.
8. *Ibid.* p. 487.
9. *Ibid.* p. 179.
10. *Ibid.* p. 179.
11. *Ibid.* p. 183.
12. Center for Field Research and School Services, Boston College, *Issues of Aid to Nonpublic Schools,* Newton, Mass., 1971, p. 16.
13. *Ibid.* p. 17.
14. *Ibid.* pp. 20 and 23.
15. John L. McKenzie, *The Roman Catholic Church,* Doubleday Image Books, 1971.
16. Neil G. McCluskey, S.J., *Catholic Viewpoint on Education,* Doubleday Image Books, 1962.
17. Victoria C. Krause, editor, *Lutheran Elementary Schools in Action,* Concordia, 1963.
18. National Catholic Educational Association, *A Statistical Report on Catholic Elementary and Secondary Schools for the Years 1967-68 to 1969-40,* Washington, D.C., 1970.
19. Office for Educational Research, *op. cit.,* p. 491.
20. N.C.E.A., *op. cit.*
21. U.S. Department of H.E.W. news release, January 4, 1970.
22. Office for Educational Research, *op. cit.,* p. 485.
23. U.S. Commission on Civil Rights, *Racial Isolation in the Public Schools,* Washington, D.C., 1967.
24. Office for Educational Research, *op. cit.,* p. 548.
25. National Educational Finance Project, *op. cit.,* p. 111.
26. Decided with *Earley v. DiCenso* and *Robinson v. DiCenso.*
27. The Committee for Public Education and Religious Liberty, a coalition of 32 religious, educational, and civic groups.
28. Article XI, Section 3. See Edd Doerr, *The Conspiracy That Failed,* Americans United, Washington, D.C., 1968, p. xiii.

29. Religious News Service, April 20, 1972.
30. *Church & State*, June 1971, and July-August 1971.
31. *New York Times*, April 21, 1972.
32. A Gallup-*Catholic Digest* poll in 1966 registered opposition by a 50% to 38% margin, while a 1969 poll by A Study of the American Independent School, Cambridge, Mass., showed opposition at 59% to 37% (*Church & State*, Dec. 1969). A Maryland poll by Americans United Surveys in 1970 showed opposition at 62.5% to 35.3% (*Church & State*, May 1970). A 1970 Illinois poll by Americans United Surveys showed opposition at 59% to 39.2% (*Church & State*, July-August 1970). Parochiaid referenda in Michigan and Nebraska in November 1970 registered opposition by a 57% to 43% margin (*Church & State*, January 1971).
33. Bureau of the Census, *op. cit.*
34. Prince Georges County, Md., Board of Education.
35. Fairfax County, Va., Board of Education.
36. Bureau of the Census, *op. cit.*
37. Report of the New York State Commission on the Quality, Cost and Financing of Elementary and Secondary Education, Chapter 5, pp. 2-6, February 1972.

CHAPTER 9

Educational Vouchers: Pro and Con

FREDERICK O. GODDARD*
IRVING J. GOFFMAN

In recent years, the concept of tuition vouchers for education has gained increasing attention and support. This attention and support has come from widely separated and diverse groups within the political spectrum, groups that one would not normally expect to find in agreement. Closer inspection of the specific voucher proposals by these different groups reveals that indeed they are not in agreement upon either the goals of education reform or upon the means to obtain it. The term voucher has been used loosely to name a wide variety of quite different institutional arrangements. This paper has been written to sort out these differences and to indicate to the reader just what various "voucher" schemes can really be expected to accomplish.

The public choice of which scheme to adopt, if any is to be adopted at all, will be seen to rest primarily upon the public choice concerning the goals of public education. A voucher system is not then just another experiment in methods of financing—one that can be adopted or discarded at will—but rather may involve fundamental reforms in the very nature of public education, its goals, its accomplishments and its institutional framework.

University of Chicago Professor Milton Friedman is per-

*The authors are respectively: Associate Professor and Professor of Economics at the University of Florida.

haps the father of modern education voucher proposals. Friedman introduced this idea in his 1955 article, "The Role of Government in Education."[1] Friedman's proposal was not designed to improve the financial basis of public schools but rather to divert public funds away from public education and into private educational institutions. This objective is very different from that of the Center for the Study of Public Policy (CSPP) which would require that: "No public money should be used to support private schools."[2]

The proposals by Professor Friedman and the CSPP are not reconcilable because they rest upon very different educational goals. This paper will investigate these and other proposals in later sections with particular emphasis upon the specifiic type of systems most likely to promote various goals. The section immediately following sets the stage for the investigation by examining the current crises in public support, financial and other, of our educational system.

TAXPAYER REVOLT

Prior to the 1966-67, fiscal year, voters consistently approved school bond proposals in about 72 percent of elections representing from 70 to 80 percent of the proposed dollar value. The year 1966 marked the beginning of a downward trend, however, so that by 1968-69, only 56.8 percent of school bond proposals were passed, representing only 42.6 percent of dollar value proposed.[3] The actual amount approved fell from $2.65 billion in 1966 to $1.70 billion in 1969 even though enrollments, income and prices had risen. Clearly the American voter was less willing than ever to vote new property taxes for the support of education.

The revolt by local property taxpayers against school bond issues after 1966 was not the only symptom of a taxpayer revolt. State governments have been under increasing pressure for parsimony, and in 1969, with national interest and support, Congress voted wide reforms and reductions in Federal taxes. More recently, the people of New Jersey have turned down tax reforms and increases, while both Senator McGovern and Governor Wallace gained some support in primary campaigns on the basis of tax relief proposals. There are two possible sources of taxpayer dissatisfaction that might underlie this revolt.

First, the revolt may be against too high or inequitable

taxes. Certainly taxes at both the federal and state levels have increased absolutely and as a percent of income in the past six years. This is due partly to the inflation accompanying the Viet Nam conflict and partly to increases in government programs at all levels. During 1970-71, for example, while overall GNP grew at 7.4 percent, state expenditures grew at 16.2 percent.[4] A general belief that the tax system is unfair has also been evident in recent years. Comment has already been made about widespread support of political candidates who have promised reform. When people believe that they are being asked to pay more than their fair share, we can expect them to resist expanding the program that treats them unfairly.

The refusal of communities to vote school bond issues can be interpreted in part as a revolt against the inequities of a specific tax—the property tax. This tax yielded up to 99 percent of local school districts' tax revenue in 1969.[5] Certainly distribution of the burden of the tax bears little relation to the benefits acquired from education. In addition, this tax amounts to a particularly discriminatory excise on an important essential of the household budget—housing. Economist Dick Netzer has estimated that this excise averages from 17 to 27 percent of annual use value of residential property.[6] Compared to a 3 to 4 percent excise on other goods, this is indeed high!

A second possible source of taxpayer dissatisfaction leading to rejection of school bond proposals is that the preferences or objectives of individual taxpayers have changed. That is, taxpayers have voted against new school programs not simply because they object to the taxes involved, but because they want less, or at least less growth, of the educational programs in question. Several important factors might have led to such a change in preferences.

First, the widespread occurrence of student rebellion has undoubtedly brought forth public dissatisfaction with the results of the use of their tax dollars for education. Regardless of the extent to which the education establishment is to blame for current disorders, taxpayers tend to place the blame upon it. The average taxpayer reacting to student disruptions may not in fact have reduced his support of education as it *might be* operated. But when he is asked to support education, he is limited to supporting what exists, not what he might wish to exist. In the long run his wishes for change in the operation of schools might be realized, but in the short run his only means of control lies with his control of the purse.

The second factor is the inherent liberalism of the educational process. In the best of times this factor leads to some antagonism between the taxpayer and the educator. By its very nature education promotes more liberal values than those held by many citizens. Education must place high values upon individual and intellectual freedom, and the study of our culture's history leads to an increased humanistic orientation. In recent years this normal gap has been widened by a drive to make modern education more relevant to the immediate solution of social ills. Thus education has been injected into the middle of political controversy over the best means of running society. Whether or not this trend is wise, and many do not believe it is, it cannot but erode general support for education. To the extent that education joins sides in political issues it must lose the support of those taxpayers on the opposing side of the issue.

A third factor that possibly has led to a reduction of public support of education is the increasing length of stay in school. This has in effect created a new class within society. It is a new leisure class of people too old (over 17 years of age) to be constrained by rules normally governing younger students yet a class that does not bear the full individual responsibilities of adulthood, that is, the responsibilities of providing for one's financial needs. Such a class has, of course, always existed, but until recent times it was small. The enormous increase in the percent of college-age youths actually enrolled in universities, colleges and junior colleges has made this a large and significant social class and one more apt to create resentment and conflict. Again the taxpayer may support lower levels of education, but his opportunity to support or oppose them financially may only apply to the whole package of educational programs.

A fourth factor that had undoubtedly contributed to a reduction of public support for public education is the tying of education to racial integration. As Federal pressure for integration is extended to the non-South, this factor becomes important on a nationwide scale. This factor is closely related to the second factor above. Again those who oppose integration will be induced to oppose educational expenditures as part of their political strategy. The main difference between this factor and the second one is that in the case of integration the decisions are being largely made outside the educational establishment. Many would argue that this factor is a necessary cost of obtaining a social reform at least as important as increased education. The reduction of racial discrimination and conflict is undoubtedly a very important social goal and there is some level of costs in terms of loss in other goals that is justified. But rational policy-making requires that the costs be considered in judging the extent to which the tradeoff in goals will be pursued.

The fifth factor leading to reduction of support for local education is parental dissatisfaction with the results of current educational programs. There are all too many cases of the failure of the schools to teach the elementary skills in reading, mathematics and spelling. These cases are not confined solely to ghetto schools. Parents have also objected to what seems to be a failure of the schools in developing a sense of self-discipline and good work habits in students.

Resistance of taxpayers to increases in the size of the education budget may not be only a resistance to increased taxes per se but also may arise from a deep dissatisfaction with the performance of the current school system. During the first two years of the Nixon Administration, much was made of the idea that states and localities were running out of revenue sources. A study prepared for the President's Commission on School Finance failed to find evidence to support this view.[7] While some localities are experiencing serious difficulties in obtaining needed revenue, every state has enormous untapped revenue sources at its disposal.[8] John F. Due calculated that if state governments had in 1969, implemented his proposals for tax changes, none of which would have involved higher tax rates than exist in some states today, revenue representing a more than 50 percent increase in expenditures on education could have been collected, and this revenue would have grown more rapidly than GNP in succeeding years.[9] Current financial limitations do not arise out of an economic constraint on funds available to the states, but rather arise out of an unwillingness on the part of the voting taxpayer to support increased budgets. This unwillingness may be as much related to dissatisfaction with current performance of our schools as to any other causes.

However pressing it may seem to those who must budget

school operations that the current crisis in public education
is one of finance or availability of public revenues, economists
perceive a crisis from lack of performance or lack of equity
rather than a simple shortage of funds. Indeed it is not at all
evident in economic terms that we are not already spending
too much for education—that the total expenditure could not be
reduced in conjunction with a wiser allocation of that budget.
In the period 1955 to 1969, the share of GNP devoted to education has increased from 3.7 percent to 6.3 percent.[10] Few
would argue that the quality and quantity of educational output has been increasing at almost twice the rate for the rest
of the economy. Rather it would seem this growth is due to
increases in costs that are higher and increases in productivity
that are lower than is found in other areas. Indeed it may
very well be that productivity changes in some areas of education have been negative. For example, although no statistics
exist, the intuitive feeling of many college teachers is that the
learning acquired per unit of budgeted resources has declined
in recent years.

What is seen from the above is that form of voucher schemes
must be a vehicle to reform the fundamental structure of the
educational system and not simply a pipeline for revenue grants
to localities.

EDUCATIONAL VOUCHERS AND
CONSUMER SOVEREIGNTY

The original voucher proposal by Friedman had as its objective the granting of consumer sovereignty to parents in determining the kind of schooling their children would receive.
By granting this sovereignty to parents, the education industry, through predominately private schools, would more closely approach what economists term allocative efficiency.

The concept of consumer sovereignty, introduced by Adam
Smith, argues that in a competitive marketplace, the ultimate
combination of different products and services produced is
determined by the desires and tastes of the consumers. Because producing agents, in this case the schools, cannot long
remain in business unless they can attract sufficient consumers
as customers, these agents must produce those products and
services that conform to the desires of consumers. It is the
individual consumer, then, and not producers or a government agency as surrogate for the social will who determines

the character of the goods and services available to him. It is the consumer who is sovereign, and producers are his servants. This power of the consumer over the nature of productive output is lost, however, if producers do not have to compete for customers. For this reason economists are opposed to monopoly.

Today, with few exceptions, the public school system in the United States is a monopoly. While the schools are not centrally administered on a national basis (there are over 16,000 individual school districts), and there is a great deal of variation in the kind and quality of schools among districts, parents are faced with a single monopolistic provider of schools within any given market or school district. It is not the number of enterprises within a state or nation that matters, but rather the number of enterprises that are operating within a local market that determines the degree of meaningful choice that consumers face. For example, relatively few firms provide supermarkets in a given state, but a great many school districts will be found in the same state. Yet the citizens of a typical city are faced with a single monopolistic provider of public education but can choose from eight different supermarket firms, each with stores in several convenient locations. There are, as might be expected, wide variations in the kind and quality of services offered and in the prices charged by each supermarket firm. In any meaningful sense, then, the citizens of a typical city, and of a state, can be said to have a *diversity* of choices in supermarkets but no choice at all in education. It is this diversity of choices that leads to consumer sovereignty.

If the consumer is faced with a diverse set of choices, he will select that enterprise that best meets his individual tastes and preferences. In doing so, the individual consumer, along with others that share his tastes, will reward the enterprise that best meets his demands. Further, enterprises have a strong incentive to seek out consumer opinions and modify their product in ways that will improve it in the consumer's mind. It is precisely this process that Friedman sees operating to improve educational diversity and choice through consumer sovereignty via his voucher proposal.

There are, of course, limits to the degree to which consumer sovereignty will act to provide individual consumers with the kinds of services that they prefer. Two limits are particularly important. First, enterprises do not normally respond greatly to the isolated tastes of an individual consumer, but rather to the common desires and taste of an aggregate of consumers with similar preferences. Thus consumer sovereignty will work better for consumers who share tastes and preferences with a large number of other consumers. The individual with unusual and rare tastes may well find himself ignored. Some citizens, with rather ordinary tastes in supermarkets, are, for example, satisfied by the current diversity in a typical city, but are frustrated by the lack of an expensive and high quality French restaurant. This limitation, however, only constrains and does not void the advantages of competition and consumer sovereignty. A public monopoly, such as the public schools, offers no choice at all. The only way a parent can influence the school system to change and conform to his particular tastes is through the political process. But in this process he must get not just a large number of others, but a majority of the parents within the local district to share his tastes. The competitive process, while it does not respond to all individual tastes, does respond to the desires of substantial minority groups. Further, through diversity of services, each substantial minority interest can be satisfied without denying satisfaction to other interests. In a homogeneous, monopolistic public school system, minority interests, when recognized through the political process, can only be met by reducing the satisfaction of conflicting interests of other groups.

Another limit on the process of consumer sovereignty arises because the market weighs individual desires by an individual's ability to pay. In other words, rich consumers are normally more sovereign than poor consumers. In order that the poor may be offered a high degree of diversity and choice in educational opportunities for their children, public programs must be designed to reduce the disparity in market influence that arises from income inequalities.

The process of consumer sovereignty, through competitive diversity in the marketplace, is then more compatible with an ethic of individualism than is a public monopoly controlled through majority rule in the political process. Individual demands, even though they differ from the average or majority tastes, are recognized and responded to by competing enterprises. Consumer sovereignty, in addition to this provision for individualism and diversity, is also seen by economists as providing for what is termed allocative efficiency.

An efficient economy is one that utilizes its scarce resources in such a way as to produce maximum satisfaction of consumer wants. In doing so, provision must be made for determining optimum innovative activity, for selecting the least cost methods of production, and for determining and selecting the best of these resources in terms of the particular goods and services to be produced. It is this last consideration that is encompassed by the term allocative efficiency. Allocative efficiency is obtained when the scarce resources of society are, *given current knowledge, techniques, and state of the arts,* used to produce that particular combination of goods and services that maximizes consumer satisfaction. In general, economists insist that the free marketplace for final goods and services is the best mechanism for attaining allocative efficiency, and that a free market for inputs is the best way of attaining efficiency (least cost method) of production. Note the emphasis in the statement above. The claim for allocative efficiency of the free market does not rest upon a claim that the free market will somehow discover new technologies and methods of production, but rather that it will lend to choices of outputs from among the current possibilities that enhance overall welfare. This point is important in light of some recent enthusiasm over vouchers and limited parental choice (from among several "public" schools) as a means to spur discovery of better teaching techniques and tools. Such enthusiasm is based upon a mistaken notion of the operation of the consumer sovereignty. Indeed, there is every reason to believe that centralized research, perhaps federally sponsored, would be more effective in discovering new techniques than uncoordinated, poorly financed efforts of many small educational entrepreneurs.

In the economists paradigm, then, consumer sovereignty serves as a most efficient way to select the objectives of a social system and not as a means of prompting inventiveness in obtaining given goals. If society is to impose collectively determined objectives upon the education industry, the advantages of freedom of choice and consumer sovereignty are lost. What all this means is that some form of voucher system can be an effective social tool *only* if the objectives of the education system are left unspecified by social agencies and instead in the hands of individual parents.

CONFLICTING GOALS FOR STRUCTURAL REFORM

An unfortunate fact for our society is that the primary goals for the education system sought by diverse reformers are in fundamental conflict. On the one hand, some parents wish a greater range of choice in selecting the kind of education their children receive. In order for this choice to be meaningful the parent must be permitted to choose the type of education, the amount of education, including the cost per day, and, to some extent the students who will be his child's classmates. But this very freedom of choice conflicts with the goal of educational equality. A very significant force in American society seeks this equality through social, economic and racial integration and greater homogenization of the quality and characteristics of education received by the nation's youth.

Clearly these goals are in conflict, for the very act of requiring that all schools be open to everyone regardless of ability, background, motivation or interest robs the parent of consumer sovereignty or meaningful freedom of choice. This point must be emphasized. Numerous authors of reform plans, including Christopher Jencks, John Coons, Stephen Sugarman, and Judith Areen have proposed systems that allow some selection of schools by the parent. But the plans submitted by these authors all deny any meaningful choice to the parents through restrictions that require eligible schools to be integrated socially, economically and racially through quotas and lotteries. The most that a parent could choose would be the level of expenditures per student day, and even this is not an available choice in some of the plans.

Considerable evidence exists suggesting that such choices are not very meaningful in terms of educational attainment. The Coleman Report of 1965 revealed that such items as capital expenditures or teachers' salaries seem to have no detectable influence on the student's progress.[11] Coleman's findings suggest instead that the most important influence on a student's progress is his classmates. However repelling it may be to some, the conclusion is inescapable: if parents are to have a meaningful choice of schools—one that can affect significantly their children's educational progress—then they must be allowed, to some extent, to choose their children's classmates.

The better value judgment may be to opt for equalization and homogenization of education, and society may make this choice. But such a judgment should be made with the true cost in mind. Equalization and homogenization of the social, economic and racial backgrounds of children in all schools can only be obtained through denying parents any meaningful choice or control over their own children's education. Further, and perhaps more important, such equalization might be obtainable only by lowering the educational opportunity of some in order to enhance that of others. As Martin Mayer stated, "There is some reason to believe, on the basis of the Coleman Report, that the children of low-income, ill-educated parents will on the average do somewhat better in school if they are exposed to the more invigorating air of classrooms dominated by the children of higher-income, better-educated parents. The same report gives evidence (much less frequently cited) that children from more fortunate homes will on the average do worse in school if they are a minority group in classrooms where the air is that of the slums."[12]

Society is then faced with a choice of attempting to *maximize* the opportunities of individuals for self improvement and a better life by allowing full consumer sovereignty and freedom of choice in education or of attempting to *equalize* the opportunities of some while enhancing that of others, less talented or from poorer backgrounds. Economists cannot and should not make this choice involving fundamental philosophical and ethical values. All that economic science can do is indicate those institutions that best serve society's goals once the choice is made. The following sections are devoted to this purpose.

THE FRIEDMAN VOUCHER PLAN

Professor Friedman, though normally thought of as the father of the modern voucher plan, has not in any one place set out the details of a "Friedman" voucher scheme. Nevertheless, his ideas can be collected from a wide diversity of writings, speeches and private conversations, and a "Friedman" plan can then be set forth as follows:

1. Government would require a minimum level of education and finance that through ". . . vouchers redeemable for a specified maximum sum per child per year if spent on approved educational services."[13]

2. "Parents would then be free to spend this sum *and any additional sum* they themselves provided on purchasing educa-

tional services from an 'approved' institution of their own choice."[14] (emphasis added)

3. Approved schools might be run by ". . . private enterprises operated for profit, or by non-profit institutions."[15] Public, state operated schools might still exist (especially in low population areas where only one school is economically feasible) but these would receive no public funds beyond the amount of the voucher.

4. "The role of government would be limited to insuring that the eligible schools met certain minimum standards, such as the inclusion of a minimum common content in their programs, much as it now inspects restaurants to insure that they maintain minimum sanitary standards."[16]

5. Schools would be able to set the entrance, disciplinary and achievement standards they wished subject only to the pressures of the marketplace and obvious constitutional restrictions against racial or religious segregation.

On the positive side, the simple Friedman voucher plan, if implemented, would certainly promote consumer sovereignty and freedom of choice. Those parents who are today denied reasonable opportunity to increase the level of expenditure on their child's education would be able to do so under the Friedman plan. In like manner, parents would have an enhanced opportunity to choose from various kinds of educational institutions in order to fit the institution to their perception of their child's particular needs. Of course, if parents wish to purchase additional amounts of education by sending their child to a more expensive school they must pay the difference (above the voucher amount) from their own budget. But this is what freedom of choice is all about. Currently, parents who have a child in the public school can do this only by persuading everyone else (including those who have no children) that a higher budget is desirable or by withdrawing their child from the public system and thus pay not only the additional amount, but also what was previously obtained from public funds. Under the Friedman plan, then, parents would be able to entertain preferences for education budgets that differed from the community average.

This opportunity would not be confined only to the rich. Indeed, the poor would benefit proportionately more. Under the current system, it is only the rich who can afford the choice of sending a gifted child to a special and more costly school. Under

Friedman's plan this choice becomes more available to poor parents, since they would only have to pay the additional tuition and would not have to lose their public support. Additionally, under a Friedman voucher plan, total expenditures on education would undoubtedly rise significantly even if total public expenditures were not increased. Thus, the limits on education currently imposed by political constraints on state budgets would be broken. An increase in expenditures for welfare or highways would not necessarily mean a curtailment of educational opportunity as is often the case now.

Friedman's plan does, however, have many negative aspects. Perhaps the most important one is that typical schools would not have student bodies that proportionately represented the students of the whole community. Even with the prohibition of racial and religious discrimination in admissions, it is probable that parents would voluntarily send their children to schools with a student body of similar cultural background. While, for example, no school eligible for vouchers would be allowed to exclude students on the basis of religion, one would still expect to find predominately Catholic schools. Similarly, the prohibition of racial discrimination would not preclude many of the better "academic" schools from being predominately white. As long as a disproportionate number of blacks come from deprived family backgrounds, one can expect a reduced ability to compete on purely academic grounds for admission to select schools and, thus, a less than proportionate enrollment in those schools. Thus, the Friedman voucher plan would fail to promote social integration of different classes, races and religions; indeed, it might encourage the opposite.

While Friedman's plan would allow increased opportunity for individual families to upgrade their children's education through individual financial effort, inequalities in the distribution of the nation's income would lead to far more rich than poor parents doing so. Thus, one could expect some increase in levels of segregation by income class.

THE FRIEDMAN-PAULY OR CPPC VOUCHER

A variation of the Friedman plan has been proposed by several economists, including Mark V. Pauly and Jay Chambers who calls his plan the Compensation Principle-Price Competition or CPPC Voucher.[17]

Pauly and Chambers propose in principle the same scheme; in Pauly's words:

". . . a scheme in which the community agrees to pay some fraction of the cost of *each unit* of education purchased by the parents could lead to optimality. . . . The optimal structure of these payments is not, however, one in which the community pays the same fraction of the per unit cost at all income levels, but rather it is one in which the fraction paid by the community varies inversely with family income."[18]

The effect of the Pauly-Chambers modification would be to change the first two characteristics of the Friedman proposal listed above to read:

1. Government would require a minimum level of education, and finance this through a fixed minimum voucher granted for each child.

2. Parents would then be free to spend more than this minimum sum on their child's education with the State paying *a part* of the additional tuition increments above the fixed sum. The fraction of the additional tuition to be paid by the state would *vary inversely with family income.*

The exact details of the payments mechanism implementing the above are not as important as the principle involved, and several specific schemes have been proposed. Perhaps the easiest form of implementation would be to allow parents to purchase additional vouchers at a fraction of their face value with the fractional price to be determined from the family's income as reported for tax purposes. This particular form has the advantage of minimizing the administrative burden of the scheme. Families with incomes above some level would have to pay the full face value. Families at the lower end of the income scale would *always* have to pay something for additional vouchers though it might be as low as 10 to 20 percent of face value.

While retaining the positive characteristics of efficiency and consumer sovereignty in the unmodified Friedman plan, this Pauly-Chambers modification would go far towards eliminating any inequities due to income distribution, and granting more choice to poor families. Indeed, the modified voucher scheme might lead to greater equality of opportunity among children from different income classes than does the current public school system. Under the current system, children are largely restricted to attending schools on a residential basis, and children from poor families cannot transfer to better schools in rich neighborhoods. Under the modified voucher scheme, poor children would be enabled to buy into better schools.

While the modified voucher plan would largely eliminate inequities in education due to wealth, it would not eliminate differences in education arising from differences in the students' talent or ability. It would not be expected that schools would separate students on the basis of family background per se, but separation of students according to academic merit or their individual talents and ability would, de facto, tend to promote the enrollment in separate schools of children from good and bad family backgrounds. This would follow since currently a poor family background is statistically associated with low academic ability. The talented student from a poor background would, under the Pauly-Chambers voucher, be able to attend the better schools (that is, schools with high entrance requirements), but the average child from a poor background would not.

Thus the Pauly-Chambers modified voucher would promote efficiency and individual opportunity even better than the unmodified plan, but would fail to promote, indeed discourage, proportional integration of students of different racial, religious or cultural backgrounds. Schools would tend to group students on the basis of talent with talented students, regardless of background, attending one school and less capable students attending another. If the community were large enough to support several schools in each category (high and low academic achievement) then further separation along cultural (especially religious) line could be expected. Note that this would be true even though no tests of religion or background could be applied for admission. Parents would naturally tend to (other things such as academic quality being equal) place their children in schools with an enrollment of predominately the same culture as their own.

The Pauly-Chambers modified voucher could be changed in two more ways that might improve its performance with respect to the goals of social integration and compensatory education. First, as a prerequisite for qualifying as a voucher accredited school, a school might be required to take affirmative action rather than simply to refrain from discriminating in its admissions policies on the basis of race, religion, or other ethnic qualities, and in addition, might be required to assure a reasonable representation of various subgroups of the population in its student body. For example, each school might be required to have an admissions procedure which would assure that each cultural subgroup would be represented in the same proportion in the student body as it was in otherwise qualified applications. More stringently, a school might be required to actually recruit students so as to meet quotas based upon race, religion and other groupings. Such requirements, especially the use of quotas, would of course diminish the degree to which consumer sovereignty would guide the development of the nation's schools. But this reduction in the ability of consumers to determine the character of schools would take place in an area where society has already determined that consumer choice is to be constrained, for example by the 1964 Public Accommodations Act. Considerable consumer sovereignty would still remain to determine the amount of expenditure in individual schools and the character of the schools in terms of academic versus vocational programs, the level of scholastic rigor and the nature of discipline maintained.

A voucher system changed in the above manner would not only obtain the level of social integration of the current public school system, but would in addition go much further than current schools to offer opportunity to children from poor or deprived backgrounds to obtain the excellence usually associated only with wealthy school districts. Further, such a voucher system, would promote the integration of children from different income classes to a degree far exceeding anything the public, neighborhood school system could attain.

A second possible change in the above voucher scheme would be to increase the amount of public subsidy of tuition vouchers (as opposed to the parent's contribution) used to purchase special types of socially desirable education. Thus, an incentive could be provided to encourage the expansion of programs for retarded or handicapped children, or remedial education for children from disadvantaged neighborhoods or cultures. Few things work as well as the possibility of obtaining more money in inducing educators to change programs and introduce special aids.

Most voucher proposals to date have had the shortcoming of allowing if not promoting *de facto* segregation in the schools. The addition of these two changes to the Pauly-Chambers voucher scheme would go far towards eliminating this objection. The first change would, however, be obtained at a cost.

The degree of consumer sovereignty, individual parental choice and economic efficiency would certainly be reduced by restrictions on enrollment policy to assure social homogeneity of student bodies. The fundamental conflict between individual choice and efficiency on the one hand and social integration on the other is not avoided, but rather compromised by trading off some of one for the other.

SOME PSEUDO VOUCHER SCHEMES

Several attempts have been made to design plans that would eliminate the unmodified voucher plans' shortcoming of *de facto* social segregation in the schools. Foremost among these are the proposal of the Center for the Study of Public Policy (CSPP) currently being tested by the Office of Economic Opportunity and the Family Power Equalizing proposal of Coons, Sugarman and Clune.[19] Neither of these are in fact true voucher schemes since both deny any meaningful consumer sovereignty to parents. Hence, both are treated together.

The full details of the CSPP proposal are too extensive to repeat here and only an outline of the important principles is given below:[20]

1.   Schools would *not* be able to charge any tuition or fees beyond the fixed voucher given to all children.

2.   Schools would have to accept any and all applicants so long as space was available.

3.   If excess applicants existed at least half of the spaces would be filled by lottery from the applicant pool; the other half of available spaces would be subject to quotas regarding minority ethnic groups.

4.   Schools would not have control over suspension or expulsion but would be subject to uniform standards set by a government agency.

5.   A new government agency would be established to distribute vouchers to parents, pay schools for vouchers and pay parents for transportation costs to school.

The most immediate critical comment on the CSPP plan is: why bother with vouchers at all? Since parents cannot augment the voucher from their own funds and the value of the voucher is fixed, it would be far more economical to simply pay the schools an amount based upon enrollment. Vouchers in this plan serve no purpose other than to increase administrative overhead costs.

In fact the CSPP plan is not a voucher plan, but rather a plan to reform the public school systems. With the restrictions listed above, any significant degree of consumer sovereignty or variation in educational opportunity is blocked. In effect, this plan is designed to replace the neighborhood school system with a more centralized system with individual public schools, perhaps, emphasizing science, the arts or vocational skills. These objectives may well be good ones, but the plan itself is overly awkward and complicated by the "voucher" format.[21] While the CSPP plan would not significantly allow for consumer sovereignty or allocative efficiency in the schools, it might go a long way toward granting more social integration than is found in the current public school system or could be expected from a true voucher system—might, that is, with one exception. The CSPP plan, by centralizing school programs *and financing* would eliminate the current practice of well-off neighborhoods voting themselves higher than average school budgets through local property tax financing. If this opportunity is removed, we may well experience an increasing number of well-off parents removing their children from the public school system entirely and simultaneously *ending their support of the public schools and school taxes*. Thus, the CSPP plan could lead to reduced taxpayer support of public schools, increased social segregation by wealth class and a wider differential between total expenditures on rich and poor children. This danger of the CSPP plan is one shared with many other plans that attempt to force equal expenditures for all children. It is not a danger for any of the voucher plans, for these do allow individual parents to obtain higher than normal expenditures on their child's education if they so desire.

The Family Power Equalizing plan of Coons, Sugarman and Clune, while not presented as a voucher plan, has features more compatible with the use of a voucher mechanism than those of the CSPP plan. Briefly, Family Power Equalizing would:

1. Provide for a selection of public or private schools with different set costs per pupil (for example, with costs of $500, $800, $1100, and $1400 per pupil).

2. Private schools in the system could receive no funds from any other source than the government payment given above.

3. Each family would be directly taxed according to its

choice of school. That is, school taxes would be higher as the parents sent their child to a higher cost school.

4. These direct taxes would also vary with family income, so that a high income family would pay more than a low income family for each level of school costs.

5. ". . . the price (tax) to a rich family would exceed the full cost."[22] For example, a rich family might be taxed $2000 if it chose to send its child to the $1400 school.

This plan, including item number five, can only be described as naive to the point of absurdity. It is unimaginable that, in general, families would voluntarily pay $2000 to attend a $1400 school. Further, it is difficult to imagine a society that would attempt to impose all of the burden of subsidizing poor families with children solely upon upper-middle class and rich families with children, leaving those well off families without children free of any tax. The Family Power Equalizing plan as proposed simply would not work. In any public educational program, we can expect that, *unless the direct tax cost* (or voucher price) *is significantly less than the school cost per pupil,* families that would be charged an amount close to or exceeding the expenditure per pupil in the public system would withdraw from the public system and enter the purely private system. Since private schools have the reputation of offering the parent a program that more closely tailored to his individual tastes for his child, the typical parent will, dollar for dollar, prefer a private school to a public one. The more the public schools are directed to pursue social or public goals rather than accommodate parental demands, the greater will be this *ceterus paribus* preference for private schools. To overcome this preference, the typical parent must be faced with a compensating financial advantage in the public system. A program that offered this advantage to only part of the families in the population could only reasonably be expected to result in part of the families participating.[23]

Thus Family Power Equalizing, as proposed, would in fact perform much worse than the existing public school system based on neighborhood school districts. Currently, integration of children from different income classes is limited but not eliminated because of residential patterns. The Family Power Equalizing plan would assure a total separation of the children from the different income groups. Moreover, with the withdrawal of the upper-middle and upper income groups, the public system would lose financial support as well as students and the children of the poor would be absolutely worse off than in a segregated but better financed system.

Family Power Equalizing can only be made viable, then, by the elimination of item five. If this provision is discarded, however, Family Power Equalizing approaches a modified Pauley-Chambers voucher plan. This option is then made unnecessarily complicated and restrictive by such features as forbidding outside donations to private schools and limiting school budget variation to a few set figures. At best (when modified), Family Power Equalizing is inferior to the Pauley-Chambers modified voucher.[24]

SUMMARY

The use of vouchers for partially financing education is probably the best method of obtaining a larger degree of consumer sovereignty, individualism, efficiency and diversity in our nations schools. The cost, however, would be the sacrificing of the objective of widespread integration of social, racial and religious classes within the schools. Some modification through the imposition of legal restrictions upon discriminatory admissions requirements could avoid much of this cost. To do so would reduce the gains in consumer sovereignty, individualism, efficiency and diversity, but would not eliminate these. A voucher system could significantly promote these objectives, even with legal restrictions to promote social integration, provided that the voucher system encouraged a variety of per pupil school budgets by allowing parents, through the family budget, to augment their child's public support.

An integral part of any workable voucher scheme must be that parents, in determining the level of total education expenditures of their child, must pay at least a part of tuition costs above some social minimum. If social integration is to be promoted *all parents*, even the richest, must be subsidized enough to make the publically supported system more attractive than the totally private system.

Some pseudo voucher schemes, such as the CSPP model and Family Power Equalizing, by attempting to impose what amounts to punitive restrictions on the rich, would in fact, cause the well-off to desert the public system, the poor then would be worse off than before. Rather than adopt these extreme measures, society, if it chooses not to seek the objectives obtainable with vouchers, should seek to reform the current school system, with better and more equitable financing and diversity within individual public schools.

FOOTNOTES

1. Milton Friedman, "The Role of Government in Education," reprinted in *Capitalism and Freedom* (Chicago: University of Chicago Press, 1962).
2. Judith Areen and Christopher Jencks, "Education Vouchers: A Proposal for Diversity and Choice," in George R. La Noue, *Educational Vouchers: Concepts and Controversies* (New York: Teachers College Press, 1972), pp. 48-57.
3. National Goals Research Staff, *Toward Balanced Growth: Quality with Quantity* (Washington: U.S. Government Printing Office, 1970), pp. 94. A more detailed discussion of the problem of tax resources for education can be found in Irving J. Goffman and Frederick Goddard, "Revenue Limitations Related to Economic Growth: Particular Emphasis on Educational Programs," *The Concept of Education as an Investment* (Washington, D.C.: U.S. Government Printing Office, 1971), pp. 74-117. This was part of a final report to the President's Commission on School Finance.
4. U.S. Department of Commerce, Bureau of the Census, *State Government Finances in 1971* (Washington, D.C.: U.S. Printing Office, 1972).
5. John F. Due, "Alternative Tax Sources for Education," *Economic Factors Affecting the Financing of Education*, edited by Roe Johns, Irving Goffman, Kern Alexander and Dewey Stollar (Gainesville, Florida: National Education Finance Project, 1970), p. 294.
6. Dick Netzer, *Economics of the Property Tax* (Washington: The Brookings Institution, 1966), p. 30.
7. Irving J. Goffman and Frederick Goddard, *op. cit.* especially pp. 91-95.
8. This is not to say that every (or any) state could tap these revenue sources painlessly. Every tax imposes a burden upon members of the community. Rather the argument is that states find it difficult to raise additional revenue because taxpayers-voters are unwilling to bear the cost, not that they are unable to bear it.
9. John F. Due, *op. cit.* pp. 325-26.
10. Council of Economic Advisors, *Economic Report of the President* (Washington, D.C.: U.S. Government Printing Office, 1969), p. 65.
11. James S. Coleman, et. al., *Equality of Educational Opportunity* (Washington, D.C.: U.S. Government Printing Office, 1968).
12. Martin Mayer, "Improving Schools: The Sham of Distant Equality," *The New Republic*, 166 (April 1, 1972), 14-15.
13. Friedman, "The Role of Government in Education," *loc. cit.* p. 89.
14. *Ibid.*
15. *Ibid.*
16. *Ibid.*
17. Mark V. Pauly, "Mixed Public and Private Financing of Education: Efficiency and Feasibility," *American Economic Review*, 57 (March, 1967), 120-30; and Jay Chambers, "An Alternative Voucher Plan: The Compensation Principle and Price Competition," Occasional Paper in the *Economics and Politics of Education*, 72-1, Stanford University School of Education, 27 pp.
18. Pauly, p. 129.
19. Judith Areen and Christopher Jencks, "Education Vouchers: A Proposal for Diversity and Choice," and John E. Coons, Stephen D. Sugarman, and William H. Clune, III, "Reslicing the School Pie," both in George R. La Noue, *op. cit.*, pp. 48-67.
20. See Areen and Jencks, *op. cit.* for further detail.
21. The voucher format might however, be a good one for experimental purposes in obtaining data for designing public school reforms. Thus, the

current use of vouchers for the OEO tests of the CSPP plan may be worth the administrative costs.

23. It has been suggested that this scheme would amount to a user tax for education, but this is not true. A user tax is a tax on some complementary economic activity as a means of taxing users of a good of service that cannot be priced. Educational services most certainly can be priced. Moreover, even in the case of true user taxes, if the tax cost exceeds the benefits of the taxed activity, consumers will cease that activity and avoid the tax.

24. A separate proposal by Coons, Sugarman, and Clune — School District Power Equalization — is aimed at simple reform of the financing of the public school system and has much to recommend it. See Coons, et. al., *op. cit.*, p. 64.